Telecommuting: How to Make It Work for You and Your Company

Gil E. Gordon

and

Marcia M. Kelly

Prentice-Hall, Inc.
Englewood Cliffs, New Jersey

Prentice-Hall International, Inc., *London*
Prentice-Hall of Australia Pty. Ltd., *Sydney*
Prentice-Hall of Canada Inc., *Toronto*
Prentice-Hall of India Private Ltd., *New Delhi*
Prentice-Hall of Japan, Inc., *Tokyo*
Prentice-Hall of Southeast Asia Pte. Ltd., *Singapore*
Whitehall Books Limited, *Wellington, New Zealand*
Editora Prentice-Hall do Brasil Ltda., *Rio de Janeiro*
Prentice-Hall Hispanoamericana, S.A., *Mexico*

© 1986 *by*

Gil E. Gordon
and
Marcia M. Kelly

Cover photo credit for Marcia Kelly: Cecilia Capella

Library of Congress Cataloging-in-Publication Data

Gordon, Gil E.
  Telecommuting: how to make it work for you and
your company.

  Includes index.
    1. Telecommuting—United States—Management.
I. Kelly, Marcia M. II. Title.
HD2336.U5G67   1986   658.3'12   86-510

ISBN 0-13-902339-9
ISBN 0-13-902297-X {PBK}

PRINTED IN THE UNITED STATES OF AMERICA

About the Authors

GIL E. GORDON is founder and principal of Gil Gordon Associates, a human-resource management consulting firm in Monmouth Junction, New Jersey. He specializes in the implementation of telecommuting programs for business and industry.

Mr. Gordon's experience includes almost ten years with Johnson & Johnson in several areas of personnel work including recruiting, training and development, employee relations, and manpower planning. His education includes a B.S. degree in Business Administration from Northeastern University and an M.S. in Organizational Behavior from Cornell University. His earlier work experience included marketing research duties at General Foods Corporation.

As one of the pioneers in the field of telecommuting, Mr. Gordon has done extensive research into the practical aspects of the field and has spoken on the topic at numerous professional conferences including the International Communications Association, the Office Automation Conference, the National Computer Conference, the Organization Development Network, the Data Entry Management Association, and The Conference Board. He has been widely quoted in trade and business publications and is acknowledged as an expert in this developing field.

He is editor of "TELECOMMUTING REVIEW: The Gordon Report," a monthly newsletter published by TeleSpan Publishing in Altadena, California.

MARCIA M. KELLY is founder and president of Electronic Services Unlimited (ESU), a New York-based firm devoted entirely to research, consulting, and training services in the telecommuting field. ESU's clients include major corporations in the banking, financial services, computer and telecommunications industries, and government organizations. ESU conducts telecommuting feasibility studies, provides pilot program planning, and trains managers and remote workers for a variety of telework applications.

Ms. Kelly conceived, organized, and directed the multiclient study, *Telecommuting: Its Potential Effects on Profits and Productivity*, which was   **iii** sponsored by 30 leading U.S. corporations and is considered the bench-mark study in the field. She is also publisher of the "TELECOMMUTING REPORT—The Monthly Newsletter of Trends and Developments in Loca-tion Independent Work." In addition, she heads an annual conference on telecommuting sponsored by ESU as a regular forum for bringing together program managers, vendors of telework products and services, and others interested in this new way of optimizing human resources.

She began her business career on Wall Street and participated in the building of two other leading edge information companies before starting ESU. She has been written about in *Business Week, Computerworld, Forbes, Fortune, InfoWorld, The New York Times,* and *The Wall Street Journal,* and has appeared on the *"CBS Evening News,"* the *"Today Show,"* and other televised programs.

In August, ESU became a wholly owned subsidiary of LINK/Inter-national Data Corporation, the leading market research, analysis, con-sulting and publishing firm for the information processing and electronic services industries. Its worldwide resources include offices in the United Kingdom, France, Germany, Sweden, Hong Kong, Japan and Australia, giving the phrase "working from anywhere" a broader meaning for ESU staff members, who until now have telecommuted only from U.S. locations.

One of the challenges of work at home is merging work and home life successfully. The support and patience of our families who have had to learn to live and work with us has been unfailing—most of the time. We dedicate this book to them, with deepest thanks.

Contents

Contents

Acknowledgments

We thank Bette Schwartzberg, our editor at Prentice-Hall, for helping us develop what we believe is a practical, useful book for the manager. Her criticism was always constructive and very much on target.

Also, we appreciate the comments we received from Donald M. Falken-stine, Assistant Vice President for Systems Humanics at CIGNA. Don's review of the manuscript was comprehensive and insightful, and we thank him for taking time from a busy schedule to help us.

Introduction:
Sardines in the Subway

Did you ever stop to think how much you take some things for granted? How you don't even question certain traditions but just assume that things have to be that way? That's probably how you feel about your decision to go to work every morning. It's so much of a habit that you don't even think of it as a decision. But today, you and people in your company *do* have a decision to make about going to work and about a fundamental change in how and where you do your work.

It's about time we had an alternative to the commuting problems that most people face. Whether it's crowded subways, late trains, bumper-to-bumper freeway traffic, or just the high cost and general aggravation of any of these, few people enjoy commuting. It's a drain on the person and it hurts the employer as well; it's not unusual for office workers in metropolitan areas to take 15 to 30 minutes in the morning—on paid company time—to unwind from the commute before beginning work.

This is part of the hidden subsidy your organization pays so everyone can work in the same central location. Depending on your location you may also pay for parking lots or garages for employees' cars. Add to that the high but uncounted cost of seemingly harmless idle gossip and socializing in any office and you can see how the traditional office location reduces profits and productivity. This book will show you how to implement an exciting new idea that can help trim these costs and have real bottom-line impact.

You're in the midst of a technological revolution that makes it possible for many office workers to work from home or other remote locations using a concept called *telecommuting*. Simply stated, it's a way to bring the work to the workers rather than the reverse, which is what we've been doing for years. This book will tell you what telecommuting is, how it works, what's in it for you and your company, and how you can implement it in your office. It's not for everyone or every company, but when properly applied, it can be a powerful tool to help staff and manage today's and tomorrow's offices. This book is addressed to *you* as the manager responsible for implementing telecommuting, and also perhaps as a manager of telecommuters yourself.

People such as sales representatives, artists, writers, doctors, and lawyers have been working at home for years. And it's a rare businessperson who never brings home a briefcase full of work for the evenings or weekend. So what's new about telecommuting? you might ask. Well, the answer is simple: *more people* doing *more kinds* of jobs for *longer periods* away from the office. This isn't the nightly briefcase on the dining room table or the occasional day spent at home working on a key project. We're talking about the home (or other remote sites) becoming the *primary* work location with only periodic visits back to the central office.

Not sure this will work for you? Stop and think about your job and your office. If you're like many people, you deal with information and ideas. You deal with others in person but primarily by phone and memo. And, if your office is like most offices, you're relying on a personal computer or terminal more and more for access to information, to solve problems, and to communicate with others. There's almost nothing in this scenario that (with planning) isn't "portable" or can't be done from outside the office. For example, look how much you do today on a business trip: You take the files you need and your calculator and dictation machine and put them in your briefcase, stay in touch via telephone, and work very efficiently from your "office" on an airplane or in a hotel room.

Telecommuting means that more and more people will be able to spend part of the work week at some remote work location, generally (but not always) the home. This has some big plusses for them, but it also can mean a lot for you in terms of cost savings, higher productivity, and the ability to do a better job of recruiting and retraining key employees. You'll learn exactly how to plan for and implement telecommuting with long-term success and payoffs in mind. The key to getting these benefits is in careful evaluation and planning to tailor telecommuting to your company's situation. Here's how this book is organized to help you do that.

Chapter 1 will give you a quick look at the four trends behind telecommuting's growth and potential: changes in computers and related technology, changes in corporations, changes in employee values and preferences, and the exploding growth of personal computers in the office. You'll then see in Chapter 2 how you and your company can benefit from a well-planned telecommuting program. You'll see how the concept is used to hire and retain talented employees who otherwise might not want or be able to work in the office, and how firms can beat the growing costs for office space by shifting some of the work to remote locations. Once you learn about these and other benefits of telecommuting, you'll be able to pick the right reasons for starting a telecommuting program that helps solve business problems. Telecommuting isn't a pie-in-the-sky idea—it's a practical approach to the kinds of problems that you *and* your top management face every day.

Next, Chapter 3 takes you on a tour of the full range of remote work locations. You'll see that the home is a good choice in most cases, but far from the only one. The pros and cons of satellite offices, neighborhood work centers, and other facilities will be covered, along with the unique managerial challenges of each. Chapter 4 gets you started on a program in your organization by giving you an overview of six key steps for implementation plus tips on how to organize a planning team or task force to help guide the project. You'll see exactly how to get off to a good start by getting the right people working on the right tasks from the very beginning.

The next six chapters give you detailed guidance for each of the implementation steps:

Chapter 5 will help you spot the jobs that are best suited for remote work, and you'll see that they range from paper-and-pencil tasks to telemarketing to data processing and almost everything in between.

Chapter 6 gives you information on how to choose the right people to work from a remote location. Telecommuting is a unique kind of work arrangement and it's not for everyone. You'll learn how to make the right choices to help insure success.

Chapter 7 looks at the special requirements for the person managing telecommuters and lays out an outline for refining the skills for "long-distance management." You'll learn how to get your managers *ready* for telecommuting and *able* to supervise it effectively.

Chapter 8 is directed at the training and orientation needs of the telecommuters themselves. You'll see why it's important to give them some special skills for working independently and managing their jobs and careers from a distance. You'll also learn about some of the surprising challenges and situations that come with working at home—and how telecommuters can cope with them.

Chapter 9 lets you see how to keep the telecommuters tied into the office so they remain productive and keep their work on schedule. You'll learn why it's important to build and maintain social and information "networks" to keep everyone linked to a common purpose.

Chapter 10 addresses the technical and logistical planning details in telecommuting. Without resorting to computer jargon, you'll be able to understand the technical requirements and, most important, learn how to involve the right people to handle these details.

As with any innovation, there are some risks and traps for the unwary. Chapter 11 gives you the tools to spot these potential problem areas and helps you get around the obstacles. These can include legal and regulatory challenges, labor union concerns, and even zoning issues. You'll see how to avoid the trouble spots and steer clear of possible pitfalls.

Chapter 12 gives you a detailed and eye-opening look at the many choices you have for recruiting and staffing your organization. Telecommuting lets you make better use of part-time and retired employees, for example, in addition to being well suited for permanent full-time workers. You'll see the pros and cons of the various employment options and learn how a blend of several might be best for the years to come.

Chapter 13 is devoted to the productivity implications of telecommuting. With gains reported in the 15%–30% range for office workers, it's no wonder that telecommuting is catching the attention of more and more employers. You'll see how to use telecommuting to help increase productivity—and how some of the management practices involved can help office-based workers as well. Finally, you'll take a glimpse into the future in Chapter 14 as we look at the implications for telecommuting in 1990 and beyond. If it continues to grow at its current rate, we can expect some broad changes in business, society, commerce, and family life in the years to come. You'll also see some projections for new technologies that will help spur the growth of alternate work locations.

You can be on the leading edge of this exciting change in traditional work and commuting patterns as you explore the world of telecommuting. This book is designed to take you step by step through all aspects of the field. You'll find it easy to decide how to best apply what you read in your company since there are checklists throughout to focus your thinking and lead you to the best course of action.

To help you see the full scope of telecommuting at a glance, here's a "master checklist" that summarizes all the key issues. Note the chapter references and subheadings—these will help you pinpoint specific areas of interest. The chapter sequence is designed to give you a step-by-step guide to telecommuting. You can refer back to this chart to precisely locate desired additional information on certain topics, or to remind you where you are in the "big picture" of telecommuting and remote work.

THE MANAGER'S TELECOMMUTING CHECKLIST

A. UNDERSTANDING THE FOUR TRENDS BEHIND TELECOMMUT-ING'S GROWTH (CHAPTER 1)

  ✔ Changes in computers and related technology

  ✔ Changes in corporations

  ✔ Changes in employee values and preferences

  ✔ Exploding growth of personal computers in the office

B. LEARNING HOW TELECOMMUTING CAN BENEFIT YOUR ORGANIZATION (CHAPTER 2)

  ✔ Improved recruiting of staff

  ✔ Improved retention of trained, valuable employees

  ✔ Reduced office space costs

  ✔ Increased productivity

C. CONSIDERING AND SELECTING AMONG THE FULL RANGE OF REMOTE WORK LOCATIONS (CHAPTER 3)

  ✔ Understanding pros and cons of the home as a work site

  ✔ Understanding remote supervision options at various work locations

  ✔ Using branch offices and neighborhood work centers

  ✔ Taking a "mix and match" approach to work locations

  ✔ Using teleconferencing and other technologies for remote-site communications

  ✔ Using one remote site versus several: the use of dynamic schedules

  ✔ Knowing when on-site supervision is needed

✔ Assessing the new office space choices: teleports, mixed-use and shared-service buildings, planned communities, renovated malls, and schools

D. ORGANIZING YOURSELF AND OTHERS TO IMPLEMENT TELECOMMUTING (CHAPTER 4)

✔ Learning how innovations are adopted in large organizations
✔ Getting off to a good start and building in success factors
✔ Choosing the right people to help with the planning
✔ Previewing six key steps for implementing telecommuting

E. SELECTING THE RIGHT JOBS FOR TELECOMMUTING CHAPTER 5)

✔ Keyboard jobs and beyond
✔ Using a job-selection profile
✔ Taking advantage of cycles in jobs and projects
✔ Taking advantage of available technology
✔ Redesigning jobs or departments

F. SELECTING THE RIGHT PEOPLE TO BE TELECOMMUTERS (CHAPTER 6)

✔ Relying on volunteers: pros and cons
✔ Using job previews to help screen telecommuters
✔ Using work performance information for selection
✔ Working with examples of selection criteria
✔ Using work personality information for selection

G. TRAINING THE MANAGER TO MANAGE FROM A DISTANCE (CHAPTER 7)

✔ Understanding the manager's resistance
✔ Learning from other remote-supervision examples
✔ Developing five key skills for remote supervision
✔ Coaching the manager on career mobility issues for telecommuters
✔ Helping the manager "spotlight" telecommuters' performance
✔ Selecting the managers of telecommuters

H. TRAINING THE TELECOMMUTERS TO BE PRODUCTIVE
   AND EFFECTIVE (CHAPTER 8)

   ✔ Helping them adjust to a less structured setting
   ✔ Training them to choose and organize a work location
   ✔ Encouraging them to set schedules, manage time, and adopt
     "rituals"
   ✔ Finding ways to move work to and from the office
   ✔ Training them to take more responsibility for their own work
   ✔ Helping them tame the comforts of home
   ✔ Helping them understand and cope with legal and tax issues
   ✔ Training them to deal effectively with family, friends, and
     neighbors
   ✔ Helping them manage their jobs and careers from a distance

I. KEEPING TELECOMMUTERS LINKED INTO THE OFFICE
   (CHAPTER 9)

   ✔ Understanding why it's important to be part of the office's
     social and information networks
   ✔ Determining how often telecommuters should come into the
     office
   ✔ Drawing a blueprint for linking the telecommuters (collecting
     information and using it to build a plan)
   ✔ Understanding the role of electronic mail and voice mail
   ✔ Spreading the office news to telecommuters
   ✔ Using meetings effectively to maintain contact
   ✔ Using the telephone and teleconferencing to supplement face-
     to-face contact

J. TAKING CARE OF TECHNICAL DETAILS
   (CHAPTER 10)

   ✔ Knowing where to get the best technical advice
   ✔ Watching out for equipment service and maintenance problems
   ✔ Identifying and dealing with steps with long lead times
   ✔ Understanding basic objectives for technical support
   ✔ Using mechanical and electronic delivery systems
   ✔ Selecting other telephone-based equipment and services for
     telecommuters

K. STEERING CLEAR OF POTENTIAL PROBLEMS AND OBSTACLES (CHAPTER 11)

✔ Understanding resistance to change in general

✔ Understanding and dealing with resistance or problems from managers, telecommuters, and other employees

✔ Understanding possible security risks and finding ways to manage the risks

✔ Taking a realistic approach to four potential technical barriers

✔ Understanding the employer's potential liability and taking appropriate preventive steps

✔ Coping with labor laws and the reactions of unions

✔ Taking a positive approach to employee relations

✔ Making the right choice on employment status for telecommuters

✔ Using a "telecommuter's agreement" to clarify responsibilities and prevent problems

✔ Making the right decision on pay and benefits for telecommuters

L. EXPLORING NEW OPTIONS FOR EMPLOYMENT STATUS (CHAPTER 12)

✔ Understanding how alternate work arrangements will pay off today and in the future

✔ Understanding the link between alternate work *arrangements* and alternate work *locations*

✔ Making the best use of the seven major work options

M. ACHIEVING AND TRACKING PRODUCTIVITY IN TELECOMMUTING (CHAPTER 13)

✔ Understanding the sources of increased productivity

✔ Understanding why it's important to track productivity

✔ Planning for effective productivity measurement

✔ Learning why and how to use control groups

✔ Choosing the right control group

✔ Finding ways to sustain productivity gains

✔ Finding ways to extend telecommuting's productivity gains to office-based workers

N. LOOKING AHEAD TO THE FUTURE
    (CHAPTER 14)

✔ Understanding the possible limits on telecommuting's growth

✔ Estimating the projected numbers of telecommuters nationwide

✔ Understanding and acting on telecommuting-based projections
   in five areas:

   Urban structure

   Business organization and staffing

   Effects on existing businesses and opportunities for new
   ones

   Six new or developing technologies

   The "virtual office"

✔ Learning about the future from the lessons of the past

Looking for Alternatives: Four Converging Trends

Since the Industrial Revolution there has been a continuing trend to move work out of the home and into central locations. This implies travel to and from the work site, something that many people take for granted. But this book will tell you how to use telecommunications (with and without the use of computers) to substitute for travel. To understand why this shift is happening you'll need to take a look at four key trends in business today: changes in technology, changes in the "ground rules" under which most employers operate, changes in employee values, and the dramatic rise in the use of microcomputers* in business.

CHANGES IN TECHNOLOGY

It's no secret to anyone today that something profound has happened in the use of technology for office work. The field of microelectronics has

---

*NOTE: Throughout the book, you'll see the terms microcomputer, personal computer, PC, and terminal often used interchangeably. These terms can have different meanings, and a terminal in particular has no true computing power. The common idea is that all give a person convenient, easy-to-use access to information and computing power.

given us the "chip" that's at the heart of many of the new office products. As the capacity and processing power of the chip grow and its cost drops, its application spreads. Industry experts expect a continuing pattern of cost and efficiency improvements as new generations of chips are developed and manufacturers progress along the learning curve.

With this kind of computing power becoming more widespread, it's easy to see how the nature of office work is changing. Your firm has used computers for years, but their widespread use (that began in the 1960s) was based on large centralized installations that rarely, if ever, were useful to an individual. They were designed to handle large-scale business processing tasks—accounts receivable, payroll, and general ledger work, for example, that ran on "batch" systems where the computer would grind away sometimes for hours on single tasks.

Compare that with today's situation where you can reach over to a truly personal computer and do sales forecasting using a popular spreadsheet program, after having downloaded current sales data from your company's mainframe computer. You now can have direct access to a tool that can be used to help meet your personal business needs.

Think what would happen if everyone had to rely just on mass transit to get around. You'd be limited by when and where the bus or train was going and would have to sacrifice your need to run a short errand in favor of the "common denominator" needs of everyone else. When the "personal transportation system" (better known as the automobile) enters the scene, you have the flexibility to go where you want, when you want, at reasonable cost.

This is exactly the impact of the PC—and, unfortunately, the analogy holds down to the effects of crowded highways (or communications networks), tradeoffs between the luxury of individual cars versus mass transit economies (or PC use versus multiuser shared systems), and the risk of accidents (or PC users who make or contribute to poor decisions because they make errors in using software).

Information Centers and Computer Literacy

Another factor is the growth in "information centers," which have been described as the retail side of corporate data processing. You can use these on a walk-in basis since they're staffed by professionals trained to help you select and use the right computing resource.

The implication of these centers for the first time for telecommuting is that nontechnical managers and professionals are learning how to apply today's technology to their jobs. You don't give a thought anymore about how much you rely on the telephone and the pocket calculator to help with your job—they're taken for granted. The same is beginning to happen with PC use; the net effect is that entire jobs or parts of jobs now become more "portable" because they take advantage of this personal computing power. You're no longer bound to the office because that's where the computer printout book is, or because you need to rely on the DP staff for a special report. You can often do it yourself because you have the knowledge and the tools to do it virtually anywhere.

Telecommunications Changes

The second major change in technology is in the "glue" that holds everything together—the telecommunications system. This is a good news–bad news situation; the good news is that there have been great advances in telecommunications, but the bad news is that they haven't kept pace with the changes in computers and with the demands of managers.

The spread of PCs and the growth of distributed access and processing means that a lot of equipment somehow has to be tied together. As many firms have learned, it's not quite as easy as the television commercials imply; you don't just "plug it in." The equipment and the way it communicates often varies from brand to brand. Also, many companies have internal telecommunications networks that were designed to carry voice signals. Sending computer data on these systems can cause problems—the quality of a line that was adequate for voice isn't good enough for data, for example.

But fortunately you're now benefiting from advances like these:

- The familiar switchboard is being upgraded to a sophisticated "private branch exchange" (PBX) capable of handling voice and data simultaneously.
- The telephone operating companies are converting to all-digital networks, although this will be a slow process.
- The growth of fiber optics as a transmission system—with capacity that is as much as 250 to 500 times that of traditional copper wire—will allow faster and better-quality information flow.
- The range of software and hardware solutions to the problems of connecting dissimilar equipment is growing.

The telecommunications landscape has changed much over the last two years because of technological advances and the AT&T divestiture. The combined effect of the AT&T breakup and growing demands for data transmission has created headaches for corporate DP and telecommunications managers. You'll find that the growth of telecommuting will depend in part on how fast these electronic highways catch up to the growth in PCs themselves. Fortunately, you can look to your vendors and your own technical managers to help tackle these problems for you.

Growth of Online Databases

You'll also find that telecommuting is aided by the spread of online databases. These electronic libraries have put almost unlimited information at your fingertips. Today, over 2,400 of these are available to the public plus countless other internal ones that contain proprietary information. Examples of what's available range from Dun and Bradstreet credit reports and the LEXIS legal information database from Mead Data Central, to more specific ones such as COFFEELINE (abstracts of news and research reports on coffee culled from over 5,000 journals) and FAMILY RESOURCES, which includes citations of sociological and psychological literature about family studies.

Some of these are available only online; there is no print equivalent. Others include the full text of printed works, while some are citation services that help you identify sources for further research. The number of users of these services is skyrocketing; for example, Dow Jones News Retrieval (including a range of financial, business news, and other databases) has over 200,000 subscribers. Another popular service is DIALOG, which allows access to over 275 separate databases.

What difference does it make if you can sit down at your PC and find out that a Circle Line cruise boat took an inflatable octopus on a cruise around Manhattan on July 31, 1984—an actual item from the NEWSEARCH database? It means that jobs relying on access to specific information are now more portable since they aren't tied to the shelves of a library. Functions like market research, forecasting, policy analysis, and others that rely on access to facts and information now can be done in different ways and from different places than before. Chapter 5 will tell you how to consider jobs like these for telecommuting, either in part or in whole.

These are the main factors in the technological forces behind telecommuting. There are others you'll want to consider but which as yet have seen limited application in remote work. Perhaps the most important is teleconferencing, which includes a range of products and services from a simple three-party conference call (to discuss some sales forecasts) to a computer-based conference (to gather opinions about product development strategies) to a multilocation full-motion videoconference (to discuss a new product introduction with marketing managers across the country). Teleconferencing will play a growing role in remote work because it will allow the kinds of interactions that you normally assume must happen face to face. (See examples of teleconferencing use in the section "A Teleconferencing Case Study" in Chapter 9.)

CHANGES IN OPERATING PRESSURES

The "ground rules" in your organization are changing. Years of high infla-tion in the 1970s, followed by a recession and the growth in worldwide competition mean that it's no longer business as usual. The days of abun-dant staffs, loose spending, and less-than-disciplined business planning are long gone for most companies and even for many organizations like hospitals and government agencies.

Cost-Saving Pressures

These changed conditions force you to make do with less, to justify spend-ing plans more carefully, and to get the most out of investments in all resources. Expenses that used to be taken for granted are now checked carefully. This means you're forced today to look beyond the easy ways to trim budgets and find innovative approaches to make do with what you have. Also, some observers note that the thinning of the middle manage-ment ranks—caused by headcount cuts due to economy moves or to emu-late the "flatter" Japanese organizations—means that much of the work that used to be done by people will now be done by machines—PCs, to be exact. Telecommuting becomes appealing because of its cost-cutting potential and its technological base.

As these pressures grow, the role of telecommuting also grows. It's not surprising that managers in companies with electronic mail systems find that they can often draft and send their own memos; it's faster and cheaper than relying on a secretary. This means that you now can work anywhere you have access to that electronic mail system since you're no longer tied to access to the secretary.

As you'll see in Chapter 2, one of the main reasons for getting involved with telecommuting is to save your company money. Some of the costs involved are sometimes hidden and don't get as much attention but ac-count for a big part of the human resource budget. These include costs of hiring, training, and relocating staff, and the opportunity of improving productivity. Further, when it comes to cutting costs, the easy steps in-clude slashing budgets across the board or laying off staff; it's usually harder to find those next dollars once you're down to a leaner operation. This is part of what's behind the growing attention to white-collar productivity improvement programs.

Demand for DP Services

Another change in operating pressures relates back to the changes in technology. The spread of PCs and computer literacy courses have made more managers aware of data processing concepts in general. They often see how DP can help improve the way the business is run, above and beyond the standard business applications. In many cases managers are becoming aware of the strategic value of information management; American Express, American Hospital Supply Corp., Citicorp, and Sears are four companies often cited for their skill in using information to improve their competitive position.

The result is a growing demand for centralized DP services. This increased workload for already overworked DP staffs results in what's called the "applications backlog," which is another way of saying that many DP departments are from one to two years behind schedule. There's growing pressure on DP to deliver the goods while the supply of talented programmers is short and budgets for expansion are often tight. The problem is becoming more severe because some of the applications that are being delayed are those with high strategic value (and thus more visible to your top executives). Here's another case where you can look to telecommuting to help ease staffing problems and thus keep these critical projects on schedule.

In summary, these and related changes in the way business does business mean that managers are often searching for new solutions; telecommuting is one of them.

CHANGES IN PEOPLE

The third major change that drives telecommuting is the different makeup of today's work force. If you sometimes get the feeling that your employees aren't as they used to be, you're absolutely correct. The employee population today bears little resemblance to that of ten years ago.

Women in the Work Force

The most profound change is the rise in the number of women in the work force today. As of 1984, 54 percent of American women were in the labor force, up from 43 percent in 1970; this number is expected to grow to 58 percent by 1990. More important, women held close to 20 percent of the management jobs in 1980, up from 11 percent in 1970. This is due to two changes: more women going through the educational pipeline and changes in family status that result in more women entering or reentering the work force. For example, recent figures show that women now represent 52 percent of all undergraduates, 15 percent of engineering students, 33 percent of MBA students, and 50 percent of law school students.

Changes in Family Status

Changes in family status are even more significant. Overall, they indicate that our traditional idea of the family is no longer typical—the classic arrangement of Dad going out to work while Mom stays home with the kids is the exception, not the rule. This "nuclear family" accounts for about 20 percent of the population today, and some estimates put the number at below 15 percent. Instead, we see that just over 50 percent of today's work force is people from households where both spouses work, and fully 10 percent of the work force consists of single parents. Experts expect the portion of dual-income households to rise to 60 percent by 1990.

Also, about one out of six families is headed by a woman, and in 1984 roughly 60 percent of mothers with children under age 18 were in the work force, up from 40 percent in 1970. According to Dr. Dana Friedman of The Conference Board, the fastest growing segment of the work force is mothers with children under three years old. These changes in family status coupled with the number of women coming from college mean that about two thirds of all new entrants into the labor force through 1990 will be women. Of them, 80 percent will be of child-bearing age, and 93 percent (of the 80 percent) would be expected to become pregnant.

What do all these numbers mean? You'll need to pay more attention to the role of women in the work force. Also, the task of balancing family responsibilities with work is quickly becoming an issue that affects large numbers of workers—and their employers. However, telecommuting is not only for women or for parents with young children, and it's not the answer to the problem of finding quality day care for young children. As you'll see in Chapter 2, there are some cases where the parent at home can be an effective telecommuter and care-giver at the same time, but these are the exceptions. The image (often suggested by some media reports on telecommuting) of the parent in the den with a keyboard in one hand and baby bottle in the other is simply not feasible in most cases.

Changes in Employee Values

A more subtle change in the work force is a change in employee values and preferences about the terms and conditions of work. You've no doubt noticed that today's newer workers often are quick to let you know about their preferences for the content and nature of their work and even about work schedules. It's not the kind of "palace revolt" that some managers remember about the late 1960s and early 1970s as that crop of college graduates entered the work force. If those years gave us the "me" generation, then today we have the "you *and* me" generation—workers who are more accepting of company goals but at the same time are clear about what kind of work environments they prefer.

This doesn't apply to the entire work force, but when it involves the workers who might be in short supply you have a challenge. Firms recognize these people are a critical resource and may have to adapt standard policies to attract and retain them. The need to accommodate these values can be a motivating force behind telecommuting.

THE MARCH OF THE MICROCOMPUTER

The fourth and final reason why the time is right for telecommuting is the tremendous spread of PCs through U.S. organizations. Although it's hard to believe, the first commercially available microcomputers used widely in business didn't come on the scene until late 1980 and began to get wider distribution in 1981. The growth in the last few years has been dramatic; these numbers from LINK Resources show how quickly PCs have spread throughout U.S. business:

TOTAL NUMBER OF PCs
INSTALLED IN U.S. BUSINESSES

1983—3,160,000
1984—5,544,000
1985—8,834,000 (est.)

What's even more significant is the phenomenon of multiple orders for PCs. In the early days—way back in 1982, for instance—stories would surface regularly about the devious methods used to order a PC in the face of corporate policies that severely restricted their purchase. PCs were described on purchase orders as typewriters or file cabinets to sneak them in under the noses of corporate watchdogs. Today, single companies order hundreds (or in some cases thousands) of PCs—with staggered delivery schedules in most cases.

PC USE AND PURCHASE PLANS BY SIZE OF COMPANY

Number of Employees	% of Firms in This Category Using PCs	% of Firms Planning to Order More Than 100 PCs in 1984
100–499	27%	n.a.
1,000–4,999	62%	n.a.
5,000–24,999	66%	17%
25,000 and over	80%	60%

For some organizations in information-intensive industries (such as banking, insurance, or financial services) there may be one PC or terminal for every two or three office employees. It will be used to access corporate information files, for routine tasks like budgets, special projects, and as a communications link for electronic mail and database research. As noted earlier, this proliferation of PCs means that they will be accepted as commonplace work tools. They become an integral ingredient for many telecommuting applications.

Now you have a good appreciation for the four forces behind telecommuting. These combine to make telecommuting a practical reality of the mid-1980s and beyond. It's up to you to take advantage of this workplace innovation.

2

What's in It for Me and My Company?

You may have mixed feelings about telecommuting so far; the concept interests you, but you're not sure if it makes sense for you personally or for your company. You'll see in this chapter why many firms have gotten over this skepticism and implemented telecommuting once they understood the payoffs.

Telecommuting is *not* all things to all people or all companies. It's a tool that has significant payoffs when used the right way under the right conditions. This chapter will help you decide how well it fits your situation by outlining its key benefits. Once you understand these payoffs and match them up with your own organization's needs, you can make the best use of telecommuting.

PAYOFF 1: IMPROVED RECRUITING

It's rare that a manager doesn't have problems finding enough of the right kinds of people to fill openings. This is especially true in those job categories where demand exceeds supply due to local or national conditions. The key to effective recruiting is to have a large enough pool to select from; without enough applicants it's hard for you to make a good choice.

Let's look behind the scenes at your organization's recruiting process to see why you can't always readily find the people you need. Competition with other employers can be stiff, and recruiting is often a high-volume operation with hectic activity for the professional recruiters. If the volume itself isn't enough, there are added pressures to balance timeliness, cost control, affirmative action goals, and other employment objectives.

Telecommuting can help manage these pressures by expanding the pool of available candidates. Recruiting is like any other marketplace—it requires a satisfactory match between buyer and seller. As in other marketplaces, buyers who put limits on what they're willing to consider often are disappointed. This is what many managers do when looking to hire someone. They set very rigid criteria for whom they're willing to consider—and wind up eliminating potentially good candidates who might fit in well. Telecommuting can help by adding more candidates to the labor pool and giving you more choices. The net effect, if all goes well, is that your job opening gets filled faster and the work is more likely to stay on schedule.

Expanding the Labor Pool

Let's look at how this works. The traditional labor pool considered in most cases includes only those people willing and able to work five full days a week in the office. This isn't surprising because you've been conditioned to expect that pattern of work. But look at who is excluded from the labor pool if you limit it to those "regular" applicants:

- People who are unable to work full time because they have to care for young children or aging relatives at home;
- People who are unable to come in to a central work location every day because of a short-term or permanent disability, or because they lack easy access to reliable transportation;
- People who simply want (and can afford to ask for) more flexibility in work schedules. Sometimes these are people who will gladly trade off salary for more free time; others may be willing to work a full-time job but want to do it more on their own terms if possible.
- People who live outside the traditional recruiting (and commuting) range but are more qualified than those available locally. With telecommuting, the radius of the recruiting "net" can increase; a telecommuter might not mind a 90-minute commute if it's done only once or twice a week on days when he or she has to be in the office.

This might appeal to people who've moved (or want to move) farther away from the close-in suburbs to get away from the congestion, yet still have access to center-city job opportunities.

New Hires Versus Existing Employees as Telecommuters

As you reach out to hire these people, though, remember that there are pros and cons of hiring new employees as telecommuters versus taking existing employees and having them become telecommuters. It's clear from reviewing the experiences of employers with telecommuting programs that there's a risk in hiring new employees specifically to work at home. While they may be technically qualified they just don't know the ins and outs of how your organization works. Also, it's an added burden to supervise someone remotely who's never been supervised in the office. It requires a level of trust above and beyond what's normally required in remote supervision.

In general, it makes sense to select telecommuters from your current work force. If that's not possible you can hire them from the outside as long as there's some kind of orientation period. Ideally, the new telecommuter would work in the office full time for several months. The new employee would then begin to telecommute if the work quality was satisfactory and if he or she had learned the ropes of the organization. You

---

RECRUITING CHECKLIST

✔ Do you have certain jobs that are usually hard to fill?

✔ Do you know of current or anticipated labor shortages for key jobs?

✔ Do white-collar job openings remain unfilled for more than three to four weeks? If so, is this disruptive or costly to your operation?

✔ Are you spending more than you like for employment agency fees?

✔ Do you know of job candidates who are qualified but can't work in the office five days a week?

✔ Are you having problems attracting good people to your location?

If you answered "yes" to several of these, consider telecommuting as a way to improve your recruiting efforts.

might have to accommodate disabled hires who can only come into the office one day a week; their orientation period would have to be designed differently.

This caveat about hiring from the outside isn't as restrictive as it might seem. A good way to approach it is to set up a program where telecommuters are drawn from the existing work force, which is constantly replenished with potential telecommuters hired from the outside. At any time, you'd have people in the early stages of the in-house orientation, others almost ready to begin telecommuting, and others actually working off-site.

PAYOFF 2: IMPROVED RETENTION

Just as it's important to *find and attract* key people, it's important to *retain* them once they've been hired. Most firms don't do an accurate job of tracking or even estimating the costs of turnover. Here's a list of the major direct and indirect costs of turnover, taken from a classic article on the subject ("Estimating Turnover Costs" by Thomas E. Hall, *Personnel*, July–August, 1981, published by the American Management Association):

DIRECT COSTS	INDIRECT COSTS
1. Employment advertising	1. Cost of management time per hire
2. Agency and search fees	2. Cost of other employees' time per hire
3. Internal referrals	3. Cost of training per hire
4. Applicant expenses	4. Cost of learning curve and productivity/business losses
5. Relocation expenses	
6. Employment staff compensation	
7. Other employment office costs	
8. Recruiter travel expenses	

The article listed estimated figures for an unnamed company for exempt-level employee hires as follows: direct costs of $8,252, indirect costs of $6,180, for a total—*in 1981 dollars*—of $14,432 per hire. Assuming 10 percent inflation per year, the figure would come to $21,130 in 1985. Multiply this number times the turnover among your professional-level employees and you might be shocked.

It costs money to lose employees, and the costs of losing well-trained, valued employees are even greater. Many turnover causes can't be controlled and a certain amount of turnover is good. But the worst kind of turnover—losing someone you wanted to keep for reasons that could have been controlled—is where telecommuting may help.

Reducing Turnover with Telecommuting

Let's look at the five major kinds of turnover that might be reduced with telecommuting:

1. *Child Care Needs.* The growth of the numbers of working women cited in Chapter 1 leads to another phenomenon: the problems of child care when many of those women choose to have children. A very typical pattern today is for a woman to go to work after undergraduate or graduate school and work for a number of years before having her first child. With more women waiting until their late twenties or early thirties to do this, they're able to get well into their careers before motherhood.

Very often these women strongly prefer or need to continue to work but are faced with inadequate child-care resources. Even though some firms offer child-care leaves for fathers as well now, there's still a problem of finding reliable, quality care before the child enters school. Telecommuting may help the woman, her husband, *and* the employer all come out ahead by enabling the parent to work (at least part-time) while caring for the child. Note that this isn't just a women's issue; the woman happens to be the one having the child, but both parents have to face the decision of how best to juggle work and family responsibilities.

It's pure myth to assume that someone can work at home full-time and care for a young child or two at the same time. Those who have tried experience as much stress as parents who leave home to work and hope they've found suitable day care. The compromise solution might be to work part-time at home and share child care duties with the spouse or others, either in the home or outside.

This compromise can occur most easily when the job in question is not "time-sensitive." In other words, it doesn't make much difference if the work gets done from 8 to 10 A.M. or to 8 to 10 P.M., or on weekdays or weekends, within reason. In this case it's easier to sandwich in the work between the child's rest periods and the availability of other care-givers. Even in the best cases, though, this means part-time instead of full-time work, though part-time might be up to 30 hours a week in some cases.

The other case where telecommuting might help retain a valued employee/parent is when the child is older and in school but the parent still chooses to be at home. Some employers—most notably banks—have instituted part-time schedules called "mother's hours" that usually run from 9 A.M. to 2 P.M. or similar periods. These work out well for the mothers (or fathers, for that matter) and for the employer who needs to cover lunch periods of full-time workers or handle peak loads that don't justify full-time help.

There's no reason why you couldn't use telecommuting this way just as well. The parent could work away from home for several hours, at home a few more, or a combination of both. All tasks don't offer this kind of flexibility, but it's surprising how creative and adaptable you can be if you want to retain the talents of a trusted subordinate.

Finally, there's another alternative that might be the best of all worlds—the neighborhood work center, to be discussed more fully in Chapter 3.

2. *Disability.* Just as telecommuting can help attract and employ disabled workers, it can help retain people who become disabled while employed. There can be many reasons for disability: recovery from surgery or from an accident, physical problems that limit mobility, and emotional problems related to work or outside events. Telecommuting might help you retain the services of these people while they're recovering or for the duration of the disability.

The key point when considering telecommuting for disabled employees is that the employee's health is your primary concern. The goal isn't to try to squeeze every productive moment out of someone home in bed. But in cases where the employee's physician determines that he or she is *medically able* to work at home, and the employee *willingly* agrees to do so, and the work won't interfere with or slow down the recovery, telecommuting can be considered. You might change some aspects of the job if you decide that the employee's job exactly as done in the office isn't suited to remote work, and have the disabled employee handle only portions of it, or perhaps even do a different job.

The disability situation is a perfect example of the need to rethink basic assumptions about *what* work is and *where* it gets done. One of the assumptions behind disability insurance is that employees who can't go to work can't work. If telecommuting lets you take the work to the worker, instead of the reverse, you're no longer bound by that assumption. Nobody wins in the long run when an employee is paid 50 percent or 100 percent of salary to do nothing just because he or she can't commute to the office or otherwise be a part of the regular, full-time work force. Useful employment can be designed for the disabled in this way, always keeping in mind that the employee's health and, if possible, recovery have to be your primary considerations.

3. *Relocation.* It's no secret that relocation can be one of the most difficult and costly aspects of corporate life today. According to figures from Homequity the average cost to relocate an employee in 1984 was $51,000, up from $42,000 in 1983, and $30,000 in 1980. There are these direct costs, the indirect costs of lost productive time, and the emotional costs often associated with resettling in a new community. Relocation has been and will continue to be an important method to develop and deploy talent throughout most organizations. But it doesn't always go smoothly; a 1983 study by Catalyst put the refusal rate for transfers at 24 percent, and the Employee Relocation Council notes that 43 percent of its 600 member companies surveyed in 1983 reported some problems with employee resistance to transfer.

Telecommuting gives you a chance to look at relocation differently: instead of moving the person to the new job, why not move the new job to the person in his/her existing location? This obviously won't work in many cases where the person must be located with subordinates, in a specific territory, or managing an operation that requires a "hands-on " presence. But in jobs that require more managing of information, rather than people or things, this reverse twist on relocation might work. You can save company money for the right kinds of moves and save employees who might opt to resign instead of relocate.

Telecommuting won't put the moving companies out of business, but it might help retain good people and save money at the same time in the right situation. Even with some additional telecommunications and travel costs for visits to the distant office, there should still be room to recapture some of those costs that now top $50,000 per move.

4. *Personal Preference.* Have you ever worked with or interviewed someone who was talented as an accountant, programmer, analyst, or whatever, but just didn't fit into organizational life? They're labeled as square pegs in round holes, and it's often a shame that this talent is out of the reach of the corporate world.

Not everyone is cut out for the routine of work in large organizations. (An enlightening and enjoyable book on this topic is *Working Free: Practical Alternatives to the 9 to 5 Job* by John Applegath.) Some of these "misfits" never get near a corporate headquarters but others give it a try. As the manager, you give them a try also—especially if they happen to have skills that are in short supply. But these trials rarely have happy endings because there's a kind of cultural gap between both parties. Like someone traveling in a foreign country, certain employees are confused and uncomfortable having to conform.

Telecommuting might be the buffer between the two cultures. By allowing the person to do the job where and when he/she sees fit (within reason), both sides are spared the uneasiness or even the friction that can develop when square pegs are forced into round holes. The periodic visits to the office aren't long enough to allow problems to develop, and everyone is happier.

5. *Retirees.* A well-documented change in the U.S. population is the projected rise in the number of older people. When a long-time employee retires, many years of experience walk out the door with the retiree. Many people look forward to retirement and the freedom it brings, but for some it also brings boredom and constant worry about finances.

Retirees who are willing to work part-time and keep their earnings below the Social Security cap might be good prospects as telecommuters. Unless they left on bitter terms they can continue working, though perhaps at a different job. Look at the advantages of retaining retirees as part-time employees: they know your organization, the quality of their

---

RETENTION CHECKLIST

✔ Are your turnover rates and costs higher than you think they should be?

✔ Are you losing good people because of personal or family needs?

✔ Does your department's work lend itself to part-time schedules?

✔ Have you lost good people due to short- or long-term disability where the *main* problem was mobility?

✔ Have you lost good people who stated they'd simply prefer to work on more flexible terms—and who could continue to be productive?

✔ Is there a pool of retirees you can tap to supplement your work force?

You might be able to cut the costs and disruption of turnover and retain your good employees via telecommuting if you answered "yes" to several of these questions.

work is known, and they usually live within reasonable commuting distance to the office when on-site visits are needed.

Because they're often receiving pensions and Social Security, their income requirements might be reasonable enough so they'll be a "bargain" compared to the skills they have. If you have the choice of paying one of your retirees $6 to $8 an hour for clerical work, for example, or paying the same amount to an untrained, untested worker from a temporary-help agency, whom would you prefer to hire? If you choose the retiree, then telecommuting might be one way to do it—though obviously not the only way.

PAYOFF 3: OFFICE SPACE COST CONTROL

For years you've accepted as a given that "more people" meant "more space." Large firms go through elaborate space planning projections keyed to changes in headcount for the next five or ten years. But with today's business climate of cost control, these same firms are feeling the pinch of this one-to-one link between people and space.

Perhaps the most tangible benefit of telecommuting is its ability to help cut office space costs, which is one of the main reasons why firms get into remote work. There are several cases where telecommuting might be the most appealing:

- Quickly expanding new firms that are outgrowing their current space and can't afford to allocate scarce funds from R&D, for example, to office space;
- Firms that want another alternative to squeezing more people into cubicles and offices, yet can't do without additional staff needed to support the business;
- Firms that want to shift some space from high-cost midtown locations to lower-cost suburban or even rural areas (to be discussed in Chapter 3);
- Firms that have new space under construction but need a stop-gap solution to overcrowded existing facilities for the interim months;
- Firms that want to look at office space creatively and treat it as an asset with income-producing potential. For them, telecommuting might free up some space that can be profitably leased or subleased, even including out-of-pocket costs of setting up the telecommuting program.

Mounting Costs for Space

These and similar needs can be sound reasons for implementing telecommuting. Today it's not unusual to pay from $40 to $60 per square foot for office space in desirable midtown areas. Multiply that times the 100 square feet considered minimally acceptable for office workers, and you'll see that it can cost between $4000 and $6000 just to house someone. These figures include heat and light but not electricity (which can run another $2 to $3 per square foot) and real estate and other taxes.

As if these numbers aren't high enough already, they're actually higher because of a quirk in how floor space is measured. According to an article titled "The Incredible Shrinking Square Foot" in the August 5, 1984 *New York Times**, renters are charged for more space than they can use because landlords need to spread the cost of nonusable floor space and services among all the tenants. Space for elevators, bathrooms, and even building columns get built into the calculations; tenants usually pay for up to 25 percent more space than they can use. New York City leads the nation in the premium charged over actual usable space, but the problem exists across the country.

Space-Saving Potential

If you use telecommuting to shift some work out of the central office, you get an immediate reduction in office space requirements. But it's not a one-for-one savings; as you'll see in Chapter 9, effective telecommmuting means that people still come into the office for some time each week. This might be as little as a half-day or as much as three days—it depends on the job, the person, and your preferences as the manager.

The savings can still be significant. If you head a department of ten people and half become telecommuters with each person at home three days a week, you can cut your space needs by 30 percent. This might require some careful planning to stagger the days in the office; the five telecommuters might be sharing two offices or cubicles. Also, the space savings won't happen immediately because most firms will implement telecommuting in a pilot program that allows for several months of trial and fine-tuning.

---

*Copyright © 1984 by the New York Times Company. Reprinted by permission.

It's interesting to speculate about the changing definition of office space for these "transient" telecommuters. If you look around your office, you'll see a layout designed for people who work there five full days a week. Isn't it possible that people coming in for only a day or two a week would need less elaborate space—maybe a simple work area without extensive space for files and chairs for guests? The telecommuters' in-office work space might be a cross between the traditional individual work areas of today and some kind of open-space area that can be used for small conferences, access to a number of terminals or PCs spread around the room, and a central filing area, for example. The advantage of this plan is that firms might be able to get by with less than the 100 square feet per person, or at least use space more flexibly.

OFFICE SPACE CHECKLIST

✔ Is your organization growing quickly—too quickly for the space available?

✔ Are you projecting a growth spurt in the next 12 to 24 months that will force you to build or lease more space?

✔ Are you under pressure to cut overhead costs?

✔ Does the office space near where your employees live cost much less than your current space?

✔ Can you lease some of your own office space to outside tenants who want to be at your location?

Telecommuting can help if you answered "yes" to several of these questions.

PAYOFF 4: INCREASED PRODUCTIVITY

Productivity is the watchword of American business today, especially in terms of office workers. Not too many years ago, the term was generally applied only to production workers whose output could be easily counted in pounds, units, widgets, or whatever. Since most companies are spending increasingly large proportions of the payrolls on office workers, the need to pay more attention to their productivity is clear.

There are some encouraging signs in what people working at home are able to produce. Although white-collar productivity measures aren't always precise, productivity increases averaging between 15 percent and 30 percent seem to be typical.

These productivity gains are based on seven key factors:

1. *More Hours Worked per Day.* Most commuters count their commuting time as part of the workday, whether or not they actually do any work while traveling. Telecommuters working at or near home can return part or most of that dead time to productive work. Someone who left home at 7:15 A.M. but didn't arrive at work until 8:00 A.M. might start work at home at 7:30 A.M., for example.

Similarly, your telecommuters won't need the "decompression" time many commuters spend getting ready for work once they arrive at the office. Given the grueling nature of mass transit or auto commuting in many cities, that 15- to 30-minute break might correctly be called a recuperation period. Even though it might be necessary, it's still a drain on your department.

Try an experiment in your office: come in very early one morning and watch how much time passes between arrival time and the actual start of work for your staff and coworkers. Do the same thing before and after lunch and at the end of the day. If your office is like most, you can count on 20 to 30 minutes per person per day, and longer in some cases. Add that up over the course of a week and you'll see how your company is funding some worthwhile but nonproductive socializing.

Telecommuters often work *different* hours than they might in the office, but they're generally working *more* hours as well. All else being equal, more hours worked means more work produced. There's no indication that telecommuters mind the extra hours. In fact, one characteristic of telecommuters is that they're often strongly task-oriented people for whom commuting time is a waste and an annoyance. This devotion to duty isn't all good news, though; as you'll see in Chapter 11, this has implications for nonexempt workers who must be paid overtime and for hard workers who might not know when to stop. As one observer noted, telecommuting might be the "workaholic's dream."

2. *More Work Done per Hour.* This goes with the previous point; telecommuters get more done in the hours they work, so they're ahead of the game even if they only work as many hours as they would have in the office. The normal everyday distractions and interruptions in every office just don't exist—at least to the same degree—at home. As you'll see in

Chapters 6 and 8, it's essential to select people who are less prone to distractions at home and to train them to cope with the three D's of working at home: doorbells, deliveries, and dog barks.

Don't get the impression that office socializing is all bad or that telecommuters should work hours on end without a break. The problem is the cumulative effect of those interruptions and distractions on work output in the office. If, on the other hand, you're concerned about the possible loss of productivity for people working unsupervised at home, here's another experiment: try to count how many actual working hours there are in the average work week at your office. You can do this for yourself, your staff, or your peers. Even giving people the benefit of the doubt (since some of that daydreaming is really thinking time), you'll probably find that the total falls far short of the 35 or 40 hours they're being paid to work.

There's another reason why remote work hours are often "better" hours. Many people carve up the office work day based on some artificial constraints, such as getting to the cafeteria before it gets crowded or leaving in time to catch the 5:18 train at night because it's more reliable than the 5:36 train. These constraints take their toll in a very subtle way. If it's 4:45 P.M. and you want to catch that 5:18 train (and it's going to take you almost a half-hour to clean up your desk, get out of the building, and get to the station), you're just not going to touch one more piece of work. Even though you might be mentally ready to tackle another project, your workday comes to a grinding halt.

Telecommuters generally don't face these kinds of problems; they have much more control over their schedules and—unless they're working at the kitchen table—don't have to take time to go through the ritual of setting up and breaking down the work area in the morning and at quitting time. This means that you can count on a more steady flow of work from your remote workers.

3. *Ability to Work at Peak Times.* As you've gathered from the last two sections, telecommuters generally have lots of flexibility in setting their work schedules. Tradition dictates that office workers are expected to be at the desk and working at or near the normal starting time every day. The phenomenon of flexible work hours is not new and yet it's far from standard practice across the country.

The fact is that everyone isn't an early bird. Everyone isn't up to full speed at 8:30 A.M. even though this might be the "official" time to start work. Telecommuters report they use their flexible work hours to their advantage, working at times that best fit their internal clocks. There are limits on this for remote workers who have to coordinate with coworkers or customers; few key clients would welcome a call at 10 P.M. just because the telecommuter is a night owl. But if you can let people build their schedules around their own preferences and needs, they'll be able to work at their peak (and thus more productive) times more often.

Let's look at this question of shifted work hours from another viewpoint—the need to provide extended hours of service to your customers. With the growth of inbound (the familiar "800" call-in numbers) and outbound (using phone calls instead of face-to-face or other kinds of selling) telemarketing, the workday no longer ends at 5 P.M. for everyone. Next time you get a mail-order catalog, look at the hours of operation for their telephone ordering number. More and more firms offer 18- or 24-hour service; wouldn't it be nice if those order-takers could work at home? Think of the convenience for them and the savings for the employer. Remote work lets your company extend its hours of service (and improve its marketing) without having to bring employees in at all hours of the night.

4. *Faster Access and Turnaround Times.* For jobs that rely on a central computer (such as timesharing applications) telecommuting can help spread some of the work around the clock. Moving work away from the peak first-shift hours means that your employees will be competing with fewer other users for that central computer; their turnaround time and access improves. If they can get faster response and faster processing during less busy hours, they can turn out more work per hour.

Sometimes this happens because the telecommuter shifts the work day voluntarily (as noted earlier) or it can be by design. You can set up a second-shift operation (perhaps with part-time telecommuters) and equalize computer usage around the clock. This can have a big payoff; if computer capacity can be "stretched" by shifting the workload, you may be able to delay planned lease or purchase of more computing power needed to handle the peak first-shift workload.

The telephone companies have been doing this for years with lower rates in the evening and on weekends. This shifts calling volume and reduces the need to invest in plant and equipment that would be idle at night and on weekends. Telecommuting can serve the same function for employers and be a boon for employees who work better on the off-hours.

5. *Group Norms as Productivity Drains.* Anyone who ever worked on or around a production floor knows how workers can set their own standards for a fair day's work. Pity the ambitious, conscientious employee

who works hard and exceeds that norm—he or she is labeled a "rate buster" and feels the brunt of group pressure to cut back to the acceptable level of output.

Although there's been no reported evidence of this, it's reasonable to assume that one reason telecommuters produce more is that they're free from similar pressures that exist in the office. Telecommuting allows them to work up to the level they'd like to in the office—but don't for fear of being ridiculed or ostracized.

6. *Less Incidental Absence.* When most people think of absenteeism they tend to think of health problems serious enough to confine someone to bed, or other legitimate reasons for missing work. You also know that there are other kinds of absenteeism, ranging from the proverbial mental health day ("If I don't get away from this office for a day, I'll go crazy!") to doctor visits to waiting around for a delivery.

If people are sick, they should be at home and at rest so they can get better. But an interesting poll in the *Detroit News** a few years ago confirms what you may have suspected: there are lots of borderline reasons why people stay home. People in 500 homes were asked if it was okay to stay home for the following reasons; the percentages are the number that agreed:

Fever	60%
Sprained ankle	59%
Arthritis	28%
Stomach ache	18%
Visible bruises	12%
Sunburn	11%
Lack of sleep	9%
Hangover	8%
Headache	7%
"Blah" feeling	7%
Runny nose	3%

Some of these certainly are legitimate excuses for being home and others are questionable. Add to this list the kinds of necessary chores like doctor visits, deliveries, or home or car repairs and you can see that people often miss part or full days of work for a range of reasons.

---

*Reprinted by permission of *The Detroit News*, a division of Evening News Association, copyright 1985.

The advantage of telecommuting is that the whole work day isn't lost for problems that take one or two hours to resolve. Remote workers can often salvage a big chunk of the work day since they don't have to invest the round-trip commuting time for a few hours of work. This in itself isn't enough of a reason to begin telecommuting, but it's one of the hidden benefits and it's part of the productivity issue.

7. *Use of More Productive Tools.* Finally, there is the gain that comes from using work "tools" that have built-in productivity increases. The best example here is electronic mail, a system for sending messages, memos, and reports among workers having access to a mail system and suitable terminals or PCs. Once the users get accustomed to the system, they find they can shortcut the normal work cycle of passing assignments and drafts to and from a secretary, since they do their own typing and editing. They are also free from the tyranny of schedules—theirs and others'—for getting information and exchanging messages.

If telecommuters use electronic mail and become more efficient, you

---

PRODUCTIVITY CHECKLIST

✔ Is your organization under pressure to increase office worker productivity?

✔ Are you concerned about the amount of nonproductive time and distractions in the office?

✔ Do your people do the kind of work that benefits from longer periods of concentration with few distractions?

✔ Are your work schedules at the mercy of mass transit or highway congestion?

✔ If any of your jobs rely on timesharing access to a mainframe, is first-shift usage much heavier than off-shifts?

✔ Do you get the feeling that some of your employees would work harder and better if they weren't concerned about how it would look to their peers?

Telecommuting could be the key to productivity gains if you answered "yes" to several of these questions.

can't really say it's the telecommuting that leads to the gains. But if these same workers hadn't been using this tool in the office, then telecommuting is at least the catalyst that helps your organization derive the benefits.

As you've seen, there are four big reasons why you should seriously investigate telecommuting: improved recruiting, improved retention, office space cost control, and increased productivity. It's much more than a fad or an interesting innovation; it's a practical business tool with bottom-line impact for your organization.

3

Practical Ways to Mix and Match Work Locations

The popular image of telecommuting is that it means work *at home.* So far, this book has focused on this definition and little has been said about other remote work locations. Although the vast majority of telecommuters today do in fact work at home, there's a range of other alternatives available. Saying that telecommuting means working only at home is like saying that cars can only be used for trips to the grocery store. Cars mean transportation and telecommuting means alternate work locations, of which the home is only one.

PROS AND CONS OF WORKING FROM HOME

It's not that there's anything wrong with working at home. People have done it for years, especially as entrepreneurs and small-business owners. But you should be thinking about the pros and cons of working at home, especially in terms of telecommuting and and not self-employment:

Advantages. Many of these have to do with the personal benefits of working where you live:

- You spend less for food because you eat at your kitchen table instead of a restaurant or cafeteria, and clothing costs are less because you need your work "uniform" less often—perhaps two days a week instead of five.

- You're spared the time, rigors, and costs of commuting five days a week. Unless you live close enough to walk to work, you probably won't miss the ordeal of rush-hour commuting.

- You have the opportunity for more and often better contact time with your spouse or family members. Instead of being like "ships passing in the night," you can enjoy something that more closely resembles normal family life.

- You have a chance to work more independently, away from direct supervision, away from the social hubbub of the office, and in surroundings that are likely to be more comfortable.

Disadvantages. These are also based on working and living under the same roof; commuting only as far as your den can be a mixed blessing:

- Because you're not in the office as often, you might be out of touch with what's going on—both the official news and the grapevine. As you'll see in Chapter 9, good implementation of telecommuting means careful planning to link the person to the office in many ways. But there still can be some residual loss of contact and a feeling of being on the fringes of activity.

- Social hubbub isn't all bad; annoying distractions and interruptions are problems, but there's such a thing as too much peace and quiet. This can be relieved by visits to the office, contact by phone and electronic mail, and joining the gang for lunch or a drink now and then—but it still can be a problem.

- More contact with the other people who live under the same roof can be a mixed blessing. Some couples or families look forward to the morning rush for the front door as everyone goes separate ways. People considering telecommuting from home need to give careful thought to relationships with the spouse if he/she will also be at home. If both partners are at home, one of three things will happen: good relationships will probably get better; weak ones will be tested, perhaps to the breaking point; and borderline ones will probably change for the better or worse. People who choose to be at home with a young child (under the conditions described in Chapter 2) may face even more challenges.

- Being away from close contact with your supervisor is a good arrangement for someone whose work doesn't require close supervision and who enjoys being able to exercise more independent judgment. There may be limits to how well this works over the long run. Even though there will be continued periodic contact in person and by phone or electronic mail, it's not the same as being able to drop in for an impromptu chat.

These lists are just the employee's side of it—Chapter 2 has already covered the general benefits of telecommuting for the employer. Many of them have some downside risk as you'll see in Chapters 6 and 7. There's more known about remote work at home because that's where most remote work has taken place. But it would be a mistake to let that familiarity blind you to other remote work alternatives.

KEY ISSUES IN REMOTE SUPERVISION

The single biggest factor that separates home-based telecommuting from the other alternatives (at least as seen by many managers) is the possibility for on-site supervision in other remote locations. Home-based remote work means working alone; other sites will allow contact with other workers at minimum and on-site supervision in many cases. You might be drawn to these other alternatives because of concerns about what will happen if telecommuters work without supervision. "How can I tell if someone is working—how am I going to make sure I get a fair day's work out of them?" you might ask.

While this is an understandable reaction—and one that some observers feel accounts for the relatively slow spread of telecommuting to date—it's not necessarily valid. Consider these points:

1. *It's Not New.* We have lots of experience with remote work and remote supervision already. Virtually every employer has some portion of the work force that works with little direct supervision—sales and service representatives, delivery people, and meter readers, to name a few examples. These workers see their supervisors anywhere from once a day to once every few weeks, yet they manage to work effectively and to the satisfaction of their employers.

2. *The Skills Can Be Taught.* Drawing on the experiences of these "old" remote workers and adding some sound management theory, it's possible to *teach* managers to supervise from a distance. Chapter 7 will

cover this in detail; for now let's just say that managing by remote control isn't impossible at all. It does require somewhat different approaches for the managers who are used to *monitoring activity* instead of *planning for and measuring results.* More on this in Chapter 7.

3. *Not a Simple Choice.* There's more to the decision about which remote work site to choose than just the question of ease of supervision. Some of the cost savings and staffing advantages that go with work at home may shrink or even disappear at other sites. This doesn't mean you should always choose the home for your remote site; it means that a number of factors must be considered and weighed.

REMOTE WORK ALTERNATIVES

With this in mind, let's take a look at some of the other alternatives. Much of the theoretical work on these and other alternatives comes from Jack Nilles at the University of Southern California and Richard Harkness's work done when he was at Stanford Research Institute and Satellite Business Systems. Nilles led a study team that produced a landmark report in 1976 called *The Telecommunications/Transportation Tradeoff: Options for Tomorrow*, and coined the term "telecommuting" as a shorthand version of the report title.

The use of alternate work sites is part of the process by which organizations grow. More growth means more people, more markets served, and more diverse operations; it becomes harder and harder to do everything from one central location. The growth can take the form of decentralization—the formation of branch offices or plants across the country, for example. These branches can either be single-purpose (such as a sales office or a manufacturing plant), full divisions with several functions, or smaller-scale versions of corporate headquarters with a full range of functions.

There are pros and cons for all these—control over large distances is a problem, employees might not be willing to relocate, and cost of doing business may escalate. But this kind of decentralization has been with us for a while and will continue; it's rare to find any major firm operating just at one location today.

A Remote-Site Case Study

Here's a case study to help you see how this "geography of office development" (as Richard Harkness calls it) affects your use of telecommuting. It's set in the limited scope of a single city (New York) and shows how a hypo-thetical firm (Amalgamated Computer Supplies) might decentralize its workplace.

First, some background information:

1. Let's assume there's a single midtown corporate headquarters that houses all the individual functional departments themselves, or at least the management groups responsible for them. Roughly, 150 employees work here in functions such as marketing, sales, accounting, person-nel, operations management, and new product development.

2. Amalgamated set up a 200-employee production plant for printer ribbons and diskettes in a northern New Jersey community. There's also a warehouse for the full line of supplies (including the many items purchased from other manufacturers for resale) not far from the George Washington Bridge, also in northern New Jersey. Both facilities are less than five years old and both have some vacant space for possible expansion that is as yet unplanned.

3. Amalgamated set up 60 employees in a telephone order-taking center and telemarketing group to make calls to smaller accounts. These employees work in an office park in Nassau County on Long Island, about 45 to 60 minutes from the midtown Manhattan offices.

As you can see, this firm has already decentralized quite a bit. But the remote operations are single-function sites and employ only people who work in manufacturing or warehouse operations (New Jersey) and telephone sales and service (Nassau County). Let's add a twist to the scenario now and assume that Amalgamated's landlord in Manhattan has just informed company management that rent will rise $25 to $45 per square foot as of the lease renewal date nine months later. Assuming that the corporate offices include a total of 27,000 square feet (including the "incredible shrinking square foot" penalty noted in Chapter 2), the rent hike will cost the firm $540,000 per year. Top management says this is un-acceptable and begins to think about its alternatives.

What Can Be Done?

What can Amalgamated do? It has three choices:

1. *Stay in Town.* It can look for lower-cost space in Manhattan and move the entire office. This would keep costs down, but there's the dis-ruption and cost of the move to consider, and no guarantee that the same kind of rent increase wouldn't hit them in a new location.

2. *Move Out.* It can think about moving everyone out of Manhattan entirely, joining other firms that have gone to the greener pastures of the suburbs. This idea appeals to the top management group who, after all, would like to work closer to their homes in northern New Jersey. But there's the cost and disruption to consider again, let alone the probable loss of a third to a half of the office staff who live in Manhattan and wouldn't relocate or commute to the suburbs.

3. *Mix and Match.* Finally, Amalgamated can consider a different way to decentralize. Amalgamated tries to be a good model for the industry it services and has computerized most of its day-to-day operations. Not only are the customer service and telephone sales people working on terminals directly linked to the mainframe computer, but most of the professionals at headquarters rely heavily on PCs or terminals to support their work. All routine accounting functions are on the system, sales and marketing managers track results and do forecasts on their PCs, and even the Personnel Department has a sophisticated human resource information system for all employee files and records.

This gives Amalgamated the opportunity to shift some of the work around to its other locations and at the same time keep its current headquarters. The top executives decide to keep the midtown headquarters because they want to present a stable image to customers and don't see much sense in going through the aggravation and cost of moving ten blocks. But they decide to slash their space needs by two thirds, keeping only certain people in the existing office.

The Plan

All other employees will move to one of these locations:

1. Some of the staff involved in production management and inventory control will move into extra space at the plant or the warehouse in New Jersey. It makes sense for them to be there and many of them live in the northern New Jersey suburbs anyhow.

2. Others will take over a suite of offices two floors below the telephone staff in the office park building in Nassau County. Some of these transferees are accountants, some are in sales promotion, and others are in various staff functions.

3. Others will work at home in Manhattan, New Jersey, Long Island, and Westchester County (New York) for three or four days a week. These include more of the staff group people as well as several of the sales managers.

4. Finally, a group of eight people will work at a "neighborhood work center" near Stamford, Connecticut. The number of elementary school-age children in that area has been dropping and is projected to stay low for the next ten years. A building-management firm recently converted an unused elementary school into an office building; each classroom became an office able to hold six to ten people, and the cafeteria has been converted to a pleasant dining room. One classroom was reserved for a day care center for children of the office workers. The gym was divided into three conference rooms on one side, and the other half was turned into an exercise center.

This arrangement is ideal for some Amalgamated employees who live around Stamford and can drive to the "school" in 15 minutes or less, instead of commuting via train and subway of over an hour. The rent is $22 per square foot and the building manager includes sophisticated voice and data transmission capabilities in each classroom. Amalgamated only needs to move some terminals from its existing office space to classroom 3A—Amalgamated's new Connecticut office.

Can It Work?

Is this scenario a fantasy? Not really, although there's been no discussion of the logistics of making all these moves, the costs of furnishing the vacant space in the warehouse and factory in New Jersey, and the need to sort out which employees end up where. These aren't minor details, and the feasibility of the whole relocation would depend in part on the costs and on employee reactions.

The purpose of this case study is to show you how to expand your thinking about work locations by blending available space and traditional uses with new concepts about office space and decentralized work. The notion of a dispersed work force isn't new; as noted earlier, companies have had branch offices for years.

What *is* new is the interchangeability of these various workplaces. Instead of having only salespeople in a branch sales office, for example, you might have multifunction branch offices with several departments. In its most well-developed form, decentralization might include a network of full-function satellite offices in a ring around a central location. These would be supplemented by a number of the neighborhood work centers that would house several employers *and* a number of functions for each employer. The final piece is the home as the ultimate decentralized work site.

The essential ingredients in Amalgamated's case are the well-established information systems that allow these jobs to be moved from location to location. The better-developed these systems and the telecommunications network are, the more location-independent the work becomes. The underlying assumption in considering the full range of remote work locations is that the work will follow the workers wherever they go. Few companies have automated their operations to this extent yet, and even the leaders are sometimes hampered by gaps in communications technology and/or excessive cost of some of the solutions at this time.

MULTI-LOCATION CHECKLIST (PART I)

✔ Is the geography of your organization like Amalgamated's, with a midtown central office and several suburban or rural sites?

✔ Are you facing a "trigger point" in office space as Amalgamated was, such as a lease renewal, a major tax increase, or a transportation change, thus making it harder for your people to get to work?

✔ Are your information systems well-developed enough to allow some degree of "portability" of work across different locations?

✔ If you have other locations within a comfortable radius of your central office, do any of these have extra space available?

Your operation could be suited for multilocation telecommuting if you answered "yes" to at least one of these questions.

MOVING AMONG VARIOUS LOCATIONS

Let's take this multilocation scenario one step further. In the Amalgamated example, you read about a fairly stable situation where employees worked at their assigned work locations almost all the time. The people in the Nassau County office park went there five days a week as did the people in Manhattan, northern New Jersey, Stamford, and at home. Except for occasional visits to the midtown office or other offices, the work force was assumed to be based in one place.

The next stage in decentralizing work is to make this scenario more dynamic. If the technology truly can allow the work to be wherever the worker is, why not also assume that the employees can circulate *among* a range of work sites and work equally well at each? This is the most advanced stage, since it requires a full network of office locations, each equipped with full-featured hardware and communications capabilities.

Implementing the at-home form of telecommuting includes the need for periodic visits to the office, but these are generally to do things that can't be done at home, for example, looking at a production machine in operation. But there's technology that may make some of these trips unnecessary. (Remember, though, that even if office visits aren't needed because technology will let you deliver more to the home, you'll still need to bring telecommuters into the office for the social and other reasons spelled out in Chapter 9.)

Available Technology

Here's a sample of current and developing technology that lets you make further substitutions of telecommunications for travel:

1. *Teleconferencing.* The cost of teleconferencing is dropping and users are becoming more sophisticated about its use. Meetings across several locations with high-quality video will soon become cost-effective, and today there's a range of proven technology available for audio teleconferencing and computer conferencing.

2. *Visual Images.* Transmission of visual images (as opposed to straight text or voice) is here today, but at fairly high cost. The technology for capturing an image (such as a drawing, a form, a signature, or a photo) and storing that image is available, but out of the reach of some users. However, an older technology—facsimile machines, or telecopiers—is dropping in price and can be an effective interim step.

3. *Data Transmission.* Technological developments and increased post-AT&T divestiture competition are making it cheaper to transmit more data at higher quality and faster speeds. This means that your telecommuting applications requiring fast access to large central files and high-volume data transmission will become much more feasible than they are today.

A More Dynamic Schedule

As the technology develops and remote work becomes more accepted, you may see a very dynamic work schedule for many workers. Instead of working *either* at home *or* in the office as you know it now, schedules may vary from week to week depending on personal preference, projects assigned, location of specific resources or people, and even the weather. A typical monthly schedule for a professional in the not-too-distant future might look like this:

> Week 1: 2 days at home, 1 day at headquarters, and 2 days at local neighborhood work center
>
> Week 2: 1 day at home, 4 days at headquarters
>
> Week 3: 2 days at satellite office (30 miles away), 2 days at headquarters, and 1 day at neighborhood work center in nearby suburb
>
> Week 4: 4 days at home and 1 day at local neighborhood work center

Making this kind of schedule work depends on three things:

- The *technology* to allow the work (or most of it) to follow the worker anywhere;
- A *scheduling system* to make optimal use of all available space without having severe overuse or underuse on any one day;
- *Management* that allows and is comfortable with these kinds of "itinerant" workers.

As noted earlier in the chapter, this kind of pattern isn't all that unusual for many of today's remote workers such as sales representatives. The difference is that widespread use of telecommuting will involve workers and functions that are traditionally based in a central office location. You're used to the idea of having a sales rep travel extensively and work from different locations, and you have the systems in place to support it. Things are different when you talk about accountants, programmers, or market researchers, for example.

The Case for On-Site Supervision

Note that in all forms of remote work, except work at home, it's possible to have on-site supervision. This may be an important consideration for certain tasks or situations. Here's a list of some of the cases where on-site supervision might be necessary, and thus you'd lean toward the use of these facilities:

1. *The Company Culture Puts High Value on Close Supervision and Knowledge of the Details of Your Subordinates' Work.* In this case, the idea of work at home would be hard to swallow and might be doomed to failure

even if a trial got underway. Right or wrong, some companies simply encourage this kind of detail-oriented management, and your choice of remote work sites would have to take that into account.

2. *The Nature of the Work Requires On-Site Supervision.* Some tasks have to be monitored closely no matter how competent the workers or how trusting the managers. Examples of this might be highly confidential work where company or external auditors won't allow unsupervised work, or new employees who need easy, frequent access to a supervisor with the expertise to answer questions or solve problems.

3. *The Employees Who Will Be Working Remotely Are New to the Company and/or Untrained.* As noted in Chapter 6, one of the criteria for at-home telecommuters is that their training and experience levels are high enough so they can effectively work on their own. But if you need to set up a satellite location or take space in a neighborhood work center and rely on a local work force that is unskilled or that hasn't worked for you, it makes sense to have a supervisor available. Once trained and acclimated, these people might "graduate" to telecommuting from home if they and the supervisor support it.

4. *There Is a Competitive or Business Advantage to Having People Work in Groups.* For example, there are tasks where workers must contribute to a group effort and simply can't do so efficiently or comfortably from individual homes. This might be true in creative work such as advertising design or in complex technical projects where close, frequent coordination is a must.

Another example is when there's a recruiting advantage to offer the facilities of a neighborhood work location. Just as at-home telecommuting appeals to people who want to enjoy the benefits of merging work and home life, others might prefer the convenience of the neighborhood center—especially if it includes a day-care facility. The employer who has this to offer stands out from other potential employers. It might help recruit people who otherwise can't or won't work at a traditional central office location.

Your decision about which kind(s) of remote work locations to use depends on these factors plus the business problem to be solved. In Amalgamated's case, it was the need to avoid the costs of the rent increase; your organization might be driven by recruiting needs or space shortages at the existing location, for example. Decentralization and telecommuting aren't always the best answer; they're useful alternatives to consider for certain business needs.

MULTILOCATION CHECKLIST (PART II)

✔ Have you used audio or video teleconferencing successfully, or is your work suited to its use?

✔ Are graphic or nontext images a small part of your work, so that restrictions on image transmission wouldn't be a problem?

✔ Is on-site supervision a must or a strong want for your work?

Look into multilocation telecommuting (more so than just in-home remote work) if you answered "yes" to one or more of these questions.

NEW OFFICE SPACE CHOICES

The use of multiple office locations depends in part on the availability of some of these newer forms of office space. The neighborhood work center as described in the Amalgamated case is a blend of several existing office space concepts. But there are six other building concepts that illustrate the range of possibilities for new approaches to office and/or residential space:

1. *Teleports.* These are being built or are planned in New York City, San Antonio, Chicago, San Francisco, and Los Angeles. They're best described as giant switchboards through which voice, data, facsimile, and video signals can be sent and received over satellite circuits. They generally include a group of satellite dish antennas and a network of fiber-optic or other cables to spread the signals to local users who may be nearby or at some distance away. Some are built or planned to include office parks nearby for large-volume users. Depending on how close they are to residential areas (or if housing is also included in the planning) these could serve as remote locations for firms heavily dependent on communications.

2. *Mixed-Use Buildings.* In the past, it was common to see walk-up apartments over retail shops at ground level, but today there's usually a clear separation between commercial and residential space. There are some current examples of buildings that might bridge the two uses and be ideal for remote work. Perhaps the best known is the John Hancock building in Chicago; the bottom portion is office and retail space and the top is

residential. In a building like this, employees could work at home, go down a few floors to a satellite office, and also travel to a central work location elsewhere in the city.

3. *Multitenant Shared Services Buildings.* A current trend in building management is to pool the needs of various tenants and offer building-wide systems for data and word processing and telecommunications. The advantage is that smaller tenants get services that normally would be available only to larger users, and the burden and cost of establishing and maintaining these systems is handled by an outside firm. If you wanted to take space in one of these buildings and use it as a satellite office, you'd have all the electronic comforts of the central location at a reasonable cost.

4. *Shared-Service Buildings.* These differ slightly from the above approaches since they're usually smaller facilities and the building manager provides the administrative services that small tenants can't economically supply on their own. These include receptionist and typing services, facsimile and copying equipment, conference rooms, and janitorial service. These are aimed at small businesses that need (but can't afford) the trappings of larger firms, or at self-employed people who only occasionally need office and meeting space or secretarial service. These might be ideal for smaller numbers of remote workers, where you don't need to lease larger space. This kind of office might be a halfway house between the home and a satellite office, providing support services for telecommuters on an as-needed basis.

5. *Planned Communities.* Some developers take a very broad approach to planning and building commercial areas. In the 1960s and 1970s there was a trend toward the "new towns," entire communities built from the ground up to include housing, office, and commercial space. Two of the best-known were Reston, Virginia and Columbia, Maryland; both are doing well today but there are few new entries in this category. An interesting twist on the idea comes from The Rouse Corporation, developers of Columbia. Rouse built a large complex in southern New Jersey named Echelon, including a large Echelon Mall for shopping, and office and residential areas nearby.

The Echelon Mall includes a day-care center for children of employees of stores in the mall and, if space is available, for other local residents. Nobody is calling this complex a "neighborhood work center," but it functions as such. Within the same complex are housing, shopping, and office space, though all the office workers don't necessarily live in the housing there. This is a good prototype for nearby facilities that cut down on commuting time and costs and help build a sense of community among residents and employees.

6. *Renovated Shopping Malls.* There's a small but growing trend of "adaptive reuse" of shopping malls that were the first generation of shopping centers. These older malls have become less popular because they pale by comparison against newer, larger malls, or because new housing growth has shifted potential customers away. By taking over these old malls, companies get quick access to a lot of space with utilities built in and ample parking—a combination that's hard to find in many popular suburban areas today. To make matters better, the malls often rent for relatively low cost and, even with renovations, are still cheaper than new space.

For example, Hewlett-Packard renovated the Mayfield Mall in Mountain View, California, and is moving 600 employees into space formerly occupied by about 40 stores. Tandy Corporation leases about 380,000 square feet at vacated grocery department stores throughout Texas and has converted them into light-manufacturing plants.

These conversions aren't without problems; there can be zoning restrictions, and the cost of renovation and maintenance for facilities in poor shape may be prohibitive over time. But they're perfectly situated as neighborhood centers and could easily be one of the many remote work sites you use in and around suburban areas.

SUMMARY: MAKING YOUR CHOICES

As you can see, there's a full range of work locations available beyond those you're used to seeing. Work at home is only one of those, though it will probably continue to be the most prominent in the short term. The others will be developed as managers, architects, and space planners continue to expand their thinking about what's available, and as the technology develops, so that more and more jobs become truly portable across a wide range of locations.

There's more to selecting alternate work locations than thinking about office space and floor plans. It requires some vision about what's possible, and an ability to break away from the idea that work is defined only as something done in a high-rise office building from 8:30 A.M. to 5 P.M. (You'll learn about a fresh look at office work in Chapter 14 when you read about the "virtual office.")

How to
Get Started:
Six Key Steps
for Implementation

4

Now that you've learned about the background and benefits of telecommuting and seen the range of possibilities for remote work, it's time to move on to actual implementation. As you've gathered by now, there's more to it than simply sending your employees home with a PC or terminal and telling them to plug it in and go to work.

THE FATE OF INNOVATIONS IN LARGE ORGANIZATIONS

Before covering the actual implementation step, let's step back from the details of telecommuting and review what's known about the spread of innovations and new ideas in organizations. No matter how much a CEO says to the contrary, most big firms simply are not that responsive to innovation or quick to change established procedures. Bureaucracies develop a life of their own, it seems, and sometimes manage to squash all but the most persistent innovators. Large companies can be like supertankers that need two or three miles of open space to prepare for and execute a change in direction.

Professor Gerald Gordon of the Center for Technology and Policy at Boston University has done extensive research on the ways in which various organizations adopt innovations like telecommuting. Professor Gordon notes that there are two major factors that affect how likely a company is to adopt a new concept. You must ask the following questions:

- "Will the innovations you hope to accomplish be viewed as desirable by many key people in the organization? If you're trying to convince top management that telecommuting will save space but corporate headquarters is only 80 percent occupied, you may have a tough sell on your hands.

- "Are you willing—and able—to measure the supposed benefits and changes, and are you willing to reward those who adopt the innovation and thus help the organization cut costs or improve service and productivity?" If you can't measure something, you can't count it; and if you can't count it, you can't tell how much it has improved. If you can't show improvement, you can't equitably reward those who took the risk to generate the improvement—and you therefore lose the opportunity to reinforce innovation and risk-taking.

Rewards and Breathing Room for Innovations

When there's no link between innovations and reward, says Professor Gordon, there's no payoff for taking the risk. He says this problem is often compounded because companies forget that managers involved in innovation need some leeway. "There are often problems and even short-term losses that occur when you try something new. The company says (or implies), 'Yes, we want to try something new—and by the way, be sure to keep your costs under control, don't increase turnover, etc.' What they give with the one hand they take away with the other. If the firm really wants to spur risk-taking and new ideas, it must provide some kind of cushion or margin for error so the managers really feel they can afford to take a chance."

Don't get the idea that telecommuting is of necessity a very risky proposition. It *is* new and different, however, and that in itself makes it a little risky. Remember that telecommuting (at least on the surface) flies in the face of our sacred tradition of going *to* work. That's a phrase that's more than just part of the language; it's shorthand for a whole economic system and a series of activities that are well established.

GETTING OFF TO A GOOD START

Keep these five points in mind while getting telecommuting off the ground:

1. *Try to Arrange Some Leeway for Those Involved in the Pilot.* The productivity gains won't necessarily come at once and, in fact, output

may drop a bit initially while the project is getting underway. If managers are expected to meet all of the same business targets while implementing a pilot program, they might be under more pressure than can be tolerated.

2. *Pick a Reasonable Target and Stick with It.* If cost or availability of office space is a hot button, shape a pilot program around that. If you can't recruit enough programmers without it costing an arm and a leg, build a program with recruiting benefits as the focus. While telecommuting can be many things to many organizations, it's best to focus on only one or two key benefits to your firm. By choosing an objective tied to a problem that everyone can understand, you'll increase the chance of success because you're more likely to be surrounded by supporters, not skeptics.

3. *Start Small with a Controlled Pilot.* When companies started to use PCs, their first orders weren't for 500 machines. Most firms ordered only a few, tried them for a while, then ordered some more, and eventually worked up to larger numbers. This makes sense for telecommuting also; your first goal should be to demonstrate the feasibility of the concept. You can always expand the program later when things go well, but it's harder to collapse a big program if it runs into problems. Some excellent pilots begin with only two or three people; others include up to twenty.

4. *Make an Early Decision About How to Publicize a Pilot and Stick with It.* There's no sense in drawing extra attention to a program in its early stages. If things don't work out you may not want a big audience; also, it can be annoying, confusing, or downright troublesome to have "sidewalk superintendents" poking around, wanting to know what's happening and offering advice. You don't have to treat telecommuting pilots like state secrets, but you may not want to advertise them with flashing lights either.

This extends to how you describe the pilot; many firms choose to say (to employees involved and others):

- It is an experiment, not a permanent program yet;
- It may or may not be extended or repeated in the future;
- It is planned to last for a certain period but can be ended sooner at management's discretion;
- It is voluntary, not mandatory;
- It is a new concept that has potential advantages and disadvantages for employee and employer.

This approach makes it less likely that lots of employees will rush in to ask when they can start working at home. It also gives you an "out" later on if things don't go as planned. Even though there's every reason to believe a pilot will work out, it makes sense to leave room for a graceful withdrawal.

5. *Pay Attention to Details.* The six steps that follow in the next section (and are explained in detail in Chapters 5 through 10) are designed to help cover the contingencies and are based on the experiences of many companies. Some extra time up front to work out the details and build in elements to help insure success will pay off in the end.

TELECOMMUTING PREPLANNING CHECKLIST

✔ Arrange for some leeway for those involved.
✔ Pick a reasonable target and stick with it.
✔ Start small with a controlled pilot.
✔ Make an early decision about how to publicize the pilot.
✔ Pay attention to the details.

Keep these points in mind as general principles before you move into the detailed planning—they set the tone for further planning and implementation.

INVOLVING THE RIGHT PEOPLE IN THE PLANNING

Before describing *what* to do in the planning, let's look at *who* should be involved with you. Telecommuting isn't in the domain of only one group; some early telecommuting pilots stumbled because there was too much attention to the technical details and not enough to the supervisory issues, for example. If your organization works with task forces, project teams, or study groups, you might want to convene a group with representatives from the following areas. If task forces and committees are frowned on where you work, make sure that you at least contact and draw on these four groups, even if it has to be done informally:

1. *Human Resources.* Specialties might include recruiting, compensation and benefits, employee relations, and training and development. All these people don't have to be involved; it depends on the nature of the pilot and the scope of existing personnel policies. Don't underestimate the

value of the contributions from some of these disciplines, since as you'll see in Chapter 11, many of the potential problems are linked to these areas.

2. *Data Processing.* Every firm organizes this function differently; the expertise you need may come from the systems and programming staff, telecommunications, systems engineering, database management, or other units. This group's involvement will depend mostly on whether PCs or terminals play a role in your program. There are some excellent telecommuting programs involving nothing more high-tech than a telephone plus paper and pencil.

3. *Line Management.* This is the "client" of the pilot program; it may be yourself, your staff, other managers, or one of the two groups listed above. It's critical to have early involvement from the group with the business need so you're doing something *with* them, not *to* them.

4. *Other Advisors or Supporters.* Once you've chosen the right people, you and they should think about how to "sell" the pilot. If you've gotten to the point of setting up a task force, you've convinced your boss that it's at least worth investigating. Or, you're at a level where you can do something like this without having to worry about convincing your boss—yet. In either case, you'll want to make some other groups aware of the plan and get their opinions, agreement, or support. These might include the following:

- Your legal advisors, since there may be questions of insurance and liability.
- Your accounting or financial people, to give you ideas on how to budget for the pilot.
- Your boss *and* his/her boss, to familiarize them with what's going on and to find out how strongly they'll be supporting you as you move ahead.
- Your most savvy and trusted coworker, who can give you a sense of how to construct a pilot to maximize the chance for success and fit it to the organization's culture.
- Your most respected "elder" in the firm, to find out whether anything like this was tried before and what the results were. The idea of people working at home has gotten more attention recently because of technological changes and other reasons, but it's definitely not a new idea. Wouldn't it be nice to know if someone tried it years ago and almost lost his/her job (or almost got a big promotion) because of it? Conditions and people change, but it's always good to know the history.

PILOT PROGRAM PLANNING TEAM CHECKLIST

Be sure to involve or at least contact these groups or individuals as you begin your detailed planning:

✔ Human resources (may include several areas)

✔ Data processing

✔ Line management of affected department(s)

✔ Legal and financial advisors

✔ Your boss and his/her boss

✔ A trusted coworker

✔ A respected "elder" of the organization

THE KEY STEPS: A PREVIEW

These tips about getting started should help you get off on the right foot. The first mission of the task force (or whatever planning vehicle you use) is to learn enough about the concept to determine if a pilot program makes sense and is cost-effective. Here's a quick preview of the six key steps for actual implementation that you'll need to consider during this planning stage:

1. *Select the Jobs (Chapter 5).* You might be tempted to choose your telecommuters from the two job categories that account for most of the trials to date—programmers and word processing operators, or jobs closely related to those two. This may artificially limit the pilot to two job categories that for a number of reasons might not be suitable in your organization.

As an alternative, the selection should be made by comparing the range of jobs in your firm with a checklist of those characteristics of jobs that make them suited to remote work. This expands the possibilities and lets you focus on the areas with the biggest payoff.

2. *Select the People (Chapter 6).* Telecommuters should be chosen, not volunteered, into a pilot. They must be willing to be involved and not coerced or forced, but mere willingness isn't enough. You have the same responsibility for selection here as in any other job placement decision. The selection should be based on information about the nature and qual-

ity of the person's work and the person's makeup—how well can he/she work in the unique conditions of remote, loosely supervised work?

3. *Train the Manager (Chapter 7)*. The goal here is to teach managers to manage from a distance and to help them answer the question "How can I manage someone I don't see?" The training will draw the distinction between close supervision and good supervision. It also refines basic managerial techniques that sometimes are optional in the office, but become essential for managing remote work.

It's encouraging that managers of remote workers almost always report that managing from a distance makes them better managers of their office-based employees as well. That's an example of some of the broader payoffs of telecommuting.

4. *Train the Telecommuters (Chapter 8)*. Most office-based employees don't realize how much they rely on the formal and informal cues in the office for help in scheduling and organizing their day. The training and orientation for telecommuters is designed to refine their time management and organization skills and adapt them to use off-site. Also, they need to learn how to be taken seriously at home by family, friends, and neighbors. Those people aren't used to seeing the telecommuter working at home and can interfere with a productive work schedule if not managed properly. Finally, telecommuters need to learn how to manage their jobs from a distance and maintain good relationships with their boss and coworkers, and to prevent the possible career impacts of being "out of sight, out of mind."

5. *Link the Telecommuter to the Office (Chapter 9)*. This is probably the most challenging part of telecommuting: How do you make sure that the remote worker doesn't feel cut off from the office? Key steps here include assuring proper flow of information and materials to the office and back, finding the right schedule for time in the office, and keeping the person linked into the formal and informal happenings in the office. If remote workers are isolated or even *feel* isolated, their performance will suffer.

6. *Take Care of Technical Details (Chapter 10)*. Last but certainly not least, arrangements must be made for any PCs, terminals, phones, phone lines, and other equipment and services needed at the remote site. This also includes plans for the logistics of ongoing support—equipment supplies and repairs, for example.

This step doesn't necessarily occur last, and in fact, will be one of your early agenda items because of lead times needed for ordering equipment or phone lines. But compared with the other five items it's generally a more predictable and manageable step and thus shows up last on the list.

CHECKLIST OF SIX KEY PLANNING STEPS

✔ Select the jobs (Chapter 5).

✔ Select the people (Chapter 6).

✔ Train the manager (Chapter 7).

✔ Train the telecommuters (Chapter 8).

✔ Link the telecommuters to the office (Chapter 9).

✔ Take care of technical details (Chapter 10).

Be prepared to handle all six steps—all are important for successful implementation.

That's a quick overview of the actual planning tasks. After they're covered in detail in the next six chapters, you'll go on to some additional planning concerns.

5 How to Select the Suitable Jobs

Selecting the jobs suited for telecommuting is like walking into an ice cream store that specializes in dozens of flavors. Even though everyone sees Chocolate Banana Spice and Triple Fudge Ripple on the board, most people order vanilla or chocolate. If you're thinking about setting up a telecommuting program, you owe it to yourself to read the full menu of choices—and don't hesitate to sample something that sounds out of the ordinary.

KEYBOARD JOBS AND BEYOND

Telecommuting is a victim of its own success. If you ask a hundred managers about the jobs suited to telecommuting, don't be surprised if most of them tell you that "it's for programming and word processing." A conservative estimate of past and current telecommuting applications would put at least two-thirds of the remote workers in those two job categories or closely related ones like data entry or systems engineering.

The Recruiting Advantage for Programmers

Why is this so? Is it because those jobs are keyboard-based and telecommuting means working at a keyboard? Absolutely not. The main reason why programmers account for so many telecommuters is simple: programmers have been in short supply in many locations for almost ten years, and longer in certain metropolitan areas. Employers adopted telecommuting because it was one of their last resorts in trying to attract trained programmers. They had tried methods like

- *Personnel agencies* that charged $5,000 to $10,000 placement fees per hire depending on experience;
- *Paid employee referrals*, or so-called "bounty" systems where employees who referred applicants got paid $500 to $2,000 when the person was hired and survived;
- *All kinds of gimmicks* to lure applicants directly to open houses and job fairs; drawings for everything from free computers to free cruise trips were among the enticements.

Telecommuting became the logical way to attract people to jobs that were usually very much like those offered by other local employers. The unstated but implicit strategy boiled down to this: "If we can't convince you that we're a better place to work and that we have the most advanced equipment and best training, we'll let you work at home most of the week." The opportunity to telecommute didn't—and shouldn't—make up for a dull job or poor working conditions, but it was a good way to appeal to certain people who found the prospects of working at home attractive.

Coping with Shortages

There's nothing wrong with this and you shouldn't get the idea that this is a *bad* reason to move ahead with telecommuting. It's important to understand that it was a happy accident that programmers' jobs were suited to work at home for other reasons. If the shortages had been for accountants or statisticians, it's reasonable to assume that those people would have been home working in *their* blue jeans instead.

Before leaving the programmers, don't assume that the employment problem has gone away. There may be good reason to continue to include programmers in your telecommuting plans if you believe some data from the National Science Foundation (NSF). According to a 1984 study titled "Projected Response of the Science, Engineering, and Technical Labor Market to Defense and Nondefense Needs," there could be a shortage of programmers and systems analysts in 1987 of between 115,000 and 140,000 people. These numbers are spread across all employers, all industries, and all locations, so they may or may not reflect your firm's situation. NSF noted that in other cases of labor shortages the labor market tends to correct itself by signaling people in other jobs to shift to the high-demand areas. This method can't be relied on for programmers and analysts because of the need for specific technical training.

Other Keyboard Jobs

So much for the programmers—what accounts for the numbers of clerical, word processing, and data entry workers in the telecommuters' ranks?

- Those jobs fit the profile of "portable" jobs quite well.
- There have been spot shortages of trained clerical workers recently, though not to the extent of the programmer shortage.
- Clerical work lends itself to part-time work and/or pay based on actual output. (You'll learn about the pros and cons of these arrangements in Chapters 11 and 12.)
- The vast majority of clerical workers are women, and women continue to be the primary caretakers of young children at home. Telecommuting lets them be at home and still be employed, at least part-time.
- Clerical work on a "value-per-square-foot-used" basis ranks low down on the list of office occupations. This doesn't mean the work or the workers aren't valuable. It means that a firm with a space squeeze will opt to move clerical work out via telecommuting first because of the perceived need for easy access to coworkers for most professional-level jobs. If space is tight, goes the argument, let's conserve it for the people who really have to work closely with each other.

These five points don't apply universally, but do account for most of the clerical-level telecommuting. As with programmers, this doesn't mean that your firm should automatically assume that clerical work is the best kind to move to a remote site.

REMINDERS ABOUT SELECTING KEYBOARD-BASED JOBS

1. Don't pick these jobs just because other companies have or because it seems "logical."
2. Use telecommuting to help cope with short supplies of qualified job applicants for these jobs.
3. Remember the potential benefits of selecting clerical jobs for your pilot.

What's the best way to select jobs for telecommuting? There are three basic guidelines plus a fourth, in case the first three aren't sufficient —or, if you're more adventurous. All four assume you have total flexibility in choosing jobs, i.e., no one has told you that your choice is limited to only certain people or departments. If that's the case, you still should follow these guidelines because the process will help you find out if those pre-selections make sense, and perhaps help you develop a sound counter-argument for choosing other jobs.

SELECTION GUIDELINE 1:
FOLLOW A PROFILE

Instead of trying to isolate a particular job, stand back from all the jobs in your company and treat this as a shopping trip. What follows is a generic list of the characteristics that make jobs good prospects for telecom-muting. Once you understand this list (and add to it if necessary), you can go "shopping" through your firm to find those jobs that match the profile most closely. This is a more involved way of making the choice, but it's likely to open up more opportunities and will help you move beyond any-one's preconceived notions.

Here's your shopping list:

1. *Tasks That Are Easily Measured.* This relates directly to the super-visor's need to know when the remote worker is producing up to stan-dard. A job that has countable (or at least observable) outputs and has discernible beginning and end points is a better bet than one with fuzzy edges and few clear "deliverables."

This does *not* mean that the job must be a unit-oriented one such as data entry work, with easy-to-count lines of input and number of key-strokes per hour. It can be a job like an *employment interviewer* (measured by the number of résumés screened or telephone interviews conducted); *financial analyst* (measured by the number of budgets prepared according to standard format by the agreed-on deadline), or *training course designer* (measured by the number of modules written according to course objec-tives by the agreed-on deadline).

Jobs with hard-to-measure outputs aren't always bad prospects for telecommuting, however. The manager and the telecommuter have to come to an understanding about what constitutes a good day's or week's work. If they can agree on that in a clear, no-quibbling statement, they're off and running. The point to remember is that the less measurable the job and its outputs, the more difficult it may be for the manager to feel comfortable supervising from a distance. If the manager isn't comfortable, you can bet that the employee will somehow feel the effects—more phone calls, more time in the office, and more direct supervision, all of which begin to defeat the purpose of telecommuting.

2. *Tasks That Require Relatively Little Unscheduled Face-to-Face Contact.* The key words are "unscheduled" and "face-to-face." If your office sometimes seems like Grand Central Station because of all the unexpected visitors you get who *must* see you, your job might not be good for telecommuting.

On the other hand, someone who has lots of contact with others on the phone or in scheduled meetings may be a good prospect. Telecommuting doesn't require purely solitary work—few people actually sit at their desks for hours on end anyhow. If much of the contact with others can be done via phone (or electronic mail), and if there are few if any crises where someone has to be seen "right now," most other contacts can occur in scheduled meetings on the days when the telecommuter is in the office.

It helps sometimes to analyze the nature of all those interruptions and crises that exist in a given job. Sometimes they're legitimate—such as in a production environment or other line operation where immediate action is needed, for example. But other times they are manufactured crises —because the person thrives on that kind of firing-line atmosphere, becuase the subordinates or coworkers have helped create it, or both. It's not a good idea to try to wean people away from a daily dose of crises by having them become telecommuters. It might be interesting to use the prospect of telecommuting to open up a discussion about the real cause of the chaos that exists.

3. *Tasks That Don't Require Frequent Access to Files, Equipment, or Supplies That Can't Easily or Economically Be Moved to the Remote Site.* Don't try to move a person who would need a small moving van to carry basic office supplies to the remote site. Some obvious examples are certain engineering jobs where frequent access to large drawings is needed or customer service jobs where row after row of file cabinets are consulted to handle customer inquiries.

Technology might come to the rescue of these jobs now or in the future. As more engineering work moves from drafting tables to PC-level computer systems that allow on-screen drawing and manipulations, some of those jobs will become portable. Similarly, more and more firms are storing customer records online so they're accessible via terminal, not filing cabinet. Departments using microfilm or microfiche for records storage can take advantage of small, portable low-cost microfilm/fiche readers at a remote site.

This is where you have to monitor the cost-effectiveness of telecommuting. While there might be a technical solution, its cost might wipe out any projected savings or other benefits. As the technology develops, more and more jobs will become portable, but in the short run, don't try to move the unmovable.

**SELECTION GUIDELINE 2:
TAKE ADVANTAGE OF JOB CYCLES**

A different angle on selecting jobs for telecommuting is to look for jobs that have peaks and valleys or other predictable cycles. The idea here is that *portions* of jobs might be suited for remote work, based either on calendar cycles or project stages.

Calendar Cycles

Looking first at the calendar cycles, most businesses have some kind of predictable pattern of work. Retailing tends to peak in the fourth quarter of the year, and companies with high volumes of transactions to process (such as policy renewals or claims) know from historical data which months are the heaviest. These can be "lose-lose" situations for employers: if you staff up for the peaks, you'll have idle workers at other times and may have to go through the disruption and cost of a hire/layoff/hire cycle. If you don't staff up, you'll almost certainly put an undue strain on the employees who are probably fully loaded even in the low cycles.

You might be able to smooth out these problems by using telecommuting selectively. There's no reason why some tasks couldn't be shifted to a remote site during the overflow periods only. Cost-effectiveness has to be considered here again; it doesn't make good business sense to equip a remote site and then have it lay idle when it's not needed. But if you could move a portion of the overload work out—even paper-and-pencil tasks—the core group of employees could concentrate on the work they're best suited (and equipped) to do.

Project-Stage Cycles

The other type of job cycle application is very different. If you look at certain staff professionals (such as market researchers, course designers, or project analysts), you'll see that their work varies based on the stage of a project. Let's use market research as an example:

- At the *beginning* of a project the researcher is in close contact with marketing people to define the nature of the research, review the design of the study, and fine-tune the approach.

- At the *end* of the project the researcher presents the results and consults with the marketing people to determine what will happen next.

- During the *middle* of the project the researcher does or supervises the actual data collection, analysis, and report-writing.

Why couldn't that middle portion be done from a remote location? The beginning and end almost always must be done wherever the marketing people are; in fact, one of the hallmarks of good market research people is that they're respected enough by the marketing folks to be included and consulted in the planning and follow-up stages. But that middle portion—including calls to suppliers of research information and the actual number-crunching and writing—is the kind of task perfectly suited to remote work.

If you've been following this example closely you might be thinking here that most market researchers don't just work on one project at a time, and there's no guarantee that the "middles" can all be scheduled to hit at the same time. The solution is that the market researcher might be on a more flexible form of telecommuting than many others. Instead of a fixed number of days off-site per week, he/she might range from a half-day one week to four days the next week. This means some juggling for everyone, but if it leads to faster or better reports because it provides blocks of uninterrupted time to work, it's worth it.

A more likely application is for a *group* of market researchers, course developers, or people in jobs that have these stages with different contact requirements. If you're managing a group of six people, you could stagger their time in the office. Or, you could redefine tasks so the people who worked remotely most of the time did most of the "middles" of the projects. More on this idea of redesigning tasks follows later in the chapter.

SELECTION GUIDELINE 3:
TAKE ADVANTAGE OF AVAILABLE TECHNOLOGY

So far you've learned about the use of PCs, terminals, and even portable microfiche readers as some of the tools useful in remote work. You've also seen that some applications don't require sophisticated hardware; telecommuting doesn't always mean sitting at a keyboard.

But there are some cases where an awareness of available technology might trigger some thinking about possible telecommuting applications. Here's a list of several items that might come in handy:

1. *Online Databases.* In Chapter 1 you read about the range of online databases available today. Some of the jobs that can be done remotely using these public or private electronic libraries include

- Literature search and retrieval—acting as a professional searcher for scientists, engineers, or others who need access to published literature as part of their jobs.

- Customer service—answering customer inquiries about billing or product features, or taking consumer questions and complaints. (See section below on telemarketing equipment.)

- Legal research—paralegals and attorneys can search through past court cases to prepare for litigation.

2. *Remote Typesetting.* There are several remote typesetting services that can accept text entered on a terminal or PC and transmitted via phone lines. These services will then prepare camera-ready typeset copy and mail it back. Firms with large-scale printing or publishing needs can have remote workers link up with these services. Also, there are some typesetting units on the market that are based on PCs with superior graphics capabilities. The PC actually does the formatting and typesetting, and the results are printed out on high-quality ink jet or laser printers.

3. *Equipment for the Disabled.* There's a growing array of special terminals or add-on equipment enabling handicapped people to use a full-featured keyboard. Also, units with Braille keyboards and Braille printers are available. While standard PCs or terminals can be used by handicapped telecommuters with physical mobility restrictions, these special units open up remote employment opportunities for those with other limitations.

4. *Telemarketing.* The technology for inbound telemarketing has improved, and some automatic call distributors (ACD's) on the market can direct incoming calls to remote sites in addition to people located at a central site. The applications here include telephone reservations, customer service, and consumer affairs.

There are many more examples of new hardware and software available to facilitate remote work, some of which is specific to one industry or occupation. This technology shouldn't be viewed as a "solution in search of a problem," and you shouldn't try to make use of every new offering on the market. But there are cases where technology can help bridge the gap between a job as it's done in the office and a telecommuter's job at a remote site.

SELECTION GUIDELINE 4:
REDESIGNING JOBS OR DEPARTMENTS

As promised, this is a very different approach from the other three. If no telecommuting job emerges "naturally" after you've followed the first three guidelines, you can step back and look for ways of rearranging jobs or sets of jobs to create an opportunity for telecommuting.

You might wonder why you should try to force a telecommuting application—why try to find a suitable job if none jumps out by itself? There are several reasons:

- You could have a real need to move some jobs out of the office because of space problems, and your preliminary planning didn't turn up any jobs that did well on the "shopping list" items;
- A key executive might be strongly in favor of telecommuting and want to see something get started, yet you just can't identify potential applications on your first pass through the organization;
- You might face a special circumstance involving an employee who needs to be able to work remotely (perhaps due to an illness or injury), but his/her job as done in the office isn't suited for telecommuting.

In these or similar cases you need to be a little creative in your search for telecommuting applications. Instead of looking for whole jobs that can be done remotely, look for *parts* of jobs that meet the profile. Sometimes, you can combine parts of two jobs into one telecommuting job. Other times you might have to do major surgery on several jobs—or even make some basic changes in how a department's work is done—to construct a good remote work situation.

Redistributing the Tasks

Think about a work unit composed of four professionals and two clerical or support workers—a section of an accounting department or a marketing support group, for example. Even though it's hard to admit it, you know that professionals don't always do professional-level work; they sometimes have clerical-level tasks as part of the job. This often happens because department tradition says that those professionals get saddled with some of those chores. This doesn't mean sitting down at a typewriter, but it can include tasks like doing routine, repetitive calculations, filling out lengthy forms, or making a series of phone calls that don't require the professionals' expertise.

This kind of work isn't only dull for the professional—it represents a waste of payroll dollars as well. It doesn't make good business sense for someone earning $40,000 a year to spend 15 percent to 25 percent of the time doing work better suited to someone earning $20,000 a year or less. It's impossible to cut out all of that lower-level work, but much of it can be transferred. Telecommuting can be the impetus to make the change.

In this example, one way to create a remote work job is to strip out as much of the clerical work from those professional jobs and bundle it into a new job. You'd like to juggle the clerical workers' tasks so that one did the work that must be done in the office, and the other (at a remote site) did the rest, plus this new work shifted from the professionals.

If the total clerical load now exceeds what two people can do, you might need to add some part-time help, ideally also at a remote site. This could mean a short-term loss because of the cost for that extra help. But don't forget about what you can gain from freeing that much time from the professionals—the value of having more of their time available should more than compensate for the extra payroll cost. This is the kind of calculation you have to make in the planning stage. Also, you could find that the need to move a person off-site outweighs the incremental salary cost; this too has to be weighed in the planning.

A Temporary Change in Duties

This first example deals with reassigning tasks *across* job categories; there's another approach that applies *within* job categories. This actually happened at a major pharmaceutical company where a Ph.D. had a seriously broken leg and would be out of work for four to five months while it healed. He was one of three Ph.D.s in a lab that also included several junior-level scientists. The Ph.D.s all divided their work almost evenly between experimental work on the bench and analysis and writing based on the results of that bench work.

When the scientist with the broken leg left, his manager was left with two unattractive choices: try to pile as much work as possible on the remaining scientists and try to stay close to schedule, or simply leave things alone and fall behind for the duration of the recovery period. Fortunately, a third option emerged that worked out well for everyone.

The work of the three Ph.D.s was reallocated so that the two remaining concentrated full-time on bench work, and their analysis and writing tasks were shifted to the person with the broken leg. The company in-stalled a terminal in his home so he could get access to the firm's com-puter center for the statistical analysis done via timesharing. His work schedule shifted to later in the day—he usually started work in mid-after-noon and continued on through late night or early morning. This was based on his personal preference, but also because he learned that the com-puter was less busy at those times. He could get faster turnaround time, which let him get the analytical work done sooner.

For the next few months this new pattern continued and the group's work stayed very close to schedule—much closer than if the scientist at home hadn't been working at all. Fortunately, this employee had the desire and was medically able to work this way at home, and his manager had the vision to make the best out of a bad situation. When the leg healed and the Ph.D. returned to the lab, everyone went back to the original job assignments.

This example shows two important features of telecommuting. First, with some creative and flexible thinking it's possible to set up a remote job even in an unlikely setting such as a research lab. Second, remote work doesn't have to be permanent; it was an excellent solution to this short-term problem, but there was no need to continue it. If you understand and take advantage of telecommuting's inherent flexibility, you can often identify opportunities that go far beyond what seems possible at first.

A Major Departmental Redesign

The final way to implement this "mix and match" approach to job design requires even more of a change. Here's how an entire function can be re-organized about the concept of telecommuting. This example focuses on the work in a typical employment function within a personnel depart-ment. Employment or hiring work has two main parts:

- Sourcing and Recruiting: in which applicants are sought out and go through some kind of initial screening;
- Interviewing and Selection: in which fewer applicants are carefully interviewed to identify the best candidate(s).

The normal procedure is for an employment recruiter to handle both phases, involving a mix of placing ads, reading résumés, doing tele-phone screening interviews, doing in-depth follow-up interviews, and working with the hiring manager to make the final selection. Telecom-muting opens up the possibility of this kind of division of labor:

- A "prerecruiter" at a remote site does the initial screening of applications or résumés and conducts short phone interviews with applicants to find those most qualified. This person might work part of the time in late afternoon or evening, since it's usually easier to discuss a new job with applicants when they're at home, not at work. This person would be in touch with the office via phone or electronic mail.

- The prequalified applicants' paperwork is then passed on to a recruiter in the office who does the actual face-to-face interviews and related follow-up work.

There are several potential benefits to this arrangement:

1. *Cost Savings.* As in the earlier example, it allows you to shift less demanding work to lower-paid staffers. The prerecruiting activities can often be done by someone with less experience than most professional recruiters have.

2. *Headcount Swaps.* Depending on the workload it might be possible to swap a prerecruiter for an interviewer. If four interviewers each spend 25 percent of the time on these prerecruiting activities, perhaps those portions could be pulled out for the telecommuting prerecruiter. All else being equal, the in-office workload would drop to the point where one interviewer might be idle.

3. *Faster Throughput.* The recruiting process can be sped up because the recruiters wouldn't need to use limited daytime hours for work that could be done remotely at night, or simultaneously during the day. This allows the time line from starting to look for applicants to making the hire to be collapsed, especially since all interviewers work on several jobs at once.

Let's add one more element to this example. There are several online databases available for applicants seeking jobs or companies seeking applicants. If the remote prerecruiter plugged into these, he/she might be able to turn up more applicants than from traditional sources alone and continue doing the initial screening work.

In this case you've seen how the nature of a unit's work can be transformed by using telecommuting. The payoffs—if all works out well—are lower salary costs, faster throughput, and one fewer office or cubicle required. This example is certainly a far cry from simply moving one person off-site while keeping his/her job (and those of coworkers) intact. This chapter has shown you that there's room for a creative approach to selecting remote work possibilities. The choices are almost limitless.

JOB SELECTION CHECKLIST

✔ Follow the profile of jobs suited for remote work.

✔ Take advantage of job cycles.

✔ Take advantage of available technology.

✔ Consider redesigning jobs or departments.

These are your four main methods for spotting the jobs that are prime prospects for your telecommuting pilot.

6

How to Select the People

This second step in your planning for telecommuting is related to, but not the same as, selecting the jobs. There might be times when choosing the job *is* choosing the person—there's only one person doing the job, for example. In most cases, a job category is identified and then you'll need to decide which of the people doing that job will become the remote workers. It's rare that you could—or would want to—have all members of a chosen job become telecommuters, especially at the pilot program stage.

PROS AND CONS OF VOLUNTEERS

Employees who get wind of a telecommuting pilot might be anxious to get involved, especially if they learn that their job category has been selected for a pilot. While this enthusiasm is encouraging, it can be a real problem if you rely on this factor alone to choose the pilot participants.

The basic premise of this chapter is that selecting people to become telecommuters is no different from any other selection decision you make. You don't allow employees to promote or transfer themselves into their next position *within* the office, and they shouldn't be able to do so for remote jobs either. The willingness to volunteer is a must—people shouldn't be *required* to telecommute. But it should be clear to the employees that they're volunteering to be *considered* for selection, not for the actual remote work situation itself.

Why the distinction? The main reason is that telecommuting has some very attractive features for the employee, as covered in Chapter 2. Most people latch onto those benefits and can even visualize themselves lounging around in the den while working in casual clothes, or simply contemplating and savoring the possibility of escaping rush-hour commuting. Even if you consider most of your employees to be rational, thoughtful people, the fact is it's easy for them to be lulled into thinking only about the good side of telecommuting and thus rush to volunteer for it.

What you'll be seeing in this chapter is a two-part approach to selection: first, a preview process to give prospective telecommuters a glimpse at both good and bad aspects of working at home, and second, a series of steps you can take to identify the best candidates. It doesn't make much difference in what order the two parts occur; you'll be able to set up the best method after you understand both.

This chapter will concentrate on the at-home form of telecommuting. That's because working at home has some particular challenges that won't be present at other remote work sites where there will be other telecommuters and on-site supervision. If your firm is considering telecommuting exclusively at satellite or neighborhood centers, you might be able to shortcut this step in the process.

THE PREVIEW PROCESS

One of the biggest causes of dissatisfaction and turnover is the difference between what an employee expected in a job versus what it actually turned out to be. This happens for several reasons: the employer stresses the plusses and downplays or hides the negatives; the employee only selectively hears or sees how the new job is being described, or both. Some employers have begun to provide what are called "realistic job previews" to raise the chances of a successful placement.

The Benefits of Previews—A Case Study

An example of this approach is the program in place in a major consumer goods company that was having high turnover among sales representatives. The turnover—made up mostly of voluntary resignations—was occurring in the first six months of the job, after the reps had their initial training and were getting their first taste of the real job. Interviews with reps who quit showed that the job was very different from what had been described in the interviews and recruiting brochures.

The company decided to build a job preview into the interview cycle. Applicants who passed the first round of interviews spent a day in the field working with an experienced sales rep. If they were still interested after this, they would continue in the interview process. If not, they could simply back out of the process with no hard feelings. The result? Turnover stayed just as high and actually *increased* in some parts of the country!

No one could understand how this could happen until someone checked on which sales reps were being selected to host these previews for the applicants. It turned out that in virtually every case the division manager had chosen one of the top-performing reps as the host. This was, on the surface, a logical move—these experienced, successful reps would be role models and they'd begin to learn about the recruiting process themselves by hosting and conversing with the applicants.

A Strategic Error

But the flaw in this thinking became clear. The applicants were getting a preview, but it was the wrong kind of preview. They saw a polished sales rep who was well organized, known and respected by customers, and able to generate large orders. The applicants (many of whom had little or no prior sales experience) got the impression that the job was a snap and that it was easy to be a success.

You can imagine what happened when they completed their training and went out into the cold, cruel world: they couldn't believe how difficult it was! Many got frustrated or depressed and decided that they didn't have what it takes to be in sales and resigned. In truth, most of them would have been good reps had they simply stuck with it and developed on the job.

The final chapter of the story is that the firm changed strategies and had the previews hosted by the *newest* reps in each division. These rookies presented a much more realistic view of the early months of the job and could also relate better to the applicants. The result was that a number of applicants pulled themselves out of the running (for the right reasons) after the preview day and the number of early resignations was reduced dramatically, which translated to cost savings and improved sales performance for the company.

As the case study shows, it usually makes sense to give the applicant a chance to back out of consideration for the job. It's a simple matter of saving time and money. Even though the selection process might take longer, the odds are that the person chosen will last longer and do better on the new job. This is very important in light of the costs of turnover outlined in Chapter 2. For telecommuting, the need for a good preview may be even greater than for most jobs. Many people have at least a general idea of what a sales rep (or accountant or scientist) does, but this isn't the case for the details of work at home.

Job Preview Alternatives

A realistic preview of at-home telecommuting can take several forms. Your choice of which one(s) to use depends on the number of employees and remote jobs involved and the time and money available to support the preview process. The list below starts with the simplest methods useful for large numbers of applicants early in the selection process and progresses to more involved preview steps useful as selection continues. It's not necessary to use all five steps, and you can come up with combinations or variations of the five.

1. *Group Meeting.* Prospective telecommuters could attend a meeting and hear a presentation on telecommuting, its general pros and cons, the firm's plans and expectations for remote workers, and (optionally) comments from actual telecommuters or experts in the company or from outside. This is a good starting point, but it probably can't do more than provide general information.

2. *Video Preview.* A variation on the group meeting is a videotape (or slide/tape) presentation covering much of the same material. Depending on your creative bent and the available budget, this could be a straightforward presentation or a very involved show including visits to homes of telecommuters. The advantage of this method is that it can be viewed as needed by individuals instead of having to wait to set up a group meeting.

3. *Visit with a Telecommuter.* This is like the sales rep example cited earlier. Applicants would go to a telecommuter's home and spend part of a day there observing how work gets done, seeing the home office layout, and getting a real feel for remote work. An added plus is that this can be the basis of a "buddy" system if the applicant becomes a telecommuter later on. The drawback is the logistics of arranging the visits—especially if your firm doesn't have any telecommuters yet.

4. *Trial Work at Home.* This is the most direct way to see what it's like to work at home. As with the last method, you'd probably want to reserve this for later on in the selection process. Employees could spend one or more half- or full days at home per week over a month's time. They might not be doing exactly the same work in the same way as if they were permanent telecommuters, but at least they'd get a sense of the pros and cons of remote work for *their* jobs in *their* homes.

One drawback here is the selective perception problem that can crop up in all preview activities. Some people may discount or even ignore the negatives if they're really gung-ho about working at home. A good way to cope with this is to arrange a debriefing interview with yourself, a peer, or someone in Personnel when the person comes back to the office. Useful also for the "visit" preview method above, this debriefing would help bring out both sides of the work-at-home experience. If the applicant was able to give a balanced view of the day, including the dog's barks and the six trips to the refrigerator, that's a better sign than someone who glosses over those problems and glowingly related only the good parts.

5. *Work-at-Home Simulation.* Simulation games and exercises have been used in colleges and industries for years to compress a day's or even a year's worth of experience into a few hours or less. If designed well they can be quite realistic and give the participant a flavor for a wider range of conditions than could be seen in real life in such a short time. Typical applications range from flight simulators for airline pilot training to computer-based business games in which competing teams make decisions about advertising, pricing, and promotion strategies.

JOB PREVIEW CHECKLIST

✔ Use job previews to educate potential telecommuters and clear up misconceptions.

✔ Don't penalize applicants for backing out or having doubts.

✔ Choose from among a variety of preview methods.

Whatever method you use, it's important to invest the time in some kind of preview activity. The best-designed pilot program will suffer if the telecommuters involved have unrealistic expectations about what their remote work experience will be like.

THE SELECTION PROCESS

Most selection decisions involve two parts: determining if the applicants have the skills to do the job, and determining if they "fit" the job and vice-versa. This selection process is no different; you'll need to be sure that potential telecommuters have the technical and personal qualifications to be successful.

Performance Information

This first source of data comes primarily from the manager. This is an indication of the person's work quality, training level, and type of supervision required. Performance appraisals and other records might help, but usually won't be sufficient by themselves. Managers of prospective telecommuters will normally have to be interviewed in person, by phone, or by questionnaire to get more current and relevant information.

Basic Selection Criteria

Your main task here is to find out if the person is able to work up to expected standards without direct supervision and without convenient, frequent access to coworkers. We can make some generalizations about the kind of people who can handle this situation best:

- A person with more time on the job will do better than someone who's relatively new in the job and is still learning the basics;
- A person with above average overall performance will do better than someone whose overall ratings are average or below;
- A person with a broader background who has handled a wider variety of assignments will do better than someone whose experience has been more limited or restricted to fewer kinds of tasks.

The rationale behind these three points should be clear: if you're looking for someone who can work independently, you want someone who's demonstrated the kind of performance that makes it easy to trust him/her. Also, the broader and more successful the range of past experiences, the more likely the person will be able to cope with problems or unusual circumstances that might arise at home.

Some firms use rules of thumb to make the first pass at selecting telecommuters from the available applicants. For example, they include only those with one year or more in the current job, and with a certain performance rating as of the last appraisal period. You can always make exceptions to these rules but they are an expedient and uniform way to narrow down the applicants.

Affirmative Action Considerations

A word of caution: Keep your firm's affirmative action status and goals in mind if you use any cutoff points like those described. Even if the tele- commuters will get the same pay and benefits as their peers in the office (which is a must if they're treated as employees), some would argue that telecommuting is implicitly an employee benefit because of the built-in advantages of working at home. Others argue that the drawbacks are just as important, so the telecommuter ends up coming out even.

No matter how you feel about these tradeoffs, it makes sense to try to match the race and sex mix of your office population (in the job cate- gories selected for remote work) in the telecommuter group. No particular group should be over- or under-represented among the telecommuters. Your goal is to avoid the perception that the telecommuters get special treatment—a perception that can cause problems if the telecommuters are mostly of one sex or race.

Choosing Top Performers: Pros and Cons

As you choose and use these cutoffs, don't be lulled into thinking that you should select only your top performers for a pilot program. This could defeat the purpose of the pilot because you'd be working with employees who'd probably do a good job if their office was in the middle of a parking lot. The objective of the pilot is to learn about the concept and use this in- formation to generalize to broader applications. If you pick the superstars only, you won't really know how well telecommuting will work for others on your staff.

Another reason to steer clear of exclusive use of the top people is their role in the office. Your better people are often the formal or informal coaches or mentors for newer or less talented employees. Even though they'd still have contact with others as telecommuters, it may be smarter to keep these valuable employees in the office where others can have very easy access to their skills and guidance.

Type of Supervision Needed

So far you've looked at the quality of the candidate's work in several respects. The final piece of performance information you'll need is about the type of supervision the person needs; you'll read more about this in the next section on work personality information. Some of the reasons why certain people need more direct supervision have been addressed above—they're newer on the job, their overall performance merits closer attention, and they haven't experienced a full range of situations on their own.

But the other reason why people need more close supervision (apart from the *manager's* preference for giving it) is that they simply need more ongoing contact with and reinforcement from the boss. This doesn't mean they're insecure or incompetent; it just means they benefit from the attention and their work often shows it.

This kind of person can be a dilemma for you if you're choosing telecommuters, especially if the quality of his/her work is strong enough to pass your other tests. Many managers have found they can learn more about why the person seeks the extra contact if they discuss this openly with the employee. It doesn't mean you have to play psychologist—just be open to learning more about what makes the employee tick. You may find that substituting more written feedback for face-to-face contact can be a good compromise. The employee continues to get what's needed, but it's now less of a burden for you—and is much better suited to remote supervision.

SELECTION CHECKLIST (PART I)

- ✔ Telecommuters should be chosen from among willing volunteers, based on skills and "fit" with remote work demands.
- ✔ Collect and assess performance information to help predict if applicants can do well remotely.
- ✔ Remember your organization's affirmative action commitments when selecting the group.
- ✔ Don't pick only the top performers.
- ✔ Match the person's supervision needs with type and amount of supervision likely to be available.

Work Personality Information

This second piece of the selection process comes from the employee, not the manager. What you're looking for here is a sense of how well the person will be able to cope with some of the unique demands of at-home telecommuting. Even though the telecommuter will spend some time in the office, he or she will still be at home for between two and four days a week on average. What exactly are those unique demands? Here are some of the major ones:

- Working alone for long stretches of time;
- Working without easy access to coworkers, manager, and resource materials;
- Working in a physically comfortable and familiar setting;
- Working without many of the formal and informal cues for time management and planning that exist in the office;
- Working with more latitude about hours of work, sequence of events, and even work habits;
- Working amidst "friendly" yet potentially serious sources of interruption and distraction—family members, neighbors, TVs, stereos, and delivery people, to name a few.

The methods available to find out how someone's work personality meshes with these demands include the job preview mentioned earlier (as a self-selection service), interviews, and personality inventories. Here are some comments on each:

1. *Previews.* These can be an excellent way to help someone assess his/her own personality. The preview has to include information not only about the "what" of telecommuting but the "how": How does it feel to work alone and how do you motivate and discipline yourself? This information can be invaluable coming from the experiences of actual telecommuters or others who are thoroughly familiar with remote work.

2. *Interviews.* The interview is best done by a skilled interviewer, preferably not the manager or anyone else in the direct line of authority. A peer manager could do this, as could someone with good interviewing skills such as a personnel department staffer, a market research professional, or an outside interviewer.

The interview (which should follow a structured format) should include discussions about the person's perceptions of his/her work habits, satisfactions and frustrations on the job, views on the supervisor and co-workers, and the role of work in the person's life. What you're after here is information such as how much the person depends (or even thrives) on contact with others in the office, how comfortable he/she is with different kinds of supervision, and what his/her expectations are about remote work.

3. *Personality Inventories.* These can be the most useful tools but also the most difficult to use. Although they aren't tests, people might see them as such. You should plan on sharing the results of any inventories or interviews with the employees. You're trying to make the selection decision *with* them and with their support; any step that's secretive or mysterious can undermine the program.

Unfortunately, there are no instruments on the market now specifically designed to measure suitability for work at home, although several are under development. The following instruments can be considered for use; be sure to get the opinions and advice of someone trained in the choice and administration of personality inventories when using these or similar tools:

- The Work Environment Scale
- The Myers-Briggs Type Indicator, or its short form, the Keirsey Temperament Sorter
- The Workstyle Preference Inventory

These can be valuable as "proxy" measures—they don't directly indicate if someone will do well working at home, but they provide information about traits or characteristics that seem to be essential for successful

---

SELECTION CHECKLIST (PART II)

✔ Find out how well the applicant can cope with the unique demands of remote work.

✔ Use job previews as self-assessment tools.

✔ Conduct structured interviews to learn about the applicant's motivation and expectations.

✔ Use personality inventories—with professional guidance—to collect more information.

remote work. These include the level of need for contact and affiliation with others and the strength of preference for certain kinds of work. Keep those two criteria in mind if you're looking for tests or inventories to use in your program.

In summary, the selection process benefits the organization and the employee when it's done well. It can be time-consuming but this is time well spent; without it, the value of a pilot program is questionable. If you're not sure that you're starting off with the right people you'll find it very difficult to measure progress and expand the pilot to a larger group.

7

Key Strategies for Training the Manager

It takes two to tango and it takes two to telecommute—the remote worker and the manager. Much of what's been written in the popular press about telecommuting has concentrated on the telecommuters themselves—who they are, how to choose them, and what it's like to work remotely. Relatively little attention has been paid to the manager who is equally responsible for the success of any telecommuting effort.

Managers are like college professors who "give" Cs and Ds to their students—while the students "earn" As and Bs. They often feel as if they're a party to the problems but just a witness to the successes. This can be a dangerous attitude to have in connection with telecommuting, because the demands on the remote manager are greater and more complex than with on-site supervision.

Think of your own experience as a manager for a moment. If you're like most managers, you rely on many sources of information about how your people are doing. The lower the level of management, the more the manager relies on direct observation of work and/or frequent meetings with subordinates to review progress. Higher-level managers spend less time in these downward contacts; they're often managing more senior people who need less frequent guidance, and their own time is taken up with peers and contacts outside of the organization.

73

REMOTE SUPERVISION OVERVIEW

Most managers share this legacy of supervising relatively closely from their early years, and it's one of the major obstacles in considering remote work. They ask, "How can I manage someone I can't see?" They wonder how they'll get the information they need when they can no longer simply walk down the hall or look out of the office door. There are two reasons why this obstacle is easy to overcome:

1. *Close Isn't Necessarily Good.* There's a difference between *close* supervision and *good* supervision, although many managers assume that both are the same. Managers can be trained to see the difference between the two and learn how to shift their focus from observing activity to managing for results. If anything, close, detailed-oriented supervision can be counterproductive since it often emphasizes and rewards activity rather than results. Subordinates have known for years how important it is to "look busy"; whether they're actually doing anything of value is another story.

2. *Remote Management Isn't New.* Managing from a distance is far more commonplace than most managers realize. Think of the range of jobs in your organization or others where the employees see their boss infrequently—perhaps as much as once a day but as little as once every few weeks. These include delivery people, meter readers, sales and technical or service representatives, installers, teachers, drivers, certain research scientists, and field auditors or inspectors—and the list goes on.

Firms have functioned very well over the years with these "remote workers" even though no one thinks of them as such. How does it work? When done correctly, the workers are given good initial training and clear performance standards. There is measurement of actual work performed at regular intervals followed by feedback from the manager, and lots of informal contact by phone or mail all along.

Overcoming the Manager's Resistance

The reason why many managers get concerned about the prospects of managing telecommuters is that the telecommuters (as defined in this book) are in jobs that traditionally have been office-based. Their managers in many cases have little or no experience with the categories of remote workers previously mentioned. Few managers of programming or telemarketing departments ever had much experience supervising sales reps

or meter readers in most companies. Their reactions—and initial reluc-
tance—are quite understandable.

The training need is to develop the manager's skills at planning work,
delegating, setting timetables, assessing progress, and giving performance
feedback. These are the basic skills used by the managers of those existing
groups of remote workers. And, they're the skills that almost all managers
were taught somewhere along the line. The problem is that the skills
often get rusty when they aren't used very often.

Managers who have the luxury of frequent, close contact in the office can easily develop the habit of letting that contact take the place of
more disciplined approaches to supervision. The result is what's known
as "hallway mangement"—you see a subordinate in the hallway and ask,
"How's that XYZ project going?" The subordinate may be caught off guard,
but replies with a "Just fine" or in rare moments of candor, something
like, "We've had a few problems, but should have them ironed out by tomorrow." This exchange is better than nothing, but it's no substitute for
good management.

MANAGER TRAINING CHECKLIST (PART I)

✔ Recognize and acknowledge the natural resistance of many
managers to managing from a distance. It's an understandable
reaction, but not a legitimate obstacle.

✔ Stress the difference between *close* supervision and *good* supervision.

✔ Stress the difference between *observing activity* and *managing
for results.*

Before managers of telecommuters can learn the specific skills
they'll need, help them assess and discuss their general attitudes
about remote supervision.

REMOTE SUPERVISION SKILLS

The five skills that follow are basic management skills. There's really
nothing revolutionary about managing telecommuters; it requires the use
of skills that most managers should be using with all employees.

1. *Planning Work.* Before you can assign work, you must have a clear understanding about the work itself. You don't have to be a technical expert, but do need to figure out how long certain tasks will take, what resources are needed, and how the various pieces fit together.

Since remote workers won't always have easy access to office resources, it's important that you know in advance what resources are needed to complete a task. This includes materials, files, and information from coworkers or clients. The objective of this skill is to help you do a good job of allocating work among your staff and making sure they'll be equipped to handle it.

2. *Delegating.* This is the logical extension of the first step. You need an effective way to actually hand over an assignment to the person who will be doing it. Many managers do this haphazardly; the result can be wasted time and effort by the subordinate and loads of frustration all around.

Proper delegation involves these steps:

- Break the task down into parts;
- Determine how well the subordinate can do each part and arrange for help or other resources if needed;
- Describe the task, its importance, and the reason why the subordinate was selected to do it;
- Discuss the amount of authority being delegated: where does the subordinate have discretion to act alone and where should he/she come to you for approvals?;
- Explain exactly what the desired end product should be in terms of due date, quality, quantity, scope, and any other relevant measures;
- Prepare and discuss a schedule for interim reviews. (See step #3.)

One way to think about delegation is to view it as a contract between you and the subordinate. Most people have experience with contracts and can readily appreciate the need to be specific about who does what by when and what to do if contingencies come up. This is the kind of thinking that goes into delegating, although it's less formal than for a real contract.

3. *Setting Timetables.* It's almost impossible to manage any kind of activity if the only contact or reviews are at the begining and end of the project. The exception is short-interval work—tasks that take less than a day where there's no logical interim review point. This might also be the case for some kinds of clerical work, for instance.

But for longer projects you need to establish a timetable that becomes the basis of the subordinate's accountability. The timetable is the list of deliverables: what must be completed by what date. This is a natural outgrowth of the work planning step described previously, but it's often necessary to develop the timetable *with* the subordinate. That person has a better idea of total workload and is more likely to accept the due dates if he/she participates in setting them.

This kind of timetable benefits the remote worker as much as the manager. It provides a clear target that helps focus the work, and lets the telecommuter make informed decisions about changes in work schedules, trips to the office, and the ability to take on more work.

4. *Assessing Progress.* This is where the care in planning and delegating pays off for both manager and subordinate. Once the job has been broken into discrete tasks (with clear standards for what constitutes acceptable work), and times assigned to each, it's a relatively simple matter to track progress. The normal way to do this is either at fixed intervals ("We'll meet every Friday to discuss your progress") or according to the key events ("Let's review where we are at the end of Parts 1, 3, and 6"). These review intervals will generally be linked to planned visits to the office, although these won't be the only times the telecommuter comes in.

5. *Giving Performance Feedback.* Finally, you have to be skilled at discussing the work and giving praise and criticism when both are warranted. This is another example of a skill that managers have been urged to use for years; it's absolutely essential that you do it and do it well with telecommuters. Remote workers simply don't have as much opportunity for contact with the manager, so you have to make the best of limited time by providing feedback that reinforces good performance and redirects unsatisfactory work.

Effective performance feedback has five features.

- *Positive and negative:* tell the person what's wrong so it can be changed, and what's right so it can be continued.
- *Limited to priority items:* nobody can fix six things at once; concentrate on the top priority items and move on to other later. Try to make the person's work better, not perfect.
- *Descriptive, not judgmental:* tell people what you observed, don't just label it with a vague term.
- *Ongoing:* don't save things for the "right time"; while you're waiting for a good time to tell the person something is wrong, he/she might

be doing it wrong again. This is very important in telecommuting—don't wait for in-office visits. Pick up the phone, send a note, or use electronic mail if you have it.

- *Timely:* give feedback at the right place (private, out of earshot of peers) and the right time (when you and your subordinate can devote attention to it, not over a drink or just before quitting time on Friday).

These are nothing more than sound management skills used by good managers. While some managers in an office setting might be able to skimp on some of them, managers of remote workers need to pay close attention to all of them. Successful telecommuting has little margin for error when it comes to the planning and execution required by the manager.

Training Methods

Your choice of methods for delivering this training will vary according to your organization's size and staffing. You might rely on internal training resources, call in consultants, or draw on the wide variety of packaged management training programs that are on the market today. Be sure to tailor whatever approach you select for its relevance to remote work. The managers being trained must be able to see how these skills will be used in the context of infrequent face-to-face contact.

One way to do this is in simulation exercises in which managers have a chance to manage (and be managed) in a mock setting where they can experience what it's like to manage from a distance. This can be done in

---

MANAGER TRAINING CHECKLIST (PART II)

Managers of telecommuters need basic or refresher training for

- ✔ Planning the work and breaking it into tasks
- ✔ Delegating specific tasks to subordinates
- ✔ Setting timetables for interim progress checks
- ✔ Assessing progress according to time and quality criteria
- ✔ Giving effective performance feedback on positive and negative points.

These are traditional management skills with a twist—be sure to stress the unique implications for remote supervision.

simple or complex ways; the key is to separate the worker and manager and have them communicate mostly by memo, phone, or electronic mail with only infrequent face-to-face contact. Simulations are excellent ways to compress real-life experiences into a few hours, and they allow everyone involved to try out new skills with little or no risk.

CAREER MOBILITY AND THE MANAGER'S ROLE

There's one more training task for managers of remote workers, and it's not quite as skill-oriented as the first five. A commonly held belief about telecommuting is that it may limit career mobility—"out of sight, out of mind," as the saying goes. The next chapter will address some of the things telecommuters themselves can do to help prevent this, but part of the responsibility is on the manager also.

Is Mobility Limited for Telecommuters?

Before talking about the manager's role, let's examine the premise about limited mobility. Telecommuting programs to date have shown very little evidence of limited mobility for remote workers, though this is probably best judged over longer time periods than many programs have been in existence. There's also the question of self-selection by telecommuters—informal comments from some telecommuters suggest they are consciously trading off the possible risk of slower promotion for the benefits of working at home. Also, data from a survey done by Dr. Charles McClintock of Cornell University indicated that telecommuters report *increased* chances for promotion. Some interview respondents reported that initiative or innovativeness were associated with telecommuting, and that this was more important to their success than its possible isolating effects. Factors like these make it hard to compare relative progression rates.

If employees are making this choice of being at home over mobility risks, one possible scenario is a dual work force. The employees who are aggressively seeking bigger and better things might shy away from telecommuting, and others who are very good performers but simply aren't as concerned about upward mobility might lean toward remote work. This means you might only be able to consider promotion candidates from among those in the office—a drawback for two reasons.

First, if significant numbers of workers are telecommuting at least part-time, it would be a plus if their managers had some firsthand experience with remote work. If those aspiring to higher positions put remote work off-limits for themselves, they might be limiting their own effectiveness to a degree. Second, there's the simple fact of narrowing the pool from which to select managers. Some very talented employees working remotely might be excellent candidates who otherwise would be encouraged to move ahead. If they make this tradeoff between moving up and moving out, so to speak, it's possible that they and the organization will lose in the long run.

Other Career Mobility Factors

There are some other factors influencing this career mobility issue. First and foremost, everyone is going to have to accept the prospects of less upward mobility in the management ranks. Organizations are shrinking their middle-management levels as cost-cutting pressure grows and as PCs begin to dq some of the work of people. If this is so, telecommuting might become one of several new kinds of developmental experiences that you can offer to people who in the past would have been marching up within the organization.

Second, very little is known about what happens over the long run with remote workers. There simply isn't a lot of experience with non-self-employed people working at home or elsewhere offsite for five years or more. It's conceivable that the academic tradition of sabbaticals might find its way to industry; telecommuters could spend six months back in the office after every 18 to 24 months away from it. If this cycle develops, the mobility issue might go away. The system would require that everyone cycle through the office and perhaps spend that time getting ready for or performing a managerial job.

For the sake of argument, let's assume now that tradition will prevail in most cases and telecommuters may in fact be slightly out of mind because they're often out of sight. After all, promotion decisions even in the best-managed organizations are influenced by perceptions and alliances that are built up slowly over time as a result of personal (and, often, face-to-face) contacts.

What the Manager Can Do: "Spotlighting"

How can you make sure that the telecommuter isn't losing out in this system? Like it or not, rubbing elbows with the brass in the hallway still counts for a lot in many organizations. Telecommuters who *are* interested in moving up shouldn't have to divert their attention from their work because they're concerned that the only elbows *they're* rubbing in the hall-way are those of their spouse, children, or dog.

The answer comes from what's been learned from other examples of remote and remotely managed work over the years, especially in large field sales organizations. When a sales representative in Arizona gets pro-moted, it isn't because the national sales manager at corporate headquar-ters in Chicago knows that rep personally and was directly involved in the promotion decision. The rep got promoted because the various levels of field sales management up the line were *made* aware of the rep's perfor-mance and potential by the first-line manager out in the field.

Some large sales organizations have formal vehicles for spotting and drawing attention to high performers—assessment centers and sophisti-cated performance review and organization planning systems are two common ones. But even in the less formal systems it's the first-line man-ager who has the responsibility to put the spotlight on the good performers. This "spotlighting" is what starts the process rolling; it may begin with a memo to the regional manager about the fine job being done by the rep. The regional manager follows up with a phone call to get more informa-tion, and then might spend a day working in the field with the rep. Now the sales rep has the support of two key people, an important first step.

Moving back to telecommuting from this example, the manager has a similar responsibility for this "spotlighting," above and beyond what nor-mally results from periodic performance appraisals and other measure-ment systems. A lot of this goes on in offices everywhere today. Managers like to show off the work of competent subordinates because it makes them proud, reflects on their managerial skills, and may even hasten their own promotion if the subordinate is a possible replacement.

Tips for the Manager

As with the five skills covered earlier, this spotlighting of performance can't be left to chance. Managers of remote workers need to

1. *Spot Trends.* Look for consistent trends in performance that show work clearly above average.

2. *Challenge the People.* Give "stretch" assignments that call on the skills and potential of better workers and give them a crack at more chal-lenging assignments.

3. *Spread the Word.* Keep higher levels of management aware of the high-quality work being done remotely, especially if there's normally little

opportunity for direct interaction with the telecommuter. You can do something as simple as sending a copy of a report done by the remote worker to your manager along with a cover note. The goal is to raise or maintain awareness of that person's work.

4. *Assure Exposure.* Take advantage of or create opportunities for exposure of the good performers to higher management. This is where the periodic visits to the office come in—a group presentation, a luncheon meeting with your boss, or participation at important task force meetings. These needn't be anything out of the ordinary; if you draw too much attention to the work of subordinates, you can raise suspicions of your manager or peers.

Some of these strategies for telecommuters can backfire if used to excess, just as they can for office-based employees. Other subordinates who do perfectly good work begin to think you're playing favorites or ignoring their work. If this happens, they might reason that they can slack off a bit since you're so busy paying attention to the "superstar." That's why it's important to realize that this spotlighting is in *addition* to the ongoing management attention given to all employees. Good managers aren't content to rest on their laurels when they have a solid performer under them; they seek to develop other subordinates to similarly high levels whenever possible.

THE MANAGER'S ROLE IN CAREER MOBILITY FOR TELECOMMUTERS

1. Don't assume that telecommuters automatically will fall behind in their careers—or if they do, that they'll all see it as a major problem.
2. Teach the manager the importance of spotlighting the telecommuter's good performance.
3. Make sure the manager knows how to spot performance trends, give "stretch" assignments, keep management informed, and create opportunities for exposure.
4. Make sure managers don't overdo it—too much attention can backfire.

OTHER TRAINING TOPICS

These six skills (the first five plus career awareness) are the basis of training managers of telecommuters. You may have to add to this list, depending on your specific applications. Other topics might include

- Use of electronic or voice mail systems if they haven't been used before;

- Policy and practices about work hours and time reporting for non-exempt level employees. This would be only a reminder since there should be no differences in the treatment of office-based versus remote nonexempt employees under the provisions of the Fair Labor Standards Act.

- Logistical concerns such as methods for getting materials to and from remote workers and arranging for repair and maintenance on any equipment at the remote site.

SELECTING THE MANAGER: MORE THAN MEETS THE EYE

Training is important, but what about choosing the managers to begin with? The last chapter described ways to select the telecommuters and you might assume that the managers are chosen by default, i.e., those who manage the employees selected as telecommuters.

It isn't always this simple. There are four other considerations in picking the managers; you should review these in your planning. These are part of a trio of key selection choices you make—which projects or jobs, which people, and which managers. All three elements must be examined together, but the actual order in which you do them is less important. In most cases, it makes sense to pick the projects or jobs first whenever possible; if the task itself isn't suited to remote work, it doesn't make much difference who the telecommuters or managers are.

The four considerations are

1. *Nature of Projects.* This has been covered in Chapter 5. In addition to the criteria listed there, you should also consider some of the polititical aspects of the tasks. "Political" here refers to the level of visibility or sensitivity associated with the task.

You should be able to look forward to successful implementation if you follow the steps in this book, but there's always some risk when working with innovative concepts. Things don't always work out as planned, unexpected delays crop up, and there can be people problems and technical glitches you never considered. That's why you should steer clear of projects that have little or no margin for error in your initial telecommuting applications.

In theory, no project has margin for error. In practice, you know that some projects or tasks have more slack than others. A project that's the pet idea of a senior vice-president—who has been checking with you every week on its progress—may not be the best bet for an initial remote work program. It's not politically wise to risk a delay, for two reasons. First, you obviously would like to stay on the VP's good side, and second, an initial (and highly visible) foul-up might ruin the chances for later use of telecommuting.

If you stay away from these sensitive situations at first, you have a much better chance of getting off to a good start. You won't have the added pressure of the top-management scrutiny that can put everyone a little on edge. It's far better to run the initial application on a less risky task and *then* be able to go to that executive and show off your results.

If you're wondering why this question of project selection is addressed in a chapter on training and selecting managers, it's because projects and managers are often closely linked. You can't realistically talk about picking projects without thinking about who's going to be responsible for them. Since it rarely makes any sense to shift project managers in midstream, you must consider this project selection along with manager selection.

2. *Managerial Style.* Earlier, the distinction was made between close supervision and good supervision. Some managers tend to be very detail-oriented in their style and maintain close contact with and control over the work of their subordinates. This isn't necessarily bad, and in fact, in some cases is a must depending on the kind of work and the skills of the subordinates.

There's some risk that managers who tend to supervise closely could unwittingly undermine a telecommuting program. They may never feel comfortable with having their subordinates at a distance where they no longer have easy contact and frequent access. No matter how many provisions are made for staying in touch or monitoring programs, this type of manager will likely find it difficult to let the telecommuter work more independently.

3. *Managerial Skill.* Telecommuting can make additional demands on a manager. Remote supervision and being involved in a new concept add to the everyday requirements of the manager's job. There's generally no room in telecommuting (especially in the early stages) for a manager with mediocre supervisory skills. The training that's being suggested in this chapter will refine and upgrade existing managerial skills, but is not intended to provide the basics. Don't handicap a pilot program with a manager who will be stretched—perhaps to the limit—by the unique requirements of managing from a distance.

4. *Willingness.* Just as the telecommuters themselves must be willing to be involved, the managers should also be willing participants. There

are many reasons why a manager might not want to supervise telecommuters: for example, he/she may feel it's contrary to personal beliefs about supervision, or the current workload may be such that one more project could lead to overload.

It's always possible that a manager who's unwilling or unsupportive on the inside may be a strong supporter on the outside. If telecommuting has the blessing of top management and is seen as a desirable project to be associated with, an unwilling manager might rise to the occasion and want to participate. There's probably not much that you can do to guard against this except some common-sense evaluation by yourself or the manager in charge of the project. If your instincts tell you that a manager has done a very abrupt turnaround in philosophy, you'd be wise to dig into the situation. Don't rule someone out because of a seeming change like this; give the manager the benefit of the doubt and discuss his/her views carefully. Your goal is simply to make sure that the manager wants to be involved for the right reasons.

**CHECKLIST FOR SELECTING THE MANAGER
OF TELECOMMUTERS**

Here are some special considerations for picking the right managers:

✔ Pick the projects or tasks first and then determine if the managers involved are the ones you want.

✔ Steer clear of managers who are detail-oriented and supervise very closely.

✔ Don't test the skill of a weak manager in a remote-work program.

✔ Look for managers who are genuinely interested in and support telecommuting.

The manager is a key part of telecommuting, and this chapter has described some of the considerations for selecting and training the managers involved. It's all too easy to focus attention on the telecommuters themselves and forget about the critical role played by the managers. They are the main link between the remote workers and all that goes on in the office, and they are the ones responsible for continued high levels of performance of the remote workers.

8

How to Train the Telecommuters

Picture this setting: It's 10 A.M. on a warm spring day, one of the first nice ones after a series of rainy, dreary days. You're working at home on some last-minute changes to a major report for your boss when the doorbell rings. It's your neighbor, tennis racket in hand, who informs you that he's just booked a court for two hours, but you have to leave right away or someone else will take the time. It's the third time this month that your neighborhood tennis pro (who's retired) has made such an offer. The last two times you said no, but today it's not so easy.

Those proverbial two voices (Good and evil? Adult and child? Worker and player?) start going through your head. If you play now you'll definitely get behind schedule and you promised to have the report done by noon tomorrow. But you're sick of being cooped up looking at the rain on the windows, and a couple of hours off would be just what you need. Besides, you can probably convince your spouse to go out shopping alone tonight for the new TV set. That wasn't your idea of a good time anyhow, and you could use the time to get caught up on the project. But then you were also supposed to stop over at the Martins' house for dessert after the trip to the store, and you haven't seen them for a while, and you all have such a great time when you get together. . . .

MORE FREEDOM, MORE CHOICES

By the time you finished this kind of mental maneuvering, your neighbor would probably have been long gone, leaving you on the doorstep thinking about all those what-ifs. This kind of a dilemma—annoying but certainly not earth-shaking—is not unusual for telecommuters. Working offsite (and especially at home) means more freedom and flexibility. More freedom and flexibility mean more choices and decisions that range from exciting to aggravating and everything in between.

Most people don't realize just how structured a day in the office can be until they're away from it for a while. There are so many subtle built-in cues and signals for how to organize time and work that you generally don't even know how well-ordered the work day is. For example, look at what happens from the moment you set foot in the door; there's the ritual of getting settled, getting a cup of coffee, chatting with some coworkers, and then "unpacking" your desk. The desk calendar plots out your day, your files are all organized in that bottom drawer, and your current projects are laid out (or piled up?) in the top drawer. Everything is right at hand and waiting for action. A few hours later the gang starts to make its move for lunch, signifying that everyone has made it halfway through the day. If you have a secretary or assistant, he/she adds to the order by handling your calls, getting materials together for you, and taking care of all those little tasks (where *is* that copying machine located anyhow?).

GETTING USED TO LESS STRUCTURE

When office workers are turned into telecommuters, most of this invisible blueprint for the day's activities is abandoned. There are no coworkers whose actions and locations help signal the pace of work, no assistant right at hand to act as a buffer or helper, and few, if any, remnants of the network of sights and sounds of the office that help orient you. For some people this shift is welcomed, but for others it can be very disorienting at first.

You'll see in this chapter that one of the biggest challenges of telecommuting is to help the remote workers deal with this relative absence of structure and support. You'll learn how to help them deal with the tennis pro, the delivery people, the dog barking, the kids, and the spouse in a way that lets them get their work done without alienating everyone within a one-mile radius. Also, you'll learn about some of the ways for telecommuters to manage their jobs and careers from a distance, in contrast with last chapter's tips on managing telecommuters from a distance. Finally, you'll see how to spot some of the "red flags" that might be early warning signs of trouble for telecommuters.

The topic of starting to work at home and being successful at it (as a telecommuter or as an entrepreneur) could be the subject of a separate book—in fact, it is. *Working From Home* is just that book, and it's subtitled *Everything You Need to Know About Living and Working Under the Same Roof.* It's by Paul and Sarah Edwards, published in 1985 by Jeremy P. Tarcher. This chapter will touch only on some of the topics covered in depth in the Edwards' book.

TELECOMMUTER TRAINING TASK 1:
GETTING ORGANIZED

Going from the physical familiarity and routine of an office to a home work area can be quite a shock. There are some very basic decisions to be made before the first day of working at home. These include questions of where to put the work area and how to furnish it, just for starters.

Picking a Work Location

The first point, location, shouldn't be taken lightly. In a crowded or small home or apartment the telecommuter might not have much choice; not everyone has the luxury of a spare bedroom, den, or open space that can be converted. As the employer, you should make every effort to encourage the telecommuter to find a *distinct* work area that can be dedicated to this purpose. This doesn't necessarily mean a separate room, but it does mean a certain space that is used exclusively for work.

Why is this so important? Working from home for a big portion of the week is totally different from working out of a briefcase at the dining room table or even sprawled out on the sofa. Those temporary work areas might be convenient and comfortable but are rarely suited to pro- ductive work over the long haul. Second, telecommuters often need some minimum amount of file space and/or work area for computer equip- ment. Third, a dedicated space gives a clear signal to the telecommuter and others sharing the home that working at home is serious business and not a casual activity.

From the employer's viewpoint, there is a liability question here also. Chapter 11 will address the potential insurance and worker's compensa- tion issues in more depth, but for now let's say that you probably won't want telecommuters to have a PC or terminal propped up on a shaky card table or being moved on and off the family meal table several times during the day. The equipment can suffer and there's added risk of injury—what if a leg on that card table collapses and the PC lands on the telecommuter's foot? Also, if there's extensive setup and breakdown time needed, some of the productivity gains from having easy access to the workspace at home might diminish.

Proper Space Is a Must

In summary, the need for getting organized is to build awareness of the space and layout planning issues involved and give the telecommuters some guidance on how to make the best use of available space. No one layout is best for everyone and every telecommuter's residence will have different types of space available. In fact, one consideration in selecting telecommuters is the adequacy of workspace in several regards:

- Is there space for a dedicated work area, including a desk and any needed file areas and space for equipment?
- Can it be separated (in terms of noise, sight, and traffic flow) from other activities in the home?

You have to get the message across to potential telecommuters that remote work at home even for two days a week is different from working out of a briefcase for a few hours now and then. A work area at home doesn't need to be as extensive (or expensive) as one in a traditional office. But it must be adequate—the telecommuter shouldn't have to spend a lot

---

CHECKLIST FOR GETTING ORGANIZED AT HOME

Make sure telecommuters understand they must

- ✓ Find a substitute for both the obvious and subtle cues for structuring time that are part of an office setting.
- ✓ Find the right place to work—the dining room table isn't suitable as a regular workspace.
- ✓ Separate the work area from the rest of the home—any kind of barrier helps provide needed physical and mental boundaries.

of time getting ready to work and juggling materials while making do with a corner of the dining room table that's been commandeered from the family.

TIME AND ROUTINES AND RITUALS

Most people are creatures of habit and this is very evident in how office workers structure their days. There's the day-long chain of events that mark coffee breaks, lunch, and quitting time as described earlier. But there's also a set of physical cues people rely on—trips to the file cabinet, a walk to a conference room for a meeting, and a walk down the hall to the bathroom. Each one adds variety to the day's work and some new sights and sounds for the senses.

When working at home, however, most telecommuters will be faced with a more uniform and routine set of events and surroundings. Except for phone or electronic mail contacts, most of the work will be done alone —at the same desk, in the same surroundings, and without much variation in what's seen and heard. It's easy to get lost in this relatively unchanging environment and have one's work suffer as a result.

That's why it's important to set up some ways to add some structure and diversity to the work day at home. These will vary by person and all won't work equally well for everyone. Here are some tips for getting into and maintaining the mindset of the office while enjoying the comforts and benefits of home:

1. *Set Up a Schedule.* Telecommuters working at home should try to follow some kind of schedule, preferably one that's quite similar from day to day. It doesn't have to be exactly the same schedule as is followed in the office. As long as the job allows it, telecommuters can vary their work hours to better fit their own preferences. The potential problem arises when each day's schedule is *radically* different from each other day's schedule. It can be hard for some people to start work at 8 A.M. one day, 3 P.M. the next, and 11 A.M. on the third. A personal commitment to start work within a certain time band (such as between 7:30 and 8:30 A.M.) might be a good way to get on a schedule and still have a sense of freedom about the exact starting time.

2. *Make a To-Do List.* Writing a daily to-do list is more than a cliché —it's a tried and true method for identifying and staying focused on the important tasks. There's no one best way to do this; different time management experts advocate blank sheets of paper or preprinted forms, and suggest it be done first thing in the morning or last thing at the end of the

day. These are matters of personal preference and are decided upon by trial and error, but the important thing is for telecommuters to make some kind of list.

It should be one list on one piece of paper, with some kind of importance or priority rating attached to each item. This rating can be "musts" and "wants," an A/B/C or 1/2/3 priority system, different colored pens, and so forth. Without some kind of list it's all too easy for many telecommuters to slip into an undisciplined use of time.

If making a to-do list isn't the telecommuter's favorite activity, one way to sweeten the task is to take advantage of working where he/she lives. There's no reason why that to-do list can't include activities like exercise, watching a favorite TV show, listening to a record, playing with the children, or having a cup of coffee with his or her spouse. As long as these activities don't cut into what must get done that day, they are truly some of the small but important rewards of working at home. These items won't always appear on every day's to-do list, but knowing they are there can be something to look forward to.

Also, integrating these activities with the to-do list can be a very effective way of keeping the proper distance between work and all the possible distractions at home. This doesn't mean that telecommuters have to account for every minute of the day in advance, or schedule exactly ten minutes from 3:00 to 3:10 P.M. to play with a child. But all the benefits of working from home can turn into time-robbers if the telecommuter doesn't consciously plan and work them into the day's priorities.

3. *Start New Habits.* Most telecommuters have to find something to take the place of the morning ritual of washing, dressing, and walking out the door to get into the car, bus, or train to work. As much as most people dislike going through this early-morning drill, it gets them ready for work by acting as a buffer between home and work. In fact, one of the objections raised about telecommuting is that it takes away this buffer period that helps clear and organize the mind in the morning and is a time to unwind at night. At the very least, it's a time to read the paper or listen to the news or music.

Mention telecommuting to most office workers and one of the first images that comes to mind is the luxury of lolling around in bed after the alarm clock rings, having a leisurely breakfast, and going to work (without shaving or putting on makeup) in a bathrobe or, if truly motivated, in an old pair of blue jeans. This is an appealing image to some people, but there is some value in those morning rituals of preparing for work and the buffer time between waking and beginning work (i.e., the commute to the office).

Good Ways to Get Started

There's a way to have the best of both worlds: the relative freedom and comfort of working at home and the benefit of getting mentally prepared for the day. Telecommuters will often benefit from some kind of daily ritual although it might look very different from the traditional ones. For example, it can be

- Reading the morning paper with that second cup of coffee while seated at the desk, and then making up the day's to-do list;
- Going out for a short walk after breakfast;
- Taking 15 minutes at the desk to do some work-related reading such as a business magazine, a technical journal, or a self-study book;
- Calling a coworker at the office to get caught up on yesterday's activities, or calling the manager to do the same plus quickly reviewing progress on outstanding tasks. This can also be done via electronic mail if it's available.

Telecommuters can be creative about adapting these tips to their own work schedules and personal preferences. For example, people who are true "early birds" might like to sit down at the desk from 6:00 to 7:30 A.M. to get organized and do some creative thinking or planning before having breakfast. Others might get in some early-morning exercise, or use the morning hours for family time.

There are some cases of what seem to be rather extreme needs to maintain a pattern. One noteworthy one was the person who showered, shaved, dressed in a business suit, had breakfast, and then walked out the front door and around the house to the side entrance where his office was. He needed that very clear signal that he was going to work. Others will set up the home office to mimic the central office, right down to the placement of items on the desk. For these people the visual cue of the desk and its layout might be the single most important way to know that "it's time to get to work."

Two words about dressing for working at home: it depends. Some people feel it's best to dress similarly to how they would in the office. "Sloppy clothes means sloppy thinking," or something like that, they would say. Others find that they're more relaxed and able to concentrate without the "uniform" of the office. There are no data on how many people actually work in their pajamas, but there are probably not too many. The novelty of the casual atmosphere tends to wear off and the pajamas tend to give way to something at least as dressy as blue jeans.

**CHECKLIST FOR SETTING UP
A SCHEDULE AND ROUTINE**

✔ Don't let your telecommuters become victims of the absence of a schedule or routine—it's too easy for casual work habits to drift into a total lack of structure.

✔ Encourage telecommuters to prepare and stick to a to-do list— and there's no reason why personal activities shouldn't be included in that list.

✔ Some kind of daily ritual at home is needed to replace the "going to work" ritual—whatever they choose, telecommuters need some way to get set for the day's work.

In summary, telecommuting forces employees to make some choices about things that previously involved little or no choice such as dress, work hours, and pacing of work. It's essential that your new telecommuters be briefed on the need to make these choices and then begin to work out their own best schedules and rituals at home.

MOVING WORK TO AND FROM THE OFFICE

The next main training task for telecommuters is teaching them how to maintain contact with the office. The manager's role in this task is covered in Chapter 9. In this section, you'll learn about the more basic logistic issues of getting supplies, materials, and finished work to and from the office.

This workflow problem will vary widely by type of job, frequency of visits to the office, and level and type of technology in use. At one extreme is a word processing operator typing long reports onto a standalone system from longhand or dictated originals. The originals have to be ferried to the remote site and the diskettes have to get back to the office for printing. This two-way link has to be routinized and predictable; if not, the remote worker risks running out of work or the finished product doesn't get into the hands of those who need it on time.

At the other extreme is a staff professional such as a market research analyst with a PC, sophisticated telecommunications gear, and a versatile electronic mail system. This telecommuter might be able to work for days on end without needing anything that must be transported to and from the office. He/she can make inquiries to databases, do data analysis, and draft and transmit reports all electronically. For this person the linkage needs are more for information and social contact, rather than simply to keep the work flowing.

Courier Methods

Most telecommuters with ongoing need to move materials to and from the office make arrangements with coworkers who live nearby, or even with a spouse or neighbor who works near to (but not necessarily in) the telecommuter's central office. Other methods include employer-sponsored van pools that can be routed near the remote site, taxis, or messenger services. The last two are obviously more costly; if used excessively they can eat into the potential cost savings from telecommuting.

When choosing among these resources you face a tradeoff among cost, convenience, reliability, and predictability. The friendly neighbor who works in the next office is a cheap (or free) solution, but one that's subject to the same problems inherent in car pooling—sickness, vacations, and errands. A messenger service is generally foolproof but more costly. Depending on the job, the post office might be the best and cheapest courier service, although it might lose some points for reliability and predictability.

The added wrinkle is that one of the reasons why telecommuters want to work remotely is to avoid long commutes, especially if they live quite a distance from the office. The more remote the home, the less likely you are to have the options of using car or van pooling or taxis. One difficult scenario would be a telecommuter doing the word processing job described previously who lives out in the boondocks. Without the right equipment or a cooperative neighbor who works in or near the telecommuter's office, the person might have to go into the office so often that most of the benefits of working remotely would be lost. You should watch out for this kind of problem in the selection and job preview step. However, it's still better to learn about it during the initial telecommuter training rather than to wait until equipment is installed when you expect everything to be operational.

Another important part of this training is to work through a "what-if" exercise with the telecommuters. They should be guided through a set of unusual but plausible problems that could interrupt the flow of work. These might include the following: the neighbor/courier unexpectedly decides to take a week's vacation; the van pool driver decides to change his/her route because of turnover in the pool; the spouse/courier changes jobs and now will be working on the other side of town. By doing some contingency planning early, your telecommuters are less likely to be left in the lurch if problems develop.

"TELECOMMUTER, INC."

People who start their own businesses often say that there's nothing like it for providing a crash course in business planning and a disciplined approach to work. Without a network of subordinates and coworkers to fall back on, things don't get done unless the person does them.

Telecommuters can take a lesson from these entrepreneurs and should do just that as part of their training. If you encourage them to think as if they're in their own businesses they should be able to work through and better cope with the day-to-day problems and challenges.

This doesn't mean that telecommuters have unlimited freedom or flexibility to change policies or work assignments. They still have to do jobs they might not like or understand, or whose purpose they don't agree with. But that doesn't mean they can't approach the task a little differently, as a private entrepreneur would do. All of these tips are useful in the office but somehow there's more motivation to apply them while working remotely. For example, they might:

1. *Look for Shortcuts.* Without other people close at hand, the telecommuter can find ways to do the work differently. Just because a monthly report includes four different (and time-consuming) calculations of year-to-date spending doesn't mean two can't be dropped and the other two portrayed with a graph for added impact. If it saves an hour a month and the value of the report isn't jeopardized, nothing is lost. You'd still want them to check with the manager for approval if needed; what's important is taking the first step to challenge the status quo.

The same thing applies to simple habits like using typed versus handwritten memos. Unless you or your organization are sticklers for having everything typed, why not encourage telecommuters to jot down responses to memos in the margins of the original? Or, better yet, why not urge telecommuters to simply pick up the phone (if no written record is needed) or send a reply by electronic mail? Telecommuting is a break with tradition and it can be an excellent excuse to challenge old habits.

2. *Focus on the Customer.* Successful entrepreneurs, perhaps more than anyone, absolutely must keep the customers' needs and requirements at the top of the list. If telecommuters begin to think of their managers or coworkers as internal "customers," they're more likely to make the best use of time and be less tempted by distractions at the remote site. After all,

nobody wants to tell a valued "customer" (especially if it's the boss) that a project wasn't done because you took time off to play with your child.

3. *Keep Asking "What Business Am I In?"* Entrepreneurs who can't focus on what they're trying to do, and for whom, risk spending lots of time and money and having nothing to show for it. If they concentrate on a limited mission statement, they avoid tangents and are more likely to be successful. Admittedly, most telecommuters won't have as much discretion about what jobs to take on or which opportunities to pursue. But if they can remember what's important, they'll make the best use of time and avoid drifting just because they know the boss isn't likely to pop in unexpectedly.

As stated above, these three tips don't just apply to telecommuters. The reason they're included here is that telecommuting places extra demands on the worker as it does on the manager. The extra demands call for extra emphasis on techniques that help insure that the telecommuter is productive and doing valuable work while removed from day-to-day direct supervision.

TAMING THE COMFORTS OF HOME

Question: How do you know when it's time to stop telecommuting and get back to the central office? Answer: When most of your clothes no longer fit because the refrigerator is *so* close at hand. More than one telecommuter has retreated back to the office after adding a few pounds while at home. There's the same risk for overindulgence in alcohol, drugs, or even exercise—the casual jogger who now finds it more convenient to run greater distances can start sacrificing work time for road time.

Paul and Sarah Edwards' book, *Working from Home*, cited earlier in this chapter, has some excellent tips for avoiding these and other excesses. They note that awareness is the first step, followed by a need to take corrective action immediately. Telecommuters have to face the possibility that these unwanted habits may develop. For example, they can watch for obvious signs like weight gain or a cocktail hour that starts earlier and earlier in the day. They can also rely on comments and observations from others around them, and avoid the tendency to become defensive about them. Once the awareness of the problem is there, they can take some of the steps listed below or consult with someone from your firm's employee assistance program if one is available.*

---

*Reprinted with permission from *Working from Home* by Paul and Sarah Edwards, published by Jeremy P. Tarcher, Inc.

The Edwards' six ways to avoid overindulging while working are

1. *Pace yourself.* Work at a relaxed and reasonable pace; don't over-work; take breaks, and learn to relax.

2. *Watch your habits.* Develop "positive" addictions to replace negative ones. For example, learn to take an exercise break instead of a snack break.

3. *Don't be a hermit.* Be sure you have enough contact with people you enjoy. Don't get in a work rut—make sure you have time for some kind of interpersonal contact each day.

4. *Build in breaks.* Treat yourself with something special each day, something you can look forward to. If you're trying to watch your weight don't use food as the treat—watch a TV show you were interested in seeing, listen to a favorite record, or have a chat with a neighbor.

5. *Watch the snacks.* If you want to have snacks, schedule them. If you want to avoid the temptations of junk food, simply don't have it around.

6. *Remove temptations.* Keep whatever you want to avoid (food, liquor, cigarettes, and so forth) as far away from your work area as possible. Make it inconvenient to indulge yourself.

This is good advice for prospective telecommuters; it's all too easy to fall into bad habits that can be very hard to break. Knowing what's involved at the outset can help head off problems later on. Covering this information in a training session is also one final selection step; it might not be until this point that an employee realizes his/her potential weaknesses and has to give serious thought to how well they can be kept under control.

THE LOGISTICS AND MENTALITY OF WORKING AT HOME

1. Arrange for a reliable way to move information and materials to and from the office as needed.

2. Encourage telecommuters to think like and manage themselves like entrepreneurs—within reason.

3. Educate telecommuters about the risks and possible pitfalls of working with the comforts of home nearby.

LEGAL AND TAX ISSUES

The final training topic under the "Getting Organized" heading is how to handle various legal and tax implications of telecommuting. Very few, if any, of these points will apply to telecommuters working at remote sites

other than the home. Other sites are likely to be employer-owned or managed and there would normally be no difference in tax or legal implications for people at these sites.

The best bet is to seek advice from your firm's tax experts, legal counsel, and accounting advisors for this area. The regulations and their interpretations are always changing; what follows are only general guidelines.

Deduction for Home Office Expenses

When this book was written, the regulations on home office deductions
(based on IRS publication 587—"Business Use of Your Home") were still
tied to the rule that the part of the home in question must be used "*exclusively and regularly* as

1. The principal place of business for any trade or business in which
   you engage, or

2. A place to meet or deal with your patients, clients, or customers in
   normal course of your trade or business, or

3. A structure that is not attached to your house or residence and that
   is used in connection with your trade or business.

If you use your home for your work as an employee, this use of your
home must be for the convenience of your employer in addition to meeting tests 1, 2, or 3 above."

What this means to telecommuters is that expenses associated with
the home work area may or may not be deductible. It would be nice if you
could provide definitive answers, but this is a case where the regulations
lag behind the times. This problem affects not only the tax code but also
zoning regulations; more about them later. The troublesome points in the
tax code are the phrases underlined above; taken very literally they
would mean that few, if any, telecommuters would pass the test.

A telecommuter would probably have the strongest case for taking
the deduction if he/she spent most of the work week at home *and* if you as
the employer didn't provide a regular, assigned work area in the office.
Those conditions would help establish both the home as the regular work
place and the "convenience of the employer" provision. For telecommuters
who spend less time at home—say, one to three days a week—it might be
very difficult to claim a full or even partial deduction.

The toughest part would be the test of the home as a place for meeting with clients; some recent tax cases have disallowed deductions for
people like reporters who "meet" with clients (or people being interviewed)
over the phone, and not in person. This was judged to be insufficient for

meeting this test. If that's the case, what about telecommuters who will be "meeting" with coworkers or even customers by phone or electronic mail?

Tax Breaks Not Likely

Remember that the actual decision in any individual's case will depend on the circumstances and on the accumulated interpretations to date. Also, given the size of the country's deficit it's probably not realistic to expect very loose interpretations of existing tax codes or even looser provisions in new tax bills. You should get updated information from the appropriate authorities and cover the current information with new telecommuters as part of the training. Unless there's a radical change in the laws, don't give your telecommuters the impression that they can count on the home office deduction as an added benefit of telecommuting.

Insurance

The initial training should address changes in insurance needs due to work at home. Some of these (such as worker's compensation) are the shared responsibility of the employer and will be addressed in Chapter 11. Telecommuters need to check on two aspects of personal insurance:

1. *Equipment Theft and Damage in the Home.* Every homeowner's policy is different, but many now include (or have as a low-cost option) extended coverage for an "incidental office" and/or for computer equipment in the home. Most homeowner policies would not routinely cover losses for this equipment whether or not it was used in telecommuting. A good starting point for telecommuters is to check with their own insurance carriers to find out what's covered under a work-at-home arrangement. Then, if supplemental insurance is required for protecting the equipment, you have three options:

- The company can self-insure for equipment losses on its own equipment installed in the home;
- The company can take out additional coverage on its own for equipment used by telecommuters;
- The telecommuter can take out supplemental coverage for equipment he/she owns, and perhaps have this reimbursed by the employer.

Your choice among these options will depend on who owns the equipment, its value, the risk of damage or theft, and the potential for finger pointing between the insurance carriers. It pays to check with your firm's insurance experts before making your decision, and the tele-commuters can also check as part of their planning.

2. *Personal Liability.* The state Worker's Compensation laws are de-signed to address injury to employees, but what about injury to others at the work site? Homeowners generally carry insurance to protect against claims by visitors who might trip on their steps, for example, and corpo-rations have similar coverage. Telecommuters should be briefed about this as part of their training.

The question is whether the home becomes an extension of your of-fice because it's your employee who works there. If so, are you liable for injuries to others that occur in the telecommuter's home? As with the equipment theft issue, this is prime territory for wrangling between the homeowner's and the employer's insurance companies. Also, the question of liability may depend in part on how closely related the injury or acci-dent is to the telecommuter's work or work area at home.

For example, let's say a neighbor drops over for a cup of coffee—a purely casual visit for reasons unrelated to the telecommuter's work. The neighbor slips on a rug in the hall and breaks an arm. The neighbor may try to blame the telecommuter for the injury, but it's hard to imagine that any liability would extend to the employer.

On the other hand, what if the telecommuter invited the neighbor over specifically to look at a problem with the telecommuter's PC (which is owned by the employer). Because the machine's wiring is defective, the neighbor gets a nasty shock and claims an injury. Here, the liability might fall on the employer, but this can vary by the situation and from state to state.

As a general rule, the more closely related the injury is to the tele-commuter's work or equipment, the more likely it is that your firm will be brought in on the damage claim. An aggressive attorney might size up the situation, quickly determine that the employer has deeper pockets than the telecommuter, and try to involve the employer even when the cause of an injury isn't clear.

As with the tax issues, it's imperative to involve your firm's experts—legal counsel and insurance pros, for starters. These people can give the kind of guidance needed to help telecommuters understand the scope of the potential problem. Most important, they can help identify the right preventive steps to take to lessen the chance of a problem.

Zoning

The final topic in the legal area for telecommuters is zoning. Specifically, is it legal for this particular person doing this particular job to work at home? The reason this is covered here and not under the employer's responsibility is that zoning is highly variable. Two adjacent towns that are similar in most respects might have very different zoning ordinances, so your individual telecommuters may face very different situations. Even so, some employers might choose to check on zoning restrictions on their own, long before telecommuters are even selected. This will help you to know early on if any of the local communities have bans on work at home.

You might be wondering why zoning plays any part at all in telecommuting; after all, it's not as if your people were going to build a manufacturing plant in the backyard. The answer goes back to the very basis of zoning and its intent over the years. In most cases zoning is designed to establish and enforce the separation between residential and commercial activities that began after the Industrial Revolution. Before then, almost everyone worked at home; as commercial enterprises grew and as cars and mass transit came on the scene, people wanted to establish a clear barrier between commercial and living zones.

Types of Restrictions

With telecommuting, of course, things are coming full cycle. But ordinances written even quite recently often are unduly restrictive. Most zoning ordinances are written by *inclusion*, since it's impossible to list everything to be *excluded*. As a result, many ordinances can be quite narrow and may exclude telecommuting even though this wasn't the original intent. The regulations are out of step with the times; telecommuters are in uncharted territory in many respects because their situation isn't addressed in the law.

The restrictions on home occupations were generally meant to rule out those jobs that could change the character of a neighborhood. The goal is to keep out anything that introduces noise, odors, extra traffic, extra demands on municipal services—and in some highly restrictive cases, virtually any and all kinds of commercial activity.

Coping with Restrictions

Zoning ordinances today are like a patchwork quilt around the country. They're administered by each municipality with little uniformity, so it's hard to make generalizations. If you don't turn up any restrictions in your preliminary checking of ordinances in areas from which you're likely to draw telecommuters, you're home free. But in many cases, there will be some kinds of restrictions in zoning, or in townhouse or condominium covenants. Depending on how specific they are and how tough the community has been in the past on violations of this nature, you and the telecommuters can choose to

1. *Ignore the Ordinance and Go Underground.* If you don't advertise the fact you're having employees work at home (and encourage your telecommuters to try to keep it quiet also) you might avoid the problem. This is a philosophy of "what the officials and neighbors don't know won't hurt them." Of course, there's always the risk that a neighbor will get wind of the arrangement and tip off the officials. In some very exclusive neighborhoods this wouldn't be too unlikely, no matter how benign or unobtrusive telecommuting is in relation to the character of the neighborhood.

2. *Apply for a Variance or Permission for Telecommuters to Work at Home.* Depending on how strongly work at home is prohibited in the ordinance, the amount of clout the employer carries in the community, and the enforcement history of zoning restriction on home work, this may or may not be an easy process. Expert advice is a must here, even though applying for and getting the variance may not be a very involved process.

3. *Petition the Zoning Board to Change the Ordinance.* This, too, might or might not be a simple process. One tip on how to do this comes from Frances O'Neil, chairperson of the Zoning Committee of the National Alliance of Homebased Businesswomen (NAHB). The NAHB has been instrumental in raising awareness of undue restrictions on home business and home work. Ms. O'Neil's committee has prepared a model zoning ordinance that may be an effective compromise between today's trend toward work at home (for telecommuters and the self-employed) and the desire to maintain a neighborhood's character.

She notes that it's wise to have the employer make the application for the change. If the employee applies and is turned down, the officials might keep an eye out for signs that the person is working at home. But if the employer applies and is turned down, the city fathers won't know whom to watch. This kind of underground tactic (and the one mentioned before about having telecommuters work "illegally") may not always be the best route to take.

It's ironic that telecommuting inadvertently gets tarred with the same brush as other home occupations that do in fact disrupt the neighborhood. Until the regulations catch up with today's realities, some telecommuters and their employers might engage in these mildly subversive tactics. Don't get the impression that telecommuters (and their employers) have to be lawbreakers. The very restrictive ordinances (at least as they would apply to telecommuters) are probably the exception and not the rule in the eyes of many experts. Your telecommuters should understand the zoning issue in order to be prepared (with your help) to work within or effectively challenge the ordinances as need be.

LEGAL, TAX, AND REGULATORY REMINDERS

1. Help telecommuters get current, accurate advice on home office deductions and insurance coverage for personal and equipment liability.

2. Make sure everyone understands at the outset where the telecommuter's liability ends and yours begins.

3. Zoning can be a major obstacle or not an issue at all—work with your telecommuters to find out what, if any, restrictions they face and jointly develop a strategy to deal with them if needed.

TELECOMMUTER TRAINING TASK 2: DEALING WITH OTHERS

Many of the hoped-for benefits of telecommuting won't be realized unless telecommuters can effectively deal with those around them at home. This section will focus on the at-home form of remote work because most telecommuters at other remote sites simply won't face these challenges.

Being Taken Seriously

The biggest single obstacle for telecommuters is the risk that they won't be taken seriously. Others might make the assumption that the telecommuter isn't *really* working, and that telecommuting is a more casual kind of work that doesn't require the attention and discipline of office-based work.

It's understandable why people would make this assumption. After all, most people correctly assume that almost everyone goes *to* work. and that office work done at home is only those extra things you didn't manage to finish at the office. Just like the title of the popular book of a few years ago, *Real Men Don't Eat Quiche* (by Bruce Feirstein, Simon & Schuster), the feeling is that *real* business people don't work at home! We play at home, entertain at home, relax at home, and maybe work on hobbies or outside interests at home—but nobody really *works* at home.

The challenge for the telecommuter is to gently, but persuasively, break down these assumptions and stereotypes in the minds of family, friends, and neighbors. Some telecommuters might do it more persuasively than gently, simply walling themselves off completely from everything and everybody around them. This tactic might be very effective for outsiders, but could backfire if used with family members.

Self-Appraisal Is a Must

The telecommuter can deal with these perceptions only after coming to grips with them internally. He/she has to believe deep inside that work at home is more *work* than *home*. The initial selection and training for telecommuters must cover this need to take work at home every bit as seriously as work in the office. This can be a tough challenge for some people, especially since the entire structure and pattern of work life so familiar in the office is missing at home.

This is why you read earlier about the need for structure and rituals at home, even if they take different forms than in the office. The ideal situation is for the telecommuter—and the manager—to have the best of both worlds: the relative freedom and self-discipline of the remote site coupled with at least as much productivity and quality of work as in the office. This ideal situation won't develop unless the telecommuter has some very clear and down-to-earth expectations for how he/she will operate at home.

The Telecommuter's Own Mindset

You can give your prospective telecommuters an interesting exercise: have them list their own ideas about the pros and cons of work at home, and the major differences about how they expect to approach their work at home as compared with the office. If they do it individually and then compare answers in a group discussion, each person can uncover and clarify his/her concerns and expectations. It's also an excellent way for the instructor or manager to spot potential problems: a telecommuter who stresses the benefits over the responsibilities, for example, might need some counseling on the facts of telecommuting life.

COPING WITH FAMILY, FRIENDS, AND NEIGHBORS

Once the telecommuter understands that the remote work site (and the work done in it) is no less important than the central office, it's time to move on to dealing with others. That can't be done until those internal beliefs and expectations are clear. If they aren't, the telecommuter will project an easygoing attitude that tells others that it's okay to take the telecommuter and his/her work less seriously.

Let's look at some strategies for how the telecommuter can be taught to cope effectively with everyone he/she encounters while working at home. The best way to do this is to consider some of the typical potential problems that arise for telecommuters. These aren't made up—they are real examples of what people working at home have faced:

1. *"Please Sign Here."* You become the neighborhood drop-off person for the UPS or other delivery trucks when your neighbors aren't home because they're out shopping or even doing *real* work.

2. *"Here's My Key."* Your neighbor is going out and is expecting a repair or a delivery person to arrive. You're asked to let the person into the house, and maybe even "just hang around until the stove is fixed/couch is unpacked/piano is tuned." This game can also be played with the spouse who asks you to attend to these things while he/she goes out.

3. *"Let's Go Out and Play."* Neighbors or family members don't hesitate to interrupt you, either to socialize or invite you to go out shopping, play tennis or golf, or go out for a meal or a drink.

4. *"But It's Only for a Little While."* Your neighbor or spouse has to run out to the bank/doctor/store and little Tommy doesn't want to go along. You're expected to pinch-hit for the babysitter who just isn't around that time of day.

5. *"Dear Dad/Mommy/Buddy, Can You Just Help Me for a Minute?"* A family member or neighbor needs help fixing a bicycle, hanging a picture, chasing a runaway pet, or doing homework.

Don't get the idea that all of these are bad. Telecommuters can rarely wall themselves off from everyone else and most probably don't want to. The problem comes up when the other people *repeatedly* and *automatically* assume it's okay to ask these favors or interrupt. Telecommuters might even welcome some of these because they're the home-based equivalent of a trip to the water cooler or a stroll down the office corridor. One of the risks of telecommuting is that the person will go to the other extreme and get so engrossed in work for so long that his/her effectiveness drops.

Tips for Coping

Here are some ways to head off or cope with these and similar problems and at the same time stay on speaking terms with friends and family:

1. *Decide What You Want.* If the telecommuter's job, temperament, and work schedule can tolerate these interruptions, then nothing needs to be done. But if not, the telecommuter must decide what kind of work schedule and environment will be best. Some telecommuters find that an "open door/closed door" policy works; when the door is open, it's okay to come in—if it's *really* important. But when the door is closed, they're not to be disturbed except in cases of true emergencies. They also have to spell out that leaky faucets, empty dog food dishes, and missing guinea pigs probably aren't life and death matters.

2. *Hold a Family Council Meeting.* With today's family dispersing itself all over the place, it might be hard to hold the kind of family gathering that Robert Young always had on "Father Knows Best." But if the telecommuter can get everyone (or just the spouse) to sit down for a while, he/she can explain about the change in work locations. This is best done before telecommuting starts and is important even if he/she will be at home only two days a week.

The agenda for this meeting should include an explanation of telecommuting, a discussion of the advantages and disadvantages for everyone involved, and some coaching for the kids so they and their friends will understand that Dad or Mom didn't get fired or laid off. Stop and think about this: most kids who are old enough to think about these things would probably associate being home with being out of work. That would square with their experiences and with what they've read about or seen in TV shows or movies.

The meeting should also cover some ground rules for the times when the telecommuter is at home. Each family has to work this out individually, but the telecommuter's preferences (as noted above) must have been clearly thought out beforehand if this discussion is going to work. Also, some "participative management" can have the same benefits here as in the office. If the telecommuter can allow the spouse or family members to help develop the ground rules, they'll be more likely to abide by them because the rules are in part *their* rules.

It's also wise to plan for a follow-up meeting several weeks after actual telecommuting starts. This is a time to see how well everything has been working, how satisfied everyone is, and what changes might be needed. But telecommuters shouldn't and probably won't wait for this second session to deal with pressing problems. Some tolerance on both sides might be needed; however, it may take a couple of weeks for everyone to settle in to this new arrangement, and it's often better to overlook minor problems for this period.

Home Office Boundaries

Another important topic for the family get-together is access to and use of materials or equipment in the home work area. Everyone must understand that the pens, papers, and PC in the office aren't for everyone to play with or use. The major concern is with papers and reports that are confidential or proprietary in nature, and with any equipment that's in use. The topic of computer security will be covered in Chapter 11; for now, let's simply say that the PC or terminal should be kept completely off-limits to family members except for a one-time demonstration to satisfy everyone's natural curiosity.

A must for telecommuters to discuss during this family meeting is the need to protect passwords used remotely. Under no circumstances should a password be posted on or near the terminal or PC. This is asking for trouble, even if there's no imaginable way that a family member (or neighbor, for that matter) could know how to use it.

Staying Friends with Friends

So much for dealing with family members—what about friends and neighbors? The same principles apply although a neighborhood meeting may not be necessary to get the message across. In fact, there might not be any need to discuss it at all with neighbors unless problems crop up. At the first sign that the telecommuter's presence at home is being taken advantage of, it's essential that he/she confront the problem immediately. The longer the requests for little favors and the unwelcomed interruptions continue, the harder it will be to convince neighbors that the telecommuter means business.

A little tact and diplomacy go a long way in these dealings with family, friends, and neighbors. The telecommuter has to understand that he/she will probably continue to live with these people and have contacts outside of work hours. A very aggressive approach ("How dare you interrupt me —don't you realize I'm busy? Go away and don't bother me!") may win the battle but lose the war. An assertive approach ("I'm sorry but I don't have time to talk now. I'm working and I'll call/see you when I'm done later.") does the same thing without causing the anger and hurt feelings.

The key is to establish the rules *early* and *assertively* to make it clear that work is important. The same approach will work well with neighbors who might tend to take advantage. A calm, frank, well-worded discussion will help head off problems. Here's one way to get the message across: "I would prefer that you not rely on me to sign for your packages/let the delivery people in/pick up your son at school. I'm working at home, but my first responsibility is to my job, just as if I was in the office." It's a little longer, but much more effective than saying, "Get your own packages and get out of my hair!"

The Benefits of an Answering Machine

One tool that can be worth its weight in gold as a partial solution is an answering machine, which serves as a mechanical "buffer zone." Neighbors and friends can be asked to call instead of ring the doorbell, and the telecommuter can shut out all calls (and people) just by turning on the machine. This also cuts down on annoying interruptions from phone calls from people selling magazine subscriptions, frozen foods, or whatever.

You may not automatically assume the need to provide an answering machine for telecommuters, but it could be worth the investment. The machine is more reliable than other message-takers, and gives the manager or coworkers a way to leave word if the telecommuter is away from the desk. If you aren't going to provide the machine, telecommuters should be told about the benefits of the purchase during the training session. Several basic models are available for under $100, which shouldn't be a big burden for most telecommuters.

A Word About the Spouse

Dealings with family, friends, and neighbors have been discussed, but not much has been said about the spouse specifically. It's a good bet that telecommuting can make strong marriages better, may push weak ones over the edge, and make those in the middle get better or worse quite quickly. This is true for the telecommuter whose spouse is at home full-time, but also applies if the spouse works away from home. It's easy for that departing spouse to expect the telecommuter to take responsibility for household chores or errands—"After all, you *are* home all day."

The telecommuter's training should include some attention to the impact of work at home on relations with the spouse. You aren't trying to pry into the quality of the marriage, but it's important to help the telecommuter know what to expect. There are several federally funded research programs underway to assess the impact of work at home on family relationships, but as yet it's anybody's guess about exactly what will happen. One thing seems certain: a person who looks forward to walking out the door in the morning and not seeing the spouse (who remains at home) until evening will be a bad candidate for telecommuting. It's hard to imagine how this person could continue to concentrate on work in an atmosphere where proximity might breed contempt.

HELPING TELECOMMUTERS DEAL WITH OTHERS

People working at home run the risk of not being taken seriously. To help them be productive at home be sure your telecommuters are equipped to

✔ Understand why family, friends, and neighbors may not respect the work-at-home situation;

✔ Assertively and positively respond to interruptions or demands that impinge on work time;

✔ Work with—not against—family members by discussing and re-negotiating the boundaries between home and work;

✔ Pay special attention to security and liability—the home work area shouldn't be public space readily accessible to everyone else;

✔ Understand and assess the impact of work at home on relations with the spouse.

You might be getting the impression from reading this section that training telecommuters is more therapy than education. This isn't the case at all. It's a matter of making sure that some of the less obvious factors that can contribute to successful telecommuting aren't overlooked in the initial orientation and training.

TELECOMMUTER TRAINING TASK 3: LEARNING TO MANAGE YOUR JOB AND CAREER FROM A DISTANCE

In Chapter 7 you read about the manager's role in helping keep the tele-commuter's career on track. Here, you'll look at the specific things the telecommuter can do to stay in touch with the job and avoid being left out or left behind.

It's essential that telecommuters be trained to understand their own responsibility for staying in touch. No matter how much the manager or coworkers do to keep information flowing, the remote workers are the best judges of how much information is enough. Chapter 9 will cover some of the general methods for keeping telecommuters linked in, but here are four specific things a telecommuter can do. All assume that the telecommuter is out of the office between two and four days a week.

1. *Make the Best Use of the Telephone.* Aside from the benefits of simply having others to talk to, the phone can be the lifeline to the central office. If used improperly, though, it can be one of the biggest time-wasters imaginable.

The telecommuter should set a goal of talking to the manager and/or a key coworker once a day. This isn't just for a newsy chat to get caught up on the gossip, but don't underestimate the value of that kind of call. This should be a somewhat structured call covering the day's progress and problems, and key events in the office which may be of interest to the telecommuter. Examples of the latter are announcements about policy changes, personnel reassignments, and business developments.

The telecommuter has to make a decision early on about his/her accessibility via the phone, and the manager might want to be involved in this decision. One school of thought says the telecommuter should be every bit as accessible as if he/she were in the office, and, if possible, that the work location is "transparent" to callers. In other words, someone calling shouldn't be able to tell if the telecommuter is answering from the office or from a remote location. This is easy to do if the office phone system allows for call forwarding, so that people dialing the office extension are automatically transferred to the remote location number.

Another Viewpoint on Accessibility

The other school of thought is that one advantage of telecommuting is that it allows someone to get away from the standard pace of the office—including all those phone calls. If you allow the telecommuter to be reached as easily as if he/she were in the office, what's the sense of using the remote site? There's no simple answer to this question—it will vary based on the job, the person, whether a secretary normally picks up and screens calls, and the features in the office phone system (i.e., call forwarding). Also, some telecommuters report that callers who know they're calling the person's home can be reluctant to do so—going back to the traditional separation of home and work. Others report just the opposite—callers assume that *because* there's less separation between home and work there's no reason not to call on business almost any time.

You should advise your telecommuters to do as follows, with some guidance or concurrence from the manager:

- Analyze the job and decide how accessible you must be at what times and to what people.
- Decide whether knowing your actual work location makes a difference to some, all, or none of your normal callers.
- Based on the tasks to be done remotely, decide whether the normal call volume would be distracting.

Telecommuters can develop a sensible plan to handle incoming calls based on the answers to these questions. They can choose from among several options—using someone to screen calls and refer only certain ones, having none or all calls forwarded, or using an answering machine. The plan can then be discussed with others who need phone access—including people who might normally drop by while in the office.

2. *Make the Best Use of Electronic Mail or Voice Mail.* For many jobs, and especially those professional-level ones with lots of ongoing contact with a range of people, these two technologies can be invaluable. Their main advantage over the telephone is that two people can exchange messages or information without both having to be available at the same time. They're like having a personal secretary, an answering machine, and a 24-hour answering service all rolled into one—and then some. It may not be possible to justify a new electronic mail or voice mail system for a telecommuting pilot program, but if either or both are available, it's crazy not to take advantage of them. (See examples of their use in Chapter 9.)

3. *Set Up a Buddy System.* It's nice to have someone in the office act as an extra pair of hands, eyes, or ears. A trusted coworker (or subordinate) can help make sure that important information is passed along, look up something in a file or manual, and even keep the telecommuter posted on the latest scuttlebutt. Telecommuters who recognize the need for this support person and who cultivate a good relationship with him/her will find that many aspects of remote work will go much more smoothly.

4. *Set Up a Social Event as Meeting Time.* The manager might choose to do this, but if not, the telecommuter can take the initiative to declare every third Thursday as the department pizza night, for example. Telecommuters who regularly spend two to four days out of the office need a session like this, no matter how well the more formal communications methods work. This kind of regular gathering helps everyone get caught

up on what's going on and strengthens some important ties between the telecommuter and the coworkers.

New telecommuters need to know about these four techniques. They may sound like common-sense or even simplistic tips, but these are the details that help telecommuting go smoothly and work out well for all involved.

Career Management:
The Telecommuter's Responsibility

Finally, let's look at long-distance career-management methods. There isn't enough information accumulated yet to say if there's a career progress penalty attached with telecommuting. The preventive steps (such as "spotlighting") outlined in the last chapter should help the manager head off most of these problems. But what's the telecommuter's responsibility in this area?

First, telecommuters should learn about the need to manage the boss. This isn't meant in a manipulative sense—it's just that subordinates can help themselves if they understand more about what the boss needs and how he/she operates. This is an important skill in the office, but takes on new dimensions for remote workers. (An excellent resource here is the book *How to Manage Your Boss* by Christopher Hegarty, published by Ballantine Books.)

Second, telecommuters have to take some responsibility for "spotlighting" themselves. This doesn't mean they should constantly be blowing their own horns, but they should be alert to opportunities to bring their work to the attention of management. This must be done with the knowledge and support of the direct supervisor so that person doesn't feel as though there's a game of oneupmanship going on. Some ways of doing this include

- Making sure that those who receive the telecommuter's work know that it's his/her product;
- Looking for opportunities to meet with management with whom the telecommuter would normally be dealing with if in the office five days a week;
- Avoiding becoming a hermit just because of the remote work done several days a week. This means staying in touch with others as de-

scribed earlier in the chapter, and perhaps even going to some extra lengths to keep one's name in the limelight.

Some potential telecommuters get excited about the prospect of being freed from the organizational equivalent of jury duty—involvement in the United Way or Savings Bonds campaigns, or with company functions like picnics or open houses. Everyone knows these jobs, like jury duty, are important, but few actually want to do them. But these are excellent ways of getting visibility, especially among senior management members who support these programs. Involvement in these while telecommuting can help keep one's name in the limelight (if that's what's intended) and also helps further demonstrate the visibility of telecommuting.

**CHECKLIST FOR HELPING TELECOMMUTERS
BRIDGE THE GAP
BETWEEN HOME AND OFFICE**

✔ Make it clear from the start that remote workers should *expect* to stay in touch.

✔ Coach telecommuters on the pros and cons of different approaches to phone accessibility. Then, encourage them to take a position and make it known to others.

✔ Use electronic mail or voice mail whenever possible to supplement phone contact.

✔ Encourage the use of a "buddy system" and regular social events as two informal ways to maintain contacts with the office.

✔ Make sure telecommuters know why and how to take some responsibility for managing their own careers from a distance.

In summary, there's a lot of information to be delivered to new telecommuters. You've seen a long list of topics in this chapter without much attention to actual methods for getting them across. This can be done in a combination of written materials and group sessions, though it's advisable to invest at least one day in a group session to discuss these ideas. Everything doesn't have to be covered at once; in fact, there's a real benefit to handling the basics initially and then covering other less immediate topics (such as career management) later. These could be done along with periodic follow-up sessions where telecommuters are brought together to share ideas about how they're handling remote work.

Effective telecommuting requires more than a simple decision to allow people to work away from the office. Managers and telecommuters themselves need some careful preparation for what lies ahead.

9

The Best Way to Link the Telecommuters to the Office

Mention the idea of work at home to many people and the first objection that gets raised is "I'd go crazy working alone at home five days a week." This is absolutely right—anyone used to an office environment probably *would* have a rough time with full-time remote work at home.

One of the most interesting challenges in telecommuting is to structure it so that people don't start climbing the four walls of their home offices. This chapter will show you how to maintain effective links between the office and the remote site so that telecommuters continue to feel a part of the office.

To some extent the need for these links depends on how much time the person spends at home as opposed to other remote sites. The other kinds of remote work locations listed in Chapter 3 all involve groups of employees, so it's the home where the potential for isolation is greatest. That doesn't mean you should necessarily steer clear of the home sites because of these potential problems; it just means you need some extra preparation.

The focus of this chapter is the telecommuter who spends up to four days at home every week. This is probably an extreme case; for many reasons that should be evident by now it's unlikely that someone will spend that much time continuously in that one remote work location. **115**

Nevertheless, the methods discussed will fit that scenario and can be adapted as needed for telecommuters whose work schedules and locations are more varied. The important thing is the rationale behind the techniques mentioned; with that in mind you can fit them to almost any situation.

THE NEED FOR LINKING

Let's first look at why it's important to be concerned about keeping telecommuters linked to the office. This isn't as obvious as it may seem; after all, aren't telecommuters people who don't mind being apart from the office hubbub, and perhaps even prefer a little isolation? This description is accurate for some telecommuters, but even they need information and resources from the office. More important, their managers need to keep them linked into* the office as one way of making sure they continue to perform up to expectations.

Here are three reasons why it's important to maintain these links:

1. *Information Flow.* Few, if any, telecommuters can work completely independently. They need a constant flow of information, materials, and other resources to be able to do their jobs effectively.

2. *Need to Belong.* Most, if not all, telecommuters want to continue to feel that they're part of the gang even if the gang is working miles away. The sense of belonging is important to almost everyone and it can contribute to improved performance. An excellent example of this is all the things most firms do to keep their field sales representatives informed and in touch. These range from bulletins and newsletters to sales meetings and "work-with" sessions with the manager. Even though the sales reps can and do work effectively on their own, they benefit from a sense of being a part of the organization.

3. *Coworker Needs.* Coworkers of telecommuters have similar needs as the first two items but in reverse. They need to be kept abreast of the telecommuter's activities, problems, and plans, and often benefit from the informal contact that normally happens in the office. This is even more true of internal "clients" of telecommuters who work in service-oriented staff groups. For example, the marketing manager for whom a telecommuting programmer is writing a computer program, wants to know how

---

*NOTE: In this chapter, the term "linked into" has nothing to do with the technical or telecommunications links between remote sites and the office. It has more of a psychological orientation—making sure the telecommuters continue to *feel* that they're part of the office.

it's progressing, what enhancements might be possible, and whether the deadline will be met.

Staying in Tune with the Office

There's a fourth reason as well. It was common practice in the early days of missionary work (before more widespread and reliable forms of communications) to periodically bring in the missionaries from the field. One reason was to keep them from "going native"—to make sure they were reminded of their links to a certain philosophy, and to keep them from adopting too many of the habits or beliefs of the local people they were serving. It's not a perfect analogy but the same needs exist for telecommuters, especially those working only at home. The more often they're kept in touch with the office and its norms and culture, the less the risk that they'll have trouble getting reestablished if they return to the office full-time. Even if that's not planned, it makes sense to keep sending signs that telecommuters are part of the office even though they're apart from it.

REASONS TO KEEP TELECOMMUTERS
LINKED TO THE OFFICE

1. Few people can work completely independently.
2. Remote workers want to feel as though they still belong.
3. Telecommuters' coworkers need access to their distant peers.
4. Telecommuters should stay in touch with office norms and culture.

Your goal is to create the expectation of continued contact, not separation.

TIME IN THE OFFICE: HOW MUCH, WHY, AND HOW?

So far you've seen references to varying amounts of time at the remote location(s). Telecommuters shouldn't be offsite for five full days a week except in rare cases, but you still have to decide how much time back in the office is right.

This is a difficult question because of the range of job types and people suited for telecommuting. Also, it depends on your organization's objectives for using remote work. For example, if a primary goal is to reduce cramped office conditions, it doesn't help much to have telecommuters spend only a day or so away from the office. However, for the purpose of this section, let's assume that this kind of space constraint isn't an issue.

You can easily build it in later once you've made decisions about these five considerations for setting the weekly schedule:

1: Employee Preference

You saw in Chapter 6 that different telecommuting candidates will have different reasons for wanting to work remotely. Similarly, they'll each have preferences about how much time will be spent remotely, especially at home. All else being equal, there's no reason why a telecommuter shouldn't work remotely for as much time as the manager and the job allow, up to his/her own personal limit.

By the same token, you shouldn't require remote workers to stay away from the office more than they'd like. The element of willingness is important all along in telecommuting; a person who wants to be at home only two days a week shouldn't be forced to stretch it to four days. If this happens, what might otherwise be an enjoyable change can become an unwelcome restriction. If you find that extended periods of near-continuous remote work will be required, you should make this clear to prospective telecommuters at the outset so they can decide on their involvement accordingly.

Another reason for avoiding mandatory remote work is the implication for employee relations. One reason the unions are keeping a careful eye on telecommuting is their concern that abusive practices might develop. An example of such a practice would be mandatory remote work as a condition of employment for employees who had no prior reason to believe this would be required.

2: Manager Preference

Some telecommuters will work as nearly autonomous professionals with little or no direct supervision from the manager. But most will continue to be responsible to supervisors who may have mixed feelings about telecommuting. Or, the manager might feel that the job can't be done well if the person is away from the office for more than a certain amount of time.

You have to be sensitive to the manager's preferences or even instincts in this regard. Remember that most managers are used to managing by observation at least part of the time and are used to easy access to the staff. If the manager feels that the quality of the work, the ability to supervise, or the level of service to the telecommuter's customers will suffer, don't force the issue.

Also remember that some of these beliefs might change as a result of the kind of training described in Chapter 7. You have to walk a fine line here: you want the manager to support the project, yet you don't want to give in to his/her wishes if they're based on faulty assumptions about remote supervision.

A Gradual Shift

A good compromise here is to start off with a very limited schedule. For example, the remote workers could be out of the office only one or two days a week during the first month or two, even though the optimal level is three or four days a week. Once everyone gets used to the realities of remote work, the schedule can be expanded.

This kind of gradual shift to remote work has other benefits:

- First, it lets you work the kinks out of the system; all the details about transfer of materials, equipment and telecommunications arrangements (if applicable), and simply the feel of remote management, without the demands of a full-time schedule.

- Second, it also allows the telecommuter to get used to remote work and learn how best to stay in touch with the office, what other materials are needed, and how to establish the schedules and rituals noted in Chapter 8.

- Third, and perhaps most important, it allows the telecommuter's family (where appropriate) to come to terms with the new blend of home and work life. Instead of an all-or-nothing transition, a more gradual implementation allows more relaxing learning and accommodation all around.

3: Organization Culture

This third factor obviously has a lot to do with telecommuting in general and its extent in particular. If your firm's culture encourages independent work and more self-reliant employees, you'll adapt more easily to extended periods of remote work. Other organizations that pride themselves in a more tightly controlled environment might do well by allowing a handful of people to telecommute one day a week at first.

One of the worst strategies is to impose a remote work schedule of three or more days a week in an organization that fits the second description above. While there might be compelling business reasons to do so, extensive telecommuting would trigger a major case of culture shock. There's no telling what might happen—the program could be undermined, the telecommuters might find their work coming under increased scrutiny, and you as program manager might be forced into a position of constantly defending the concept. If the telecommuting shoe fits, wear it; if it doesn't, don't force it to fit.

4: Project and Work Cycles

Another factor in figuring out how much time is spent away from the office is the changing nature of the tasks over time. In Chapter 5 you saw that some jobs are better suited for telecommuting during certain repetitive parts of a project cyle. Also, seasonality of the business affects the portability of other jobs.

This means some telecommuters might work best under a schedule that's based on these work patterns. A market research analyst might spend four or five days a week in the office during crucial planning periods when his/her impromptu advice is needed almost constantly. Three or four days away a week might work during the actual execution and analysis stages of research projects.

This kind of varying pattern is a good news–bad news situation. The good news is that the flexibility might be welcomed by the telecommuter but could cause problems for the manager. Also, this pattern could play havoc with space planning considerations; it's hard to budget limited space if use patterns can't be accurately projected. The counterargument for this is the possibility of more shared office space so these transient telecommuters could always have work space available—though it might not be their own personal offices as they're used to now.

In many ways this "fluid" scheduling is ideal because it fits the concept of telecommuting to the quirks of each job. Some of the most successful remote work programs are done so informally that no one thinks of them as "programs" per se; relative freedom in choosing one's own work location is akin to freedom in choosing what to wear. General guidelines are set forth but the specifics are left up to the individual. But not every employee, manager, or organization is ready to make the jump from a fairly regular and predictable set of work schedules and locations to one that's mostly up to the individual.

5: Job Requirements

This last factor is woven into the other four but deserves separate mention. The overriding concern when setting up remote work schedules has to be the ability to do the job *as required.* This is different from the ability to do the job *as it's done now.* Just because an employee makes ten trips to the file cabinet daily or drops in on the boss eight times a day, it doesn't mean his/her job isn't suited to remote work. It may just mean that it's being done a little sloppily now and with some organization and planning could be done as well or better remotely.

One of the key points here is the predictability of the work involved. A job with tasks that don't vary much from day to day or week to week, and for which the work methods are well understood and fairly routine, usually lends itself to more remote time. Good examples include clerical or data entry work, technical staff professional jobs like actuaries, statisticians, or writers, or telephone-based jobs like customer service, reservations, order-taking, or outbound telemarketing. You can look out for the next three to six months, for instance, and predict with relative certainty what these jobs will entail. Unless there are pressures to the contrary from the four prior factors, these kinds of jobs can be done remotely very well for most of the work week.

CHECKLIST OF THINGS TO CONSIDER WHEN SCHEDULING OFFICE TIME

- ✔ Telecommuter's preferences
- ✔ Manager's preferences and need for direct contact
- ✔ Organization culture and norms for/against independent work
- ✔ Project or work cycles
- ✔ Job requirements

  Be sure to weigh the organization's needs against the telecommuter's preference; remote work *must* include the right amount and type of time in the office.

Satisfying the Powers That Be

You may also have legitimate reasons for limiting the remote work time even though the tasks involved would allow more time away. One reason is the self-interest of someone who has enough clout to be listened to, even if it's someone not in the telecommuter's chain of command. To see how this applies, let's look at a case of a financial analyst responsible for doing feasibility studies on the financial aspects of new product introductions.

This person might have gained the respect of the marketing manager he/she serves and has become a valued member of the marketing planning team. Assume that the analyst's direct manager (in the accounting department) decides to allow the analyst to work at home three days a week and the analyst agrees. The marketing manager might hit the roof for purely selfish reasons. Even though everyone involved agrees that the job *could* be done remotely on that schedule, doing so would take away some flexibility and even some status from the marketing manager.

He/she can no longer count on being able to pick up the phone and summon the analyst to a quick meeting where some financial information or judgment is needed. The marketing manager might eventually learn to do things differently, but at the outset may try to block the implementation of the analyst's remote work. Maybe this seems narrow-minded, especially if there are some compelling business reasons for getting involved in telecommuting to begin with. But it's a real-life, everyday happening; most people give as much weight to self-interest as to other factors. Don't assume that because telecommuting is a good business proposition everyone will accept it with open arms.

What's the best way to cope with this situation, especially if there *is* a compelling reason to move ahead with a remote work program? Your best bet is to learn more about why the person with the veto power is willing to exercise it. It may be nothing more than a misconception about telecommuting or a bad experience in the past, either of which usually can be acknowledged and dealt with. Sometimes, though, it's more serious and you'll have to change the work schedule and bow to this person's wishes.

MORE TIPS ON WORK SCHEDULING

Here are three summary considerations in remote work scheduling—these will help you design the best work schedule to fit your situation. Don't fall into the trap of thinking that telecommuting has to be an all-or-nothing experience, and that if it can't be done five days a week it's not worth doing. Keep these points in mind when trying to figure out how many days are best:

1. *Start Off Slowly.* It's almost always easier to add more remote work time than to take it away, especially if you're taking it away for reasons having nothing to do with telecommuter preferences. Better to

start off with only a few days a week and increase it when and if it's warranted than to launch a more extensive program that might be harder to manage in its early stages.

2. *Work Out the Problems.* Remember that everyone involved (especially key members of management) will be watching to be sure that the telecommuters' overall performance is at least as good as it is in the office. One fear some people have is that the organization won't get much in return for giving employees this kind of flexibility. Until the bugs are ironed out (and there *will* be bugs, no matter how carefully you plan) it might be better to work with a more limited schedule.

Sometimes there's a cost attached to this kind of phase-in for applications where a terminal or PC is used at the remote site. If you need duplicate equipment (for both sites) the equipment costs will be double for the initial period. The best way to understand this cost is to think of it as insurance for a smooth telecommuting program in the long run.

3. *Be Aggressive, Yet Careful.* Contrary to the last two suggestions, don't be reluctant to start off with a more ambitious plan if (and only if) there's a lot of momentum building up in favor of it. If the task allows it, the telecommuters and their managers support it, and there are no naysayers taking potshots at you, by all means go full steam ahead. But don't ignore the need to *closely* monitor early progress to watch for signs of problems. That momentum could disappear overnight if you don't deal with snags decisively and quickly.

DRAWING THE BLUEPRINT
FOR LINKING THE TELECOMMUTERS

You now know the reasons for keeping telecommuters tied to the office and have some guidelines for deciding how much time is needed in the office. The next step is to find ways to extend the sense of being in the office to telecommuters at remote sites. Your objective here is to enable the remote workers to be as self-sufficient as possible while away from the office, and at the same time give them the sense that they're still part of the social and information network.

When setting up telecommuters for remote work, a good planning step is to profile their needs for information and interaction with others. If you can catalog the people, files, manuals, and other resources in the telecommuter's network, you can begin to effectively extend that network to the remote site. Here are three key questions to ask.

1: With Whom Does the Telecommuter Have Frequent Contact?

Make a list of the people or departments who interact most often with the telecommuter. If you can look at why, how often, and in what form that contact occurs (e.g., phone, memo, face-to-face) you'll begin to get an idea of what can be done to maintain that contact over a distance.

Here's a perfect example of why it's important to avoid taking things for granted with telecommuting. Just because two people talk with each other five times a day to ask or answer questions doesn't mean that they can't do their jobs if one starts telecommuting. The question to ask is how many of those contacts can be "saved up" and handled in one or two visits per week or, better yet, in a phone call or via electronic mail? Most office workers have developed habits out of convenience that don't become evident until you begin profiling these contacts.

In this respect, you can take a lesson from field sales people who come in for an assignment at the central office. Sometimes their office-based coworkers are amazed at their efficiency; they use the phone very effectively, rely on quick handwritten memos, have planned agendas for even the shortest meetings, and use other techniques to make the best use of their time. The reason? They've come out of a field environment—a *remote work* environment—where they didn't have the luxury of face-to-face contact except in rare cases.

The skills they developed were survival skills. This way of thinking extends to telecommuters who now have to deal with others at a distance. If you're responsible for setting up a telecommuting program, you can make your job easier by tapping the expertise of a seasoned field manager (sales, service, or other) even if the person is from another functional area. This remote work veteran can probably save you and the telecommuters lots of time and aggravation.

Once you profile these contacts you can begin asking some questions about alternatives. For example, do all in-person contacts have to be that way? How many of the impromptu meetings could have been scheduled in advance? How widely used is electronic mail, and is it accessible to most or all of the people in the telecommuter's network? These and similar questions lead you to answers that help define the best ways to keep the telecommuter in touch.

In doing so, don't forget that every telecommuter will be accessible via that wonderful invention called *the telephone.* Electronic or voice mail and PCs and terminals aside, the good old telephone is a basic business tool. As an interesting experiment, keep track of how often you get phone calls from coworkers who are within easy walking distance of your office; you'll probably be surprised how many there are. There's no reason why the phone can't be used just as well from the remote site.

2. What "Materials" Are Used Regularly in the Office?

This question forces you to look beyond people contact and examine the need for things—files, manuals, books, samples, and machines. The key word here is *regularly*—don't be concerned about the need to have access to bulky blueprints once every two months or other infrequent requirements.

As you gather this information be sure to determine whether or not the telecommuter needs hands-on access to the item. If a secretary, clerk, or coworker can go to a file drawer or manual and look up a specific piece of information, then the distance from that resource isn't a problem. But if the telecommuter actually needs to get in there and rummage around, you'll have to consider getting a duplicate copy for the remote site.

The idea of duplicates has some practical limits. It's one thing to get another copy of a reference manual at little or no cost, but quite another to even think of copying extensive customer files. In the latter case there are two alternatives. First, more and more firms are putting large files like this on the computer so they can be accessed via terminal. Second, there are low-cost (under $200) portable microfiche readers available for those applications where microfiche is already used in the office. Even if it's not, consider the advantages of having certain documents put on microfiche if the cost is justified by the convenience to the telecommuter.

Jobs involving frequent access to equipment, product samples, large drawings or artwork, and other items hard or impractical to transport present a different problem. It's possible they should be screened out of telecommuting applications altogether, as noted in Chapter 5. Otherwise, you need to make a decision about how much access is actually needed and compare this with the overall feasibility of the application.

If the telecommuter has to come into the office once a day or if you have to pay for a messenger service to shuttle artwork to the remote site, you may be wiping out some of the advantages of remote work. Even though the cost of facsimile transmission has dropped and quality has improved, this technology can't be relied on for large items. Other technologies for transmitting graphics (by digitizing an image and storing and sending it as a computer file) are just emerging. Most of them aren't cheap and can't be cost-justified for telecommuting applications.

3: What Other Printed Materials Are Seen Regularly?

This last question deals with the normal stream of mail that lands on the telecommuter's office desk. This includes things like internal memos and reports, letters from outsiders, and brochures and catalogs. You need a plan to make this material available if the telecommuter is going to be out of the office for more than two days a week. If it's two nonconsecutive days or less, you normally won't need to get it to the remote site. This would be the same as being out of the office for a day when traveling or ill.

Your strategy here depends on the time value of the mail and the availability of electronic transmission methods. If electronic mail is used, the problem can be almost entirely avoided if internally generated memos are prepared on terminals or PCs and sent to the remote site. This can be done even if the memo is printed and distributed on paper for in-office readers. The same is true if facsimile equipment is available, although it's unlikely that you could justify this for many individual telecommuters at home. You might see facsimile playing a much larger role at satellite or neighborhood centers where there are many telecommuters.

Even without electronic tools the mail still must go through. One option is to have it sorted in the office and forward (via courier or neighbor as described in Chapter 8) the most important items to the remote site. Another is to have the originators send the mail directly to the remote site, though this can be cumbersome and actually cause more delays. The biggest potential problem is for the telecommuter who gets a lot of mail that should be seen as quickly as it would have been in the offfice, and where there's no electronic alternative to some kind of courier system. In this case, the person's productivity and effectiveness hinges on a reliable courier method. This doesn't necessarily mean you'll run into problems, but it does add another layer of complexity to the remote work situation.

When you analyze this flow of mail, don't lose sight of internal mail other than memos or letters. Most people are on various distribution or routing lists for reports or journals, many of which have time value but aren't really urgent. If you're going to try to replicate the information flow available in the office (which is exactly what this process is all about), those items have to get to the remote site also. The advantage with these is that you can usually let them accumulate until the next time the telecommuter comes into the office.

HOW TO PROFILE THE TELECOMMUTER'S NEED
FOR INFORMATION

1. Find out who's in the telecommuter's network—whom does he/she deal with most often?

2. Find out what materials (of all kinds) are used in the office and determine whether and how to make them available offsite.

3. Find out how much mail the telecommuter gets, where it comes from, and how to economically get it to the remote site.

The telecommuter needs access to the people, materials, and mail that are part of the job. Provide the access with a mix of phone calls, physical or electronic transfer, and time in the office. Use electronic mail or voice mail whenever possible to help bridge the distance.

THE ROLE OF ELECTRONIC AND VOICE MAIL

You've seen repeated references to these technologies as being helpful in remote work. You might be wondering how important they are in telecommuting: the answer is that they can't hurt, almost always will help, and in some cases are key factors in possible productivity gains.

To understand what these are and what the benefits are, let's look at how messages flow in most offices now. If Tom wants to tell Mary about a possible problem in the agenda for next week's meeting, he can

- *Pick up the phone and call her,* hoping that she's at her desk *and* not on the phone *and* not in a meeting. If he can't get to her, he can leave a message with her secretary and hope she gets it right—*if* he wants to try to condense his questions into a short message.

- *Put it in writing.* He can jot it down himself and put the note on Mary's desk (if he works nearby) or send it to her or dictate a memo to be typed or give the handwritten note to his secretary for typing.

- *Wait until he runs into Mary* in the hallway or at lunch and mention it to her, if he remembers. Mary then will have to remember what Tom told her—and may, in fact, suggest that Tom call her or send her a note to confirm just to be sure.

The problem is clear: the odds of the message getting through quickly and correctly are often low. "Telephone tag," slow or busy secretaries, and inefficient interoffice mail systems are only three of the problems that plague many people in the office. These problems can be aggravated under telecommuting.

This is where the two technologies come in. Both use computer technology to get messages to others (in text or voice) and save time for both parties. Here's how the same scenario would look if the company had either system:

ELECTRONIC MAIL—Tom sits down at his terminal or PC at home, in the office, or on the road and types in his message to Mary, "addressing" it to her mailbox. He can edit it, store it, send it as is, or wait and send it later. He can save a file copy for himself or send electronic copies to others. He can even request the system to confirm that Mary received it.

VOICE MAIL—Tom picks up the phone—any pushbutton phone—and dials the voice mail system. He then identifies himself with a voice mailbox number via the phone's buttons. Next, he pushes the code for leaving a message and dictates it, including pushing in the numbers for Mary's voice mailbox. He has some of the same options as with electronic mail (e.g., copies to others, delayed sending, and confirmation).

When Mary either reads or hears Tom's message, she can reply immediately, reply later, or forward Tom's message—with a "cover memo," if desired—to others who might be going to the same meeting. These technologies are proven and are here today. Of the two, electronic mail is more widely used because voice mail is more costly. The process for breaking down a voice message and storing it in a computer (since voice mail is *not* an answering machine) uses a good deal of computing power and computer memory. But these costs are dropping, and some observers believe voice mail will spread very quickly because of two factors. It doesn't require the user to sit at a keyboard, and telephones are more accessible and widespread than PCs or terminals. In summary, having these tools as part of telecommuting is a big plus because of the added speed, convenience, and flexibility.

SPREADING THE NEWS

Another way to extend the feel of the office is to capture as much information as possible about general organization events and make it available to the telecommuters. Every organization has several news outlets that people rely on to stay current with at least the formal side of things. These include company newspapers or magazines, bulletin board postings, desk drops, and (increasingly) in-house videotex systems that are like a running news ticker.

Remote workers who are away only one or two days a week generally can catch up on these news sources when they come in. A bulletin board posting is usually up for a week or so in most organizations; the contents of any controversial or "hot" posting would reach the telecommuters via the grapevine long before their next visit to the office anyhow. But telecommuters who are only in the office once or twice a week need access to this information more quickly.

In some cases, you can do this via whatever courier system is being used for correspondence. If your people are used to seeing the company newspaper on the desk every Wednesday morning, it would be great if that same newspaper appeared at the remote site on Wednesday as well. It may seem like a small thing, but the regular arrival of that newspaper is one way to help remote workers feel that they aren't out of the mainstream by being out of the office.

This is also another application for electronic mail. If bulletin board announcements are prepared on word processing systems, there's no reason why a copy of the announcement can't be sent to the remote workers at the same time as it's printed for posting in the office. Also, some mail systems or other internal office automation systems have a "billboard" feature that shows important messages on the screen when users sign on. These methods would keep remote workers who have access to these systems every bit as informed as their counterparts in the office.

Using a Broadcaster

One last way to tie everyone together is to make someone in the office responsible for informing the remote workers of activities they would have learned about had they been in the office. This is a kind of fail-safe procedure to catch whatever might not be communicated via the methods described so far. In reality, a lot of this will go on very informally; you can bet that the office grapevine will extend its reach beyond the office walls, thanks to the ever-present telephone.

The problem with the grapevine is that it's unpredictable; you can never be sure what information gets passed on and how quickly. That's why you'll want to designate a more official broadcaster who can get the message out as needed. This role will often be filled by the manager as part of the ongoing discussions with the telecommuter. Appointing someone else to share this duty can't hurt, even if there's some duplication of effort.

The biggest use for this broadcaster role isn't the official notices but the unofficial or social events. These can include everything from personnel changes (actual or rumored) and key business events (possible new customers or acquisitions), to the fact that the gang in the office is going out to lunch or for a drink after work and wants to invite the remote worker(s) to join them.

To summarize, it's to everyone's advantage if there's some detailed planning to help the telecommuter continue to feel a part of the office. This breaks down the distance between the office and the remote sites, and reminds everyone that being physically dispersed doesn't mean being isolated and separated from the mainstream.

SOME SPECIFIC LINKING METHODS AND TOOLS

Here are four more tools you can use in this linking process.

1: Meetings in the Office

The most obvious method is meetings held while the telecommuter is in the office. One thing that helps determine the frequency of office visits is the need for face-to-face contact with coworkers or the manager. These meetings can serve several purposes:

- *Planning meetings* to lay out the week's work, including specific goals, timetables, and checkpoints;
- *Progress meetings* to check how well the work is going and to give corrective feedback;
- *Customer or user update meetings* to meet the needs of the telecommuter's internal clients;
- *Staff meetings* to share new information, solve department problems, agree on project schedules, and keep abreast of each others' work;
- *"Brown bag" sessions* to share ideas, kick around new concepts, and stay up to date on new techniques.

This last category addresses one of the concerns voiced about telecommuting: the remote worker's need to stay in touch with changes in methods, or to draw on or add to the pool of expertise in the department. Some of this will happen via phone or electronic mail, but it's also helpful to schedule specific meetings just to take time out and hash over a certain method or problem.

The number and frequency of these meetings will vary widely from person to person. At minimum, you'll want to build in a weekly sit-down review with the manager with interim phone meetings as needed. Meetings with internal customers or clients will follow the same pattern. Other meetings will be scheduled as needed, although it's to the telecommuter's advantage to try to cover as much as possible on the phone.

Planning and Flexibility Are Important

These meetings will account for a good deal of the time spent in the office, especially if the telecommuter is only coming in one day a week. Some careful planning is needed to make the best of this time. Also, some telecommuters might have to reserve some of the office time for impromptu or one-time meetings that aren't regular events. These include special-purpose meetings (budget reviews, planning sessions) or simply some time to drop in on coworkers for a short bull session.

On top of this, everyone has to recognize that there may be times when the telecommuter has to come in for a one-hour meeting on what would normally be a remote-work day. This can be unsettling to the remote worker and counterproductive if it happens often. If this becomes a problem, you have to address it early to see if the scheduling can better accommodate the telecommuter's schedule. There has to be flexibility on both sides; if the telecommuter is too rigid in his/her scheduling, people may criticize the whole concept of remote work. If enough people get upset by these scheduling problems, your telecommuting program may come under serious attack.

2: The Telephone

You've learned about the use of the phone here and in Chapter 8. It's a very effective linking tool as long as remote workers continue to be accessible. For some, the best approach might be to stick to announced phone times—hours when the remote worker promises to be in for calls unless there's an unusual situation. These might be 9 to 11 A.M. and 3 to 5 P.M., for instance—hours that shouldn't be hard for either early birds or night owls to maintain. With this schedule, the office people can know with relative certainty when they can reach the telecommuter. This is probably a better deal for callers than they'd have if the remote worker was in the office.

Phone access to telecommuters can be abused. If office people are picking up the phone for lots of little questions instead of saving them up and making one or two calls a day (if there's no urgency), the phone becomes a major distraction instead of a business tool. This problem can't be forecast during the planning stages, but you have to deal with it quickly if it comes up later. These pushbutton-happy coworkers have to be treated like the friendly neighbors described in Chapter 8; a calm, assertive approach will go a lot further than ranting and raving about how inconsiderate and insensitive one's coworkers are.

3: Meetings at the Remote Site

So far, it's been assumed that any meetings needed will be held at the office. This isn't a bad assumption since most of the people, files, and materials are there. But there's no reason why some meetings can't be held at the remote site.

This will depend on which remote sites you're using. If it's a satellite or neighborhood center, there might be conference rooms available and meetings will happen naturally. If you're talking about the telecommuter's home, however, it's a different story—or is it? There are some real advantages to having *some* meetings at the home:

- It gives others a chance to see what a home office looks like and how the telecommuter functions;
- It forces others to travel to the meeting for a change instead of the telecommuter;
- It can provide a welcome change of environment that might be important if the subject under discussion would benefit from a more relaxed setting.

There are disadvantages as well:

- There's usually a practical limit to the number of people who can comfortably meet in the home; most houses don't have their own conference rooms.
- It just doesn't make sense most of the time to ferry four or five people from the office to meet with one telecommuter at home.
- It can be inconvenient, awkward, or costly for the telecommuter to fulfill what may be a felt obligation to feed the crowd. There's a good side to this—why not use the home meeting as a social gathering as well and have it catered with pizza or another low-cost, easy-to-arrange menu? This is a great change to have the gang spend some time together after the business agenda has been covered.

All in all, meetings at the remote site have their good and bad sides. They might work best as an occasional alternative to meetings at the central office location.

4: Teleconferencing

Last but not least, this is one of the most promising tools for use with telecommuting. Teleconferencing is an umbrella term for a wide range of methods to bring people together electronically. It can be as simple as a conference call among three people or something as complex as a 20-location video conference with full-motion two-way color video. It also includes computer-based conferencing in which a "meeting" is conducted, often over a period of time, using a more sophisticated kind of electronic mail system.

A Teleconferencing Case Study

The interesting thing about teleconferencing is its ability to deal with many of the concerns about the relative isolation and lack of interaction of remote work. The best way to see this is to look at two vignettes* depicting what can be done to bring people together electronically. These vignettes assume a broad definition of teleconferencing and don't address costs or technical feasibility. However, there's nothing described that isn't commercially available today at costs that are reasonable if the benefits are clearly evident.

CASE 1: THE WEEKEND WARRIORS

Tom, Mary, and George learn late Friday afternoon that they have to pull together a major proposal for a key customer by noon on Monday. Mary is heading for a long-planned trip to the beach with her husband, and Tom and George just have the usual weekend errands to handle. Tom agrees to draft an outline of the proposal by 9 P.M. Friday night on his PC at home and dump it into the company's electronic mail (e-mail) system for comment. George and Mary read it later that night (Mary has packed her portable PC with built-in modem next to the suntan lotion) and Tom reads

---

*NOTE: These vignettes originally appeared in an article titled "Telecommuting: A New Opportunity Area for Teleconferencing?" in the December 15, 1984 issue of the *TeleSpan* teleconferencing newsletter, and are reprinted with the publisher's permission.

their comments after taking his dog for his 6 A.M. walk Saturday morning. He edits the outline and sends it via e-mail to the other two by 8 A.M.

They have a quick conference call at 9 A.M. to discuss the changes and divide up the work to draft the proposal. By 10 A.M. on Sunday all three have loaded their sections into a common file the others can access. Another round of e-mail messages among the three goes out as each person reads the other sections.

As they agreed, they each begin work on their assigned sections. Tom incorporates the changes and finishes the proposal by dinnertime on Sunday. He transmits the completed file to the office where his secretary can do some final editing and then print it out at her workstation Monday morning.

CASE 2: THE LEAKY BOTTLE

Acme Shampoo Company has a problem. It seems that their 16-ounce shampoo bottles have begun to spring leaks on store shelves across a three-state area. Top management is understandably concerned and quickly pulls together a task force to find the solution.

The task force members include Ralph from Engineering, Helen from Operations, and three others from Marketing, Distribution, and Public Relations. Ralph is a telecommuter who works at home three days every week, and the Marketing and PR reps are at headquarters located 150 miles from the plant where Helen and the Distribution person work.

A 30-minute conference call that afternoon leads to a decision to break the job into five tasks. Using a conferencing system that's based on the firm's computer, they quickly set up lists of key factors for each task. Everyone joins in the conference and adds to or comments on the lists. This happens over the next day, with each person reading the conference files and entering ideas through a nearby terminal or PC.

The possible cause is quickly narrowed down to a new set of molds used for the bottles. The Distribution rep checked the patterns of complaints against shipping records and constructed a graph showing how the complaints relate to batch numbers; each task force member has viewed this on his/her screen. When Ralph sees the graph he remembers some problems he had with the vendor of the new mold. He calls a co-worker in the office and asks him to telecopy the blueprints to the neighborhood work center two miles away, where he picks them up later that afternoon.

His hunch is right, he learns, because the drawings show a slight design flaw that nobody noticed before. He wants to see the mold to be sure, but it's almost 4:30 and there's no way he wants to buck rush-hour traffic to drive the 45 minutes to his office. As long as he's at the neighborhood center he calls Helen and asks her to have the suspect mold brought to the videoconference room right away. In a few minutes he's looking at a close-up view of the mold on a screen and discussing his thoughts with the full task force via audio conference. They agree to have the mold quickly modified, and chart plans for the recall of the leakers.

SUMMARY

These are realistic examples and they are consistent with today's technology. Teleconferencing and telecommuting share many features; by integrating the range of teleconferencing methods with telecommuting, it's possible to have remote workers stay in touch, attend staff meetings, and be linked to the office in more ways than one. Full-motion videoconferencing may not appear in everyone's living room for a while, but the use of satellite or neighborhood centers (or public video networks like those being put in place by some hotel chains) may bring video within reach.

CHECKLIST FOR LINKING
THE TELECOMMUTER TO THE OFFICE

✔ Use a variety of meetings with different formats and purposes to make the best use of time in the office.

✔ Don't overlook the telephone as a powerful linking tool—but don't overdo it with a steady stream of nonurgent calls.

✔ Hold meetings at the remote site now and then for a change of pace.

✔ Investigate all forms of teleconferencing as a way to bring groups of people together.

10

How to Handle the Technical Details

The last major step in planning a telecommuting program is to handle the hardware and software needs. The first five steps address the "people-ware" side of things and in many ways they take precedence over this last step.

That might be hard to understand—after all, isn't the essence of tele-commuting the technologies involved? In many ways it is, even though as you've seen repeatedly there are many paper-and-pencil tasks that are ex-cellent prospects for remote work. While technology is one of the driving forces behind remote work it can't overshadow the attention needed on the human resource management issues.

One mistake made in some early telecommuting trials was to view them as primarily technical challenges, to be managed by the technical staff. Not surprisingly, there was as much failure as success because little if any thought was given to the kinds of questions addressed in the previous five chapters. The technical planning step isn't last because it's least important; it's last because you should also focus attention on the other five. Also, for the most part, the technical issues are far more pre-dictable and have more clear-cut solutions than do the people issues. As you'll see, though, many of the technical issues will be tackled early on in the planning process; their position in sixth place doesn't mean they necessarily happen last.

This is not a technical chapter. You won't learn the fine points of communications protocols, hard disk design, or terminal emulation software. There *is* a section at the end that gives you a look at some of the major equipment and services categories that come into play in telecommuting, but it's included mostly as a thought-provoker.

You still may wonder how to keep track of technology and make the right selections for a remote work application. Your best bet is to draw on the expertise of people in your organization whose job is to stay in touch with the latest electronic bells and whistles.

HOW AND WHERE TO GET ADVICE

The specific technical guidance you'll need will come from different people, depending on the jobs you choose for remote work and on your organization's progress in implementing advanced office systems. At one extreme is a paper-and-pencil job (like telephone interviewing) that requires nothing more than a telephone. At the other is a job involving very sophisticated uses of data downloaded from the corporate mainframe and high-speed, high-volume data transmission to and from the remote site. Once you begin to settle on the tasks involved you can more easily decide whose asistance you'll need.

Here's an overview of the functions or specialties you might have to consult with; this is a master list and it's rare that you'd have to contact everyone:

Inside the Organization

1. *Data Processing.* This is a broad term; this department (and it goes by many names) may or may not include many of the seven functions that follow. Also, some of the seven may be combined into one or more departments, so you'll initially need to rely on someone who can give you an overview of how your organization separates these functions.

In a limited sense the DP people are responsible for the large-scale business or scientific computing needs that have always been done on machines other than PCs. This group is involved when the remote work involves processing that is done or passes through their computers.

2. *Office Automation.* More and more firms are setting up separate groups to guide the application of computer technology to everyday of-

fice functions. This can include everything from "plain vanilla" word processing to very complex systems that include electronic mail, calendar scheduling, data storage and retrieval, and many more functions. This group will play a role if the equipment or the software you'll need are tied to office functions, especially at the department level.

3. *Personal Computing Manager.* This is a new job title that's popping up as organizations try to put one person (or department) in charge of the proliferation of PCs. Sometimes referred to as the "micro marshal," this person is charged with an oversight role for everything from buying policies and approved brands to hands-on training. If you're going to be using PCs you should check in with this person.

4. *Security.* Depending on the application there may or may not be security considerations. Data processing security will continue to be a hot topic and shouldn't be ignored in the planning stages. Many DP departments have their own security functions although some of this work is handled by a corporate security department.

It's important to get these people involved very early because the security aspects may affect the jobs and/or people you select for telecommuting. An application that is otherwise well suited may be vetoed because it represents an unacceptable risk. There's some debate (see Chapter 11) about how much incremental risk is posed by telecommuting, but for now let's say you should bring these experts in early.

5. *DP Auditing.* This function is sometimes related to security although it fills a different role. Like auditing in general, this group makes sure that specified procedures are followed and consistent methods are used. In some ways it's an internal quality assurance check on DP and related operations. This group might not have much involvement other than to review your plans and perhaps spot-check actual remote operations later on.

6. *Telecommunications.* More and more organizations are treating this as a separate function, apart from DP or administrative services where it might have resided before. The breakup of AT&T and the rapid pace of developments in this field mean that someone has to devote full attention here. This group is likely to be involved in almost every remote work application; even for jobs using "just" a telephone, there are still decisions to be made about the type of equipment, service features, and connections to your organization's internal telephone system.

Another reason to rely on this group is to get an accurate picture of lead times required for installing new phone service. Although the installation backup that plagued many users just after the AT&T divestiture has been reduced, it still can take several weeks if any kind of special features or lines are needed. You'll need this information as you plan and schedule the actual implementation.

7. *DP Training.* This is another recent addition to many organizations—a group responsible for designing and/or delivering training for both DP staff and others who use computing resources. Your need to draw on their expertise will depend on what kinds of computing-related training is needed. This might include the use of electronic mail, communications software, applications packages, and even the PCs or terminals themselves.

8. *Database Administration.* Finally, you may need (or be required) to contact this person or group if your telecommuters will be using corporate data files. The database administration function keeps track of and oversees the central data files that are used across almost every application. It's a combined cataloging and inventory role to make optimal use of files by minimizing duplications and overlaps.

CHECKLIST FOR GETTING
GOOD TECHNICAL ADVICE

Most telecommuting applications involve office technology; unless you're an expert in this area be sure to call on the people responsible for these functions—and do it early in your planning:

✔ Data Processing
✔ Office Automation
✔ PC Purchase and Use
✔ Data Processing Security
✔ Data Processing Auditing
✔ Telecommunications
✔ Data Processing Training
✔ Database Administration

These may or may not be separate functions in your organization; contact the appropriate people depending on your structure and your program's needs.

Outside the Organization

These five groups represent most of the resources you might need for a telecommuting program. Your direct dealings with them could be limited if one or more of the eight groups mentioned previously handles it for you.

1. *Equipment Suppliers.* This includes the PCs or terminals if needed plus all the related gear—modems, cables, monitors, disk drives, and printers. This has become a very competitive marketplace and you'll probably find that someone in your organization has established a volume purchase program with equipment vendors or retailers.

2. *Software Providers.* These include the publishers themselves and the retailers, as well as custom developers if you need something special that can't be provided by your internal staff.

3. *Telecommunications Equipment Suppliers.* In addition to AT&T Information Systems, the local Bell companies have subsidiaries to sell equipment. There also are many other independent suppliers today, and you have a full range of equipment options plus choices to make about leasing versus purchasing. Once again, you can make your job easier by relying on someone whose job it is to stay up with the range of choices available.

4. *Telecommunications Service Providers.* In short, ditto the above. You should have no problem if all you'll need is basic local service. If your remote workers need long-distance service or access to any special data transmission lines or networks, be prepared to do some careful shopping.

5. *Suppliers of Other Office Equipment.* Depending on the application you might need answering machines, microfiche readers, copiers, special furniture, facsimile machines—and the list goes on. Most organizations have established suppliers for items like these so you should be able to rely on them, often working with your purchasing department.

It's been stated that you can draw on the services of staff people in your organization for help in selecting and purchasing the equipment and services you'll need. But what about the small firm without a full complement of staff people to do this? At minimum, most organizations large enough to be considering telecommuting are large enough to have a purchasing agent or department. Even though they might not be pros in the computer or telecommunications area, they still can give you some sound advice in buying practices that will make you a better shopper and purchaser.

CHECKLIST OF GROUPS TO CONTACT
OUTSIDE YOUR ORGANIZATION

Some of these contacts might be handled by your own technical people; all telecommuting programs won't require help from all groups:

✔ Equipment suppliers

✔ Software providers

✔ Telecommunications equipment and service providers

✔ Office equipment suppliers

SOME ADVICE ABOUT SERVICE AND MAINTENANCE

One thing to remember in your purchasing is that durability and service can be key issues for remote workers; there generally won't be service people on site or even nearby. Even though the equipment might be used less by a sole telecommuter at home than if it's used by several people in the office, the penalty for breakdowns is higher. People in the office can more readily move on to other tasks (or other PCs or terminals) if equipment starts to act up, but remote workers don't have as much flexibility.

How can you best protect yourself and your telecommuters against the risk of too much idle time? There are three things to do:

1. *Check Repair History.* Look at the "mean time between failures" (MTBF) data that should be available for most equipment, especially peripheral units like printers. This is a statistical measure of the average time between breakdowns serious enough to put the unit out of commission until it's repaired by a professional. This isn't a foolproof guide, but it's a starting point. There's usually the predictable relationship between durability and cost; the units with higher MTBF often cost more initially, but this could be money well spent.

2. *Investigate Service Arrangements.* The major equipment vendors with big stakes in the corporate market are usually quite reliable about providing on-site service that's prompt and effective. But what about servicing an IBM, Apple, Wang, or other unit when it's in someone's den 30

miles from the corporate office? No one has a lot of experience with this problem yet, so be prepared to do some digging.

Some vendors (and increasingly, third-party maintenance organizations) have carry-in service centers and some will do on-site service no matter where the unit is located. As you'd expect, the more convenient the service is to the user the higher the price tag for labor time and/or a service contract. This might be a good investment if you're convinced that the extra dollars will save time and aggravation in the long run.

3. *Use "Loaners."* Think about having one or more "loaner" units available in the office as backups for the remote work sites. These can be units that aren't heavily used in the office so they wouldn't be missed if loaned out for a couple of days. Some of your service organizations might also be able to provide these backup units.

Despite these comments on repairs and breakdowns, be assured that the kind of equipment likely to be used by telecommuters has had a good record of operating without problems. The units with a greater chance of problems are the ones with more mechanical (as opposed to electronic) parts, like printers and copiers. But most telecommuters will probably use these less than in central office settings if they use them at all; they probably won't be copying or printing out hundreds of pages a day.

CRITICAL LEAD TIME ISSUES

You aren't going to leave the technical planning process for last in most cases. It takes time to evaluate, order, and obtain the equipment and services discussed so far. A good way to help you pinpoint exactly where to get started is to look at a list of items on your "critical path." These are things that must be taken care of before anything else can happen or that have unusually long lead times.

Approval Processes

Depending on the size and/or equipment requirements of your telecommuting program, you might have to get approvals for capital expenditures (purchases, or even construction in some cases) or for the right to purchase PCs. Some organizations have set up rigorous approval processes for acquiring PCs that go far beyond what's required to justify purchases of equal dollar value in other areas.

Your best bet is to do some research once you know the general details of your program and find out what approval steps are ahead of you. Unless you have a magic wand or other powers, be sure to add some slack in the schedule, especially for approvals that have to go up the organizational ladder. You can count on key people being out of town or on vacation when you need them, approval committee meetings being canceled at the last minute, or having agendas that are unrealistically long, or further justifications needed when the first should have sufficed.

These facts of organizational life will sneak up on you without fail. They might even be more of a problem with requests based on telecommuting than for other uses because of the relative novelty of the concept. Your best insurance against these delays is to do your homework, get some advice from seasoned veterans of the appropriations battlefield, and don't hesitate to do some behind-the-scenes politicking with key people whose support is essential.

Construction

If you're going to use neighborhood or satellite centers or any other multi-employee sites where renovation or construction is required, give yourself plenty of time. Not only do you have the internal approval process noted above, but there are outsiders who get into the act such as building inspectors. Also, even the best-managed construction projects are subject to delays due to subcontractor problems, delivery delays, weather problems, and other unexpected snags.

Equipment Orders

This applies to equipment in the broad sense, such as hardware, software, and furniture. You have three possible sources of delays. First, is the equipment actually available in the quantity you need and ready for field use? Be wary about an item due to be released for the first time just when you need it. Vendors don't always meet their deadlines and even when they do, the first production models may have bugs that need to be corrected.

Second, watch out for the "vaporware" problem. This is a wonderful term that describes software that's announced before it's ready and sometimes before any design work has begun. Publishers use the announcement as a way to test the marketplace (to see if there's enough interest to actually produce the product), to confuse competitors, or to entice buyers who are leaning toward a competitive product but might hold off for this firm's offering. Unless you're a big risk-taker or there are some special circumstances, don't base your schedule on a program (or piece of equipment) that's not available today in working order with full documentation.

Third, be sure to get a good fix on actual delivery and installation schedules. A supplier whose product is in heavy demand or whose installation staff is stretched thin will need more time than what's promised or implied. You can talk to recent purchasers in other organizations to see what their experience has been and build in appropriate slack time if needed. Also, if the equipment is likely to need any fine-tuning or adjustment after it's been in use for a little while make sure to build this into the schedule. You'll want to figure on the date when it's working, not on the earlier installation date.

Service Orders

This applies to telecommunications services from AT&T, the Bell companies, GTE, or any of the other providers. If the service you need has a history of long lead times or unpredictable installation dates, it's wise to put in an order even before you know your exact requirements. This gets you into the queue if needed; be sure to cancel or change the order if your plans change, out of fairness to the supplier.

EQUIPMENT AND SERVICES OVERVIEW

As you do your technical planning, you'll be making some decisions about the mix of equipment and services needed by telecommuters. It's impossible here to describe the best setup for every telecommuter. However, you can rely on four general objectives as you make your choices.

Objectives for Technical Support

These "common denominators" are objectives that managers like yourself should try to achieve—and vendors interested in the telecommuting marketplace will have to accommodate.

1. *Transparent Communications.* Every telecommuting program will require simple, easy, and affordable communications. In the central office these often happen in informal meetings, discussions, and troubleshooting sessions, many on an ad hoc basis. These communications paths must be maintained and replicated in telecommuting.

It should be as easy to confer with people who are telecommuting as it is when they're in the office. Ideally, you needn't go through any unusual procedures to contact a telecommuter.

CHECKLIST FOR AVOIDING PROBLEMS WITH MAINTENANCE AND LEAD TIMES

✔ Choose equipment with proven reliability.

✔ Shop carefully for good service arrangements.

✔ Keep "loaner" units available.

✔ Don't forget about internal approvals and the time they'll take.

✔ Allow plenty of time if there's any construction involved.

✔ Be skeptical about delivery date information from vendors, especially for new products or services.

Don't jeopardize your program by relying on equipment or services that might leave your telecommuters high and dry, or by being too optimistic about meeting key dates.

---

2. *Good Value for the Money.* Telecommuting equipment and services must be cost-effective, though this doesn't necessarily mean inexpensive. Some remote workers will need nothing more than a phone line, but many others will need a modem, some kind of terminal or PC, and perhaps an answering machine and other equipment. These might be substantial investments but they should be offset by increased productivity and reduced operating expenses in other areas. There's no long-run advantage to setting up telecommuters with bare-bones support systems. The cost of everyone's time spent trying to cope with inadequate facilities will usually outweigh the initial savings.

3. *Meeting Organizational Goals.* If telecommuting is going to succeed, your organization must be able to do its work unimpaired. Reports must be produced on time, schedules must be met, and cost controls and service levels must be established and met.

Beyond this, the technology selected must match the organization's culture. If your firm has a casual, "open door" flavor, the communications channels should be just as relaxed. For instance, electronic mail often has a breezy, casual style that many managers appreciate. This style may fit an informal organization culture but not a more conservative one. The latter might do best with a dial-dictation system that produces a more traditional typed memo. Both styles are functional; they simply meet different needs.

4. *Satisfying Human Needs.* Telecommuters have to believe that their personal needs are being met or they will return to the office. Similarly, if their managers or coworkers are uncomfortable with cumbersome communications and operating methods, they'll stop supporting or even try to end the telecommuting program.

With these objectives in mind you can examine the range of equipment and services available. This isn't going to be an exhaustive list since many organizations will have unique needs that can't be anticipated in a general overview. The unifying theme for all items listed is *information management*—methods for moving, using, storing, and converting information used by remote workers.

Mechanical Delivery Systems

The first way to move information around the corner or around the country is to use mechanical systems that rely on physical movement of the information. There are four main methods:

- Human delivery—using feet, bikes, cars, or trucks
- Local messenger services
- National delivery or courier services (such as Federal Express, Purolator, or UPS)
- The U.S. Postal Service

Except for rare instances, these services will play a small role in telecommuting. The whole idea of remote work is that it's more sensible to move ideas and information than papers and people. As described in previous chapters, there may be a role for the courier-type services for things that can't be transported any other way, but in general, it's a bit illogical to put someone in a 21st-century work environment and then move information into that setting using an updated version of the Pony Express.

Electronic Delivery Systems

There are seven major electronic communication systems to consider, each with its own uses and cost/benefit considerations:

1. *Telephone Systems.* The telephone network is perhaps the most basic tool for telecommuters. It's widely distributed, reliable, easy to use, and a fairly good value for the money. The initial investment is usually low unless you need sophisticated features. The unknowns, in some

cases, will be the actual ongoing use costs; you'll have to decide whether you'll reimburse home-based telecommuters for business calls made on their own line or absorb the cost of installing a new line and pick up monthly charges. A related question is whether that new line is considered a residential or business line by the local phone company; arguments can be made on either side, and business service costs a lot more.

2. *Voice Messaging Systems.* These include answering machines, voice mail systems, and dial-dictation systems. The last allows a remote caller to dial in to a central dictation facility and dictate messages, memos, or reports to be transcribed and distributed later by an attendant at the central office.

Costs range from under $100 to over $100,000 depending on complexity, number of users, and range of features. The basic advantage of voice messaging systems is that they're the only enhancement to the basic telephone network that allow work to be done out-of-phase. In other words, both parties don't have to be involved in the conversation at once.

3. *Facsimile Machines.* These units have become increasingly well known, and the Japanese manufacturers have a full line of quality equipment with costs dropping steadily.

Fax machines scan a page of information (text, drawings, or pictures) and transmit a coded version of it over a standard phone line to a receiving unit at another location. There are some problems with incompatible formats among machines of different ages and from different manufacturers, but standards are spreading quickly. Fax is an adequate method for sending images, especially useful when words alone won't do. They're much less expensive than messenger services over the long run, but documents sent by fax can't be revised without being retyped.

It's worth noting that two hybrid services came onto the market in 1984: MCI's MCIMail uses the MCI network to transmit messages and deliver them electronically or, if preferred, via printed copy. Federal Express Zapmail uses its system of couriers to pick up documents for facsimile transmission to another city, where couriers deliver the fax-produced document as they do with packages.

4. *Photocopying Machines.* These have advanced in recent years but will generally be of little value for information delivery purposes. They create paper copies from paper originals, and the copies still must be transported to the final destination. They may have convenience value for telecommuters but probably won't see widespread use in most remote work settings.

5. *Personal Computers.* These machines, which some say are at the heart of telecommuting, are the ultimate communications tool. Aside from their powerful computing functions, they allow users to send, receive, store, and manipulate information from many sources. The cost spread between low-end business PCs and even the better "dumb" terminals is closing, so that you'll pay less of a penalty for upgrading to a PC from a terminal even if you think only a terminal is needed.

6. *Optical Character Readers (OCR).* OCR units are potentially important but not yet cost-effective for many telecommuting uses. Their value is as a link between other technologies. These machines scan a printed page and convert the image into a coded file that can be used by word processing software. The units have become increasingly powerful and can "read" a range of typefaces with a very low error rate. They still can't handle images, which is one of their drawbacks.

7. *Video Systems.* As noted in Chapter 9, these systems might have tremendous benefits but most carry a big price tag. They are the only way to transmit real-time three-dimensional images and to closely replicate the feel of being in a meeting. (Audio conferencing or computer conferencing also handle the latter but less realistically.) Component costs are dropping quickly, and the spread of higher-capacity fiber-optic networks will help trim transmission costs. For now, these will probably see limited use except in certain branch-to-central office applications where they can save travel time and cost.

RECAP OF ELECTRONIC DELIVERY SYSTEMS

1. Telephone systems
2. Voice messaging systems
3. Facsimile machines
4. Photocopying machines
5. Personal computers
6. Optical character readers
7. Video systems

You won't need all of these in every telecommuting application. This list should trigger your thinking when you're making equipment decisions. Also, remember these overall goals for getting information to and from telecommuters:

a. Transparent communications (simple, easy, affordable)

b. Good value for the money (cost-effective, but not always inexpensive)

c. Meeting organizational goals (must fit the task and culture)

d. Satisfying human needs (tools that help, not hinder)

Other Telephone-Based Equipment and Services

Here's a sampling of other equipment that in some way works with, or is connected to a telephone and the telephone network. It's easy to go feature-crazy when looking at a list like this, so concentrate on choosing only those items needed to make the remote worker effective:

1. *"Smart" Telephones.* This category is growing at a furious pace due to rapid advances in chip technology and increased competition. Compact units are available that do some or all of the following: last number redialing, automatic dialing, automatic redialing until the call gets through, a built-in calculator, a built-in speakerphone (see below) and the ability to activate "custom calling services" (see below). Smart phones can make life easier, but they can also be expensive paperweights if they aren't chosen wisely.

2. *Answering Machines.* These were included earlier under voice messaging units but deserve some extra attention. These may be among the most commonly chosen pieces of equipment for telecommuters, especially for the home location. With no secretary or coworkers to take messages, these allow incoming callers to do business even if the telecommuter is away.

They come with a range of features, but one that's usually a must for telecommuters is voice-actuated incoming recording. Instead of having a fixed amount of time for the caller to leave a message, these units will continue to record (for up to five minutes or more) as long as the caller is talking. Callers can leave messages that are long enough to make sense instead of just leaving their names and numbers.

3. *Speakerphones and Headsets.* Both units give the remote worker the luxury and convenience of hands-free conversation—and prevent a lot of stiff necks from wedging the phone between neck and ear. They're a boon to anyone who needs to work with papers or a keyboard while talking, and speakerphones allow several people to be in on the call. Speakerphones might get as much use in the office as at the remote site— they allow impromptu conferences among people who otherwise would

gather in the hallway or in someone's office. Of course, the same thing can be done if your phone system has a conference-calling feature.

4. *Custom-Calling Services.* Some or all of these are available at extra cost in most residential service areas; these or expanded features are often found in newer central PBX switchboards in offices. The most common ones are *call waiting* to notify you that someone else is trying to call you; *call forwarding* to have your incoming calls automatically routed to another phone number; *three-way calling* to set up conference calls without a conference operator; *speed calling* to let you call frequently called numbers using only a few numbers that trigger the full calling sequence out of a memory device.

Some of these are more appealing and useful than others for remote workers. Call forwarding is a nice feature because it lets a person's calls follow him/her around to various work locations. It's also a plus in the office phone system because it's the essence of "transparent communications" as noted earlier; callers will be automatically routed to the remote site.

A word of caution about the call waiting feature—your remote workers can't use this on a phone line used with a modem. The signal that indicates a waiting call will almost always disrupt the data transmission, resulting in lost time and lots of aggravation.

5. *Dial-Dictation Systems.* These offer the advantages of traditional dictation units without the burden of having to get a tape into the office for transcription. The remote worker dials a special number and dictates a message, letter, or memo. The better systems allow the caller to control the receiving unit (via the phone's pushbuttons) to replay or correct the tape. These systems might work well for remote workers who need to produce typed documents but can't type (or who can, but need the skills of a professional typist), or can't justify the cost of a PC or terminal only for word processing.

6. *Cellular Radio.* This is the ultimate portable work tool. Cellular radio is the new version of mobile telephone service that's been around for years. The difference is that cellular offers expanded service at quality that's comparable to standard phones. Remote workers could *really* work remotely—not only in their cars but with portable units that can be taken anywhere within the cellular service range of the telecommuter's city.

This service became available in 1984 in about two dozen cities; it should be available in roughly 300 cities in the next few years. Because of its fairly high initial and ongoing use charges, it will be used by only a fortunate few telecommuters until the costs drop.

SUMMARY

This overview has given you an idea of some of the major tools and services to consider when planning for telecommuting. Some products (such as printers or modems) were excluded since they're natural extensions of items that were covered. Also excluded were other technologies or services covered in more depth elsewhere (such as electronic mail and online databases). Both of these "dropouts" deserve attention in your planning.

To repeat the point made at the start of this chapter, technical planning is an important, but rarely the primary, consideration in getting telecommuting off the ground. Your main goal in handling the technical details is to be familiar enough with the planned telecommuting applications to intelligently draw on the expertise of others for current, correct guidance. Also, it's to your advantage to be aware of the lead times involved so you can do realistic scheduling. The sooner you consult with the experts inside and outside of your organization and get their advice, the better off you'll be as you move toward implementation.

11

Seven Potential Problem Areas and How to Cope with Them

Telecommuting, like almost anything else, has its advantages and disadvantages; by now you should have a balanced view of the concept. This chapter is about the major problems that might crop up as you move forward with a program. There's no way to know which, if any, will show up in your organization, but you'll be better off in the long run if you're aware of them and can take some preventive steps to head them off.

Everything in this chapter relates to the fact that telecommuting is new and different, at least when compared to how most people work in most organizations. When something is new, it's often unsettling or even threatening. For some people it can upset the status quo and they might strike out simply because you're introducing some change into their lives.

COPING WITH CHANGE—AN OVERVIEW

It's important that you're prepared to deal with the reactions that stem from the novelty of telecommuting as well as those based on some specific aspect of remote work. Most large organizations don't handle change that well. Some insight into this point comes from Paul and Sarah Edwards, authors of *Working from Home* (cited in Chapter 8) and directors of the

Association of Electronic Cottagers: "The three major obstacles to working at home are management resistance, management resistance, and management resistance. This often stems from a feeling of lack of control. Education and successful pilot projects will help influence some people, and retirement will dispose of others. Necessity—the high costs of space, increased need for productivity, and demands by valuable employees—will convert others."

Introducing Change Is Not Easy

Change in itself can cause problems, but in addition most managers don't know how to introduce change very well. That probably accounts for why the installed equipment base for a known and proven technology like word processing is behind the forecasts of several years ago. A common topic for the business press and at trade shows and public seminars is "How to Get Your Department to Accept Office Automation" or something similar. In short, most managers need better skills for helping their staffs and peers understand and accept new methods and techniques.

This problem goes beyond the individuals involved. According to Professor Gerald Gordon of Boston University, there can be subtle but powerful pressures against innovation no matter how strongly top management says it wants to encourage it. "With an innovation like telecommuting, there must be a fairly large payoff to stimulate the organization to take it seriously. If it only returns a small increase in productivity or only cuts costs a little, that's probably not going to be enough to get the managers involved to do it and to live with the culture shock that may come with it."

To help you understand this process of change and anticipate possible problems, here are seven major areas to consider. As you review each one, think about consulting with the appropriate staff experts in your organization for their views, since what follows is of necessity only general guidance.

1: CHALLENGES TO THE SUPERVISOR
OF TELECOMMUTERS

In Chapter 7 you read about the training needs for managers of remote workers. An important point was the need to manage according to results, not activity. The biggest challenge to the manager is to make this shift from judging the inputs and look primarily at the outputs. This can make some managers uncomfortable, to say the least. It suggests that they think of subordinates as "black boxes" in which the work somehow gets done, but the part to watch is what comes out as the finished product.

Management theorists suggest that this kind of managerial style will become more and more important for *all* subordinates, not just those working remotely. They point to the growing sophistication and education among many employees (and certainly those in professional-level jobs) and the shift away from anything that smacks of autocratic management. Managers will need to become coaches and facilitators more than close supervisors.

Developing New Skills

If this is true, remote work can be an excellent way to encourage this transition. It will appeal to the instincts and skills of the better managers, though it will be unsettling to the marginal ones. Some companies with telecommuting pilots have observed that nothing pinpoints a weak manager faster than the need to manage from a distance. Conversely, managers of remote workers often state that the need to manage from a distance makes them better managers of their other subordinates who are based in the office. The discipline needed to set goals and track progress based on results pays off for everyone, not just telecommuters. But the problem is that you can't always be sure that only the better managers will be involved with telecommuting, despite the guidelines given in Chapter 7 for selecting remote managers. That's why you have to be prepared to upgrade and monitor the skills of the managers involved. You also have to deal with some apprehension and resistance from them—especially those on shaky ground because they know their skills as managers aren't up to par.

The Manager's Juggling Act

The other major challenge to supervisors is to cope with being the center of attention in an innovative program. You saw this described in Chapter 4 —the difficulty of being expected to be innovative and take risks and at same time keep the operation running smoothly. A graphic way of visualizing how difficult this can be is to think of the classic variety act with the performer who has a number of plates spinning atop long, thin poles. It's not so hard to keep three or four plates spinning, but as he adds each additional one he's got to watch all the others much more carefully. If he's not very skillful, one of the plates might start to wobble a bit—and it doesn't take much for a wobbly plate to drop and break into lots of pieces.

Organizations often expect managers to keep all those plates spinning even as they add new ones. You have to realistically examine the workload and expectations for the managers of your telecommuters to make sure you haven't given them too many plates. To carry the analogy further, maybe you can make those poles a little sturdier or arrange for someone else to give some of them a twist now and then just to keep everything going smoothly.

CHALLENGES TO SUPERVISORS OF TELECOMMUTERS

1. They must make the shift from managing activity to managing results.
2. They must make the shift from being "the boss" to being a coach.
3. They must cope with being under the microscope during the pilot program.

2: CHALLENGES TO THE EMPLOYEES

These fall into two categories—challenges to the telecommuters and to everyone else. The telecommuters have to face some fairly radical changes in work and living patterns that have been years in the making. Despite everything that's done to prevent a feeling of isolation and separation, they'll still have to cope (at least initially) with something of an upheaval in their associations with others. Over time, they may establish or modify ties with others outside the office to replace those that were lost or weakened.

This is why it's so important to build in the "linking" practices detailed in Chapter 9, and to have realistic expectations for the early weeks of remote work. It's not unusual to have a drop-off in productivity in the early stages of the program as everyone gets used to the new work patterns. Those first few weeks can be trying; there's no sense introducing other strains by expecting great leaps in output, satisfaction, and work quality overnight.

Watching for Warning Signals

One way to keep an eye on things is to watch out for "red flags" that can signal budding problems. Some of these might show up early and others won't be seen until months into the program. Here's a list of trouble signs that telecommuters, their managers, and observers can watch for:

Look for telecommuters

- who show prolonged changes in mood or temperament;

- who experience problems in relationships with others at or away from work where similar problems didn't exist before;
- whose work begins to suffer in quality or quantity.

Look for managers.

- who become uneasy when discussing their remote workers;
- who become overly or openly critical of their remote workers' work and work habits;
- whose unit's work as a whole begins to suffer.

These aren't foolproof signs and each could be accounted for by a host of causes. But don't overlook them if you have reason to believe that the remote work experience is somehow related. Some thoughtful discussion and probing will help uncover the true causes and get everyone on a path to improvement.

Coworker Reactions

The other challenge here is for employees not involved in remote work. Especially at the pilot stages, telecommuting will get a lot of attention and probably will be seen as desirable by many people. The program might get so much scrutiny that office-based workers will become jealous or even resentful of it and the remote workers. This can lead to friction and lack of cooperation.

Similarly, there's likely to be some resentment in most pilots based on the selection process. A personnel manager for a Fortune 100 company once observed that his firm's job posting system invariably produced "one person with a swelled head and a dozen ingrates" every time an internal candidate was chosen from among those who "bid" on the open job.

You can deal with both these problems in part based on how you explain the program internally. You'll be on safer ground if you describe a pilot as such, with no promises for continuation or expansion, and if you spell out the selection criteria clearly. But if you treat it with a lot of fanfare and in effect create the expectation that it's another employee benefit, you might be creating problems. One good preventive step is to make sure of the "preview" methods outlined in Chapter 6. If you can present a balanced view of remote work, you should be able to dispel the myth that it's wonderful for everyone.

CHALLENGES TO THE EMPLOYEES

1. Telecommuters have to adjust to the unique demands of remote work and modify existing relationships with coworkers, the manager, and the family.

2. Other employees may feel left out or resentful, and unsure about how their own jobs may be affected.

3: SECURITY CONCERNS

Nothing strikes fear in the heart of a data processing manager faster than the prospect that someone is tinkering with the organization's computers for fun, profit, or just plain mischief. It might seem that it's asking for trouble to give an employee access to a system at home, where he/she (or a neighbor or child) theoretically can work away undetected for hours trying to get at protected information.

There's certainly some basis for this concern. Even though there were no reported cases of computer crime stemming from employees working at remote locations (as of late 1984, according to the National Center for Computer Crime Data), the possibility exists. But there's more involved than just the remote work location. You have to look at all four parts of the computer security issue:

1. *Hardware and Software Controls.* Even before (and certainly after) the adventures of the hackers, there have been many products on the market to thwart illegal access. These include data encryption (or coding) methods, programs that record every attempt of remote dial-up access, dial-back modems, and much more.

While the products are there, their use is limited, according to many security experts. Some organizations don't feel they're vulnerable or have any sensitive data; others think that since no method is foolproof it's senseless to bother with products that make life more difficult for legitimate users. *No* product is foolproof, but your goal is to throw up enough roadblocks to intruders—and also make their efforts visible to the system's operators—so they're discouraged and, with luck, eventually caught.

2. *Employee Selection.* Security experts note that employers are often lax in checking the backgrounds of prospective employees. One of the strongest arguments for selecting telecommuters from the ranks of existing employees (rather than directly from the outside) is the security

issue. It's better—but again not foolproof—to choose from among those with known work histories.

3. *Management Control and Audit.* This is the most involved and perhaps the most frustrating aspect to security experts. The most sophisticated hardware controls are almost useless unless someone is auditing the reports they generate and is willing to investigate and take action if needed. There's an old saying that "management expects what management inspects"; constant attention is required to get the message across that the organization is serious about security.

4. *Password Controls.* Finally, there's the ultimate weak link in the chain. Even if the first three items are handled correctly they can be undone by sloppy password control. Every system with remote access has some kind of password protection, and if used carefully, it serves its purpose. But the problem here is almost comical—in a tragic way.

Most people recognize the need for passwords but also are human and want to make life easy. They choose passwords that are easy to remember—like their last name. Or, they write them down in "hidden" or not-so-hidden places like on a desk blotter or even on a slip of paper posted on the screen. It's easy to see why the potential for security abuses is so widespread.

There's an added password problem for telecommuters. Given the novelty of remote work, your employees might be tempted to show their home office setup to neighbors and even give a quick demonstration. All it takes is someone looking over the telecommuter's shoulder while the password is being typed (even though it doesn't show up on the screen) and the system is open for intrusion.

Tips on Managing Security

What's the answer? Here are some general guidelines for handling security concerns in remote work. These are not all-inclusive, so be sure you get more specific advice from your security pros:

1. *Assess and Upgrade Current Program.* Before starting a remote work program, find out what your current security situation is and upgrade it if necessary. This includes all four issues cited previously.

2. *Identify Incremental Risks.* Determine what the *incremental* security risks are for remote workers and develop written guidelines for handling them. Remote work via computer isn't always a security risk by itself; ask yourself what the additional potential for abuse is, if any, compared with the same people doing the same tasks in the office. Also compare it

with your policies and practices for maintaining confidentiality in general. If you put few restrictions on what papers an employee can get access to or take home in a briefcase, you may have bigger security problems.

3. *Monitor and Control.* Don't equate sophisticated control systems and policies with sophisticated control; the latter comes only with visible, careful monitoring and follow-up.

CHECKLIST OF SECURITY CONCERNS

Computer security is based on four main principles:

✔ Adequate hardware and software controls

✔ Sound employee selection procedures

✔ Management control and audit

✔ Password control

All four have to be handled well even before you embark on telecommuting; then and only then can you pinpoint any incremental security risks due to telecommuting.

Above, all, give adequate emphasis to security when selecting the jobs suited for telecommuting. Based on present technology it appears that there's no way to absolutely prevent authorized access. There are certain tasks that are well-suited for remote work in all respects except security; look for guidance here from your auditors, appropriate regulatory bodies, and your own common sense.

Some of these tasks might include (but aren't limited to)

- Jobs involving funds transfer;
- Jobs involving access to material that by statute must be kept confidential, such as credit records;
- Work done on a service-bureau basis for clients who might reasonably assume security and confidentiality.

A good rule of thumb is that you and your management have to feel relatively at ease with remote work. If you have a nagging concern that the risks for a certain job aren't justified by the benefits, don't take the risk.

4: TECHNICAL BARRIERS

In a perfect world, organizations would be able to structure every remote-work use of technology from scratch. You'd have no preexisting equipment to match up with, no telecommunications devices already in place, and no limit on budgets. But you know this never happens. In the real world of telecommuting (as in office-based technology applications) you have to tie the new to the old—and therein lies the problem, at least sometimes. You also have to deal with the limitations of today's technology that, even with the plethora of gadgets on the market, can throw up some brick walls along your path.

What follows is a list of four general principles about technical barriers. As you read them, keep in mind that in telecommuting's short history there are very, very few cases of programs that were stopped dead because of problems like these. However, some programs required considerable creativity or ingenuity to make things work. Also, remember that time is on your side; the ever-growing list of what's available (especially in the telecommunications area) can only help make your technical life easier over time.

The Number of Technical Problems Varies Directly with the Complexity of What You're Trying to Accomplish

This probably isn't a surprising statement. Bear in mind that there's a spectrum of telecommuting applications ranging from paper-and-pencil tasks to those requiring frequent, rapid access to the mainframe. The "glue" that holds all this together, especially in the high-access kind of job, is telecommunications—and this field is in a mild state of turmoil today.

Consider just these four elements of the link-up between the office and the remote site: the equipment at the remote site, the types and quality of phone lines available, the format or "packaging" of data being exchanged, and the equipment in the office. The variations among these four are almost limitless. One way to keep this under control is to limit the number of vendors whose equipment you use. The advantage of a single-vendor approach is partly that all the pieces *may* have more in common, but there's no guarantee. Also, if you're dealing with one source you sometimes can exert more leverage on that vendor and try to get more technical support.

There are two important and promising trends. First, most of the major office equipment vendors have become more open with the technical specifications of their products. They've attempted to settle on standards or at least make it easier for other suppliers to connect their products. Second, the major equipment vendors are forging links with telecommunications firms because they recognize how important it is for their equipment to be able to "talk." The best, but not the only example of this, is IBM's 1984 acquisition of Rolm Corporation.

The Technical Problems
of Equipment Compatibility and Selection
Can Be Significant, but Almost Always Are Manageable

With some patience and *early* involvement of your technical pros, you should be able to get around most, if not all, of the problems. It helps if you're open-minded about equipment and service decisions. The benefits of sole-source purchases aside, be prepared for the possibility that the one unit you need comes from a company you've never heard of, located in a town that's not on most maps. This is a growing field and there are lots of small vendors out there who have found highly specialized niches that big firms can't or don't want to fill.

You also have to be open-minded about your choice of telecommuting tasks and the way they're done. You may find that the only way to do what you want is to change the processing sequence, the way data are accessed, or something else. Reconfiguring the task around the technology isn't always the best alternative but sometimes it may be the only one.

Some Things Won't Fit Together
No Matter How Big a Hammer You Use

There are some remote-work applications that seem possible on the surface but aren't technically feasible today. This can be due to equipment unavailability at cost or just plain technical obstinace. Here are some examples of these: note that they are based on generalizations about today's equipment and aren't ironclad rules—nor are they all-inclusive.

- *Applications like CAD/CAM* (computer aided design/manufacturing) that use sophisticated (and sometimes large) terminals, and/or that are so mainframe-dependent that remote access via phone lines is impractical. However, watch for lots of changes in applications like these. Since they represent one of the last frontiers of personal computing, they'll soon be available on the more powerful PCs coming to the marketplace.

- *Applications that involve frequent, ongoing access to files on a mainframe* where timely response is critical, such as telephone reservations or sales work. The trick here is to get the right kind of telecommunications links so that customers aren't kept waiting any longer than normal while the remote worker waits for new information to pop up on the screen.

- *Applications where history or common sense tell you that you're asking for trouble.* If, for example, you've had problems getting your equipment vendor to provide timely repair service in the office, what's going to happen when you need service at a remote site? Or, if you know that local phone lines are subject to "noise" or electrical power supplies are subject to interruptions or voltage drops, you may be asking for problems if you're going to rely on them for telecommuting.

The power and phone line problems aren't that unusual; the question is whether you can manage them well enough to avoid service interruptions and lots of headaches for the telecommuters and yourself. Going into remote work with unresolved problems like these is like going on a long trip with bald tires; you may not have a blowout, but then again. . . .

Just Take the Terminal or PC Home and Plug It In and You're All Set, Right? Well, Not Always

The vast majority of terminals and PCs on the market today run on ordinary household current. The problem comes in when the wiring in the remote site can't safely handle the equipment, or if the site—perhaps a 19th-century farmhouse—doesn't have grounded (three-prong) outlets.

If a telecommuter plugs a machine into a circuit rated for light loads and there are lots of other things on that circuit already, two things can happen. First, when another appliance on that circuit is turned on it might create a momentary voltage drop that affects the terminal or wipes out whatever is in memory at the time. Second, in extreme cases, an electrical overload can occur with dire consequences—and serious liability considerations for your organization.

Fortunately, you can head off problems like these in most cases with some preventive steps. Working with your technical or maintenance staff, find out exactly what the power requirements are and have the telecommuter check on the site's wiring. If there's any doubt, it might be wise to invest in a service fee for a qualified electrician to inspect the wiring. Also, there are units known as surge suppressors that get plugged in between the PC and the outlet and help absorb voltage fluctuations. How likely is it that you'll have problems like these? There's no way to tell in advance, but they should be the exception, not the rule.

Similarly, you'll want to learn about the phone lines at the remote site. If they're noisy or subject to problems that don't affect normal phone conservations but could hamper data transmission, you might need to get a special phone line installed. You'll have to weigh the cost of this versus the benefits of having a telecommuter at that remote site. This should be easy enough to test before you commit to the installation. If there's any question, have the employee use a portable unit for a day and see what happens when he/she dials up the office and tries to transmit or receive via modem.

CHECKLIST OF TECHNICAL BARRIERS

✔ More complex applications are more likely to run into technical snags.

✔ Equipment compatibility can be a problem; be prepared for some mix-and-match solutions.

✔ A few applications won't work at remote sites no matter what you try.

✔ Phone and electrical service at remote sites can cause problems if substandard.

In summary, be prepared for possible technical obstacles like these as you do your planning. If all goes well, they will be only temporary annoyances and not permanent barriers to telecommuting.

5: LIABILITY CONCERNS

Chapter 8 addressed some of the insurance and liability issues from the telecommuter's point of view. These generally are matters between the telecommuter and his/her insurance company. As the employer you do have a role, though, in encouraging or requiring preventive measures to avoid problems that might lead to questions of liability.

Keeping Work and Home Separate

First and foremost is the need to separate the work area from the living area for telecommuters working at home. The two should be physically separated if at all possible, even if it's only a portable partition or curtain that's drawn around the work area. They also should be "mentally" separated—work should be done in the work area, home activities in the living area, and there should be little or no overlap.

There are three reasons why this is important. First, the more separate the two areas are, the easier it is for the telecommuter to get into and stay in the right frame of mind when working. It's hard to concentrate on work when household bills, household chores, and household members spill over onto the work space. Second, the separation is a good way to reinforce the proper security awareness discussed earlier. Work papers, passwords, and equipment should be out of the convenient flow of household traffic. Third, the separation helps define the limits of the work area in case of accidents where the employer might be considered liable.

This last point is especially important in the case of Workers' Compensation (WC) insurance. There's always the possibility of accidents and the related liability creates a *perception* of risk and thus can be an obstacle. To understand why, it's important to examine the logic behind WC.

Workers' Compensation:
Heading Off Problems

WC is administered by each state with wide variations on the type of work covered. The statutes generally provide for compensation for injuries "arising out of and in the course of employment," to quote a common phrase. The question in many WC claims is how directly related the supposed injury is to the job, i.e., was the job the direct and primary cause of the injury and is the employer liable? The problem in the case of remote work is to define what constitutes the "office" and what the limits of the employer's liability are for accidents in the remote work area.

The hypothetical examples that are often cited can be plotted on a scale of increasing difficulty in assigning liability, as the scene of the injury gets removed farther from the work area. One end of the spectrum is an injury that happens in the work area involving work equipment— such as a PC falling off a table and landing on the telecommuter's foot. The other end is a case where the telecommuter trips and falls on the stairs elsewhere in the home while on personal business. These two extremes are relatively clear: in the first one most would probably decide that the employer was somehow liable; in the second one the employer would probably be off the hook.

Coping with the Unknown

But there are some fuzzier examples in between those extremes. What about the telecommuter who trips on the rug on the way into the spare room that's used for the home office? Or, what if the person gets up from work and goes into the kitchen for coffee while carrying a report that he/she is engrossed in, and absent-mindedly spills and gets burned by the coffee or gets a shock from the coffeemaker?

These aren't outlandish examples; things like this can and probably will happen. But this doesn't mean that you have to shy away from remote work. If your organization followed that logic in the office you'd spend all your time worrying about risks and never get any work done.

Imagine this situation: let's say that history reversed itself and large organizations never had used field sales forces to sell products or services; all selling had been done by mail or phone. Let's also say that someone had the bright idea to have representatives actually go out and *visit* customers in person. Can you imagine all the objections that would be raised?

- "What if they get into a car accident?"
- "How will we know if they're working?
- "How will they do their work without someone watching over them?"

The first comment is apropos this discussion about WC, but the other two relate to remote work in general. Despite all the objections that can be raised about this "new" kind of selling, you couldn't imagine doing without field sales reps today. The point is that some people will always find reasons to *not* do something. Fortunately, calmer heads usually prevail and the risks are assessed, weighed against the benefits, and preventive steps are taken to lessen the risks. This is exactly how you should approach this question of WC liability.

Controlling the Risks

At some point in the future the odds say that some telecommuter will, unfortunately, get injured at home. Some of the cases will be clear cut and will be at the extremes cited above. But others will be in the hazier middle areas and will be handled on a case-by-case basis. In the meantime, you can do several things to control the potential risks:

1. *Do Some Research.* Look into your state's WC statute and, in particular, provisions for covering workers who are normally away from the office—such as sales representatives. Also, check on past cases and precedents involving these kinds of remote workers; get a feel for how your state has interpreted and dealt with analogous situations in the past. This information gives you a framework for dealing with the WC issue based on facts, not supposition. Be sure to rely on the appropriate legal counsel for help in researching and interpreting the facts and for setting guidelines based on them.

2. *Use a "Telecommuter's Agreement."* This is a way to spell out the rights and responsibilities of employer and telecommuter. This agreement might include your right to visit the remote site to look for obvious risks such as poor wiring or a PC that's propped up on a shaky stack of books to get it to the right height. (See more information about this later in this chapter.)

3. *Enforce Separation.* Make sure your telecommuters stick to the idea of separating work and living areas as much as possible, as described earlier.

4. *Don't Cause New Problems.* Make sure you don't intentionally introduce any risks into the remote site. It might be sensible, for instance,

---

CHECKLIST OF LIABILITY CONCERNS

✔ Keep the work area as separate as possible from the rest of the home.

✔ The best defense is good education and preventive steps to identify and reduce risks.

✔ Get the facts on your state's Workers' Compensation statutes and look for remote-work precedents.

✔ Use a "telecommuter's agreement" to spell out rights and responsibilities.

✔ Be sure any equipment you provide for the remote site is safe and working well.

to have a terminal or PC inspected by a qualified engineer or electrician before it's installed to make sure it's in good, safe operating condition.

6: REGULATORY AND POLICY ISSUES

Is work at home illegal? Are telecommuters treated as employees or contractors? Do they get paid differently than their counterparts in the office? These questions often come up when employers begin to seriously consider remote work programs. Apart from the zoning concerns covered in Chapter 8, the regulatory and related policy questions in telecommuting deal almost exclusively with employee relations issues. Some are clear-cut, but others are quite vague, partly because the policies and regulations weren't designed with remote work in mind. Here are four areas of regulatory and/or policy concern, followed by some details on the role of the "telecommuter's agreement" in helping manage the relationship between employer and telecommuter.

Union Interests and the
Fair Labor Standards Act (FLSA)

This law was passed in 1938 mostly as a response to many of the abusive labor practices that had developed in the early 1900s. It set forth restrictions on many terms and conditions of work, including restrictions on work at home in a number of industries. These were motivated by years of in-home work where people were underpaid, overworked, and where young children were forced to join in the labors.

Over the years, the FLSA was modified and amended, and the only remaining restrictions on work at home applied to seven specific types of garment manufacture. These provisions became a political football in the last few years; home-based knitters in Vermont and elsewhere were trying to have them lifted while several unions, especially the International Ladies Garment Worker Union, sought to maintain them.

In November 1984 the restriction on home knitting was lifted with the stipulation that homebased knitters had to register with the Labor Department and keep up with certain paperwork. This registration allows the Labor Department to continue to monitor these home sites for compliance with other FLSA provisions such as those covering work hours and overtime payments. This deregulation of the knitters was hailed as a victory by many groups who had been fighting on their behalf, although as of late 1985 it seemed likely that the unions would continue to press for tighter rules.

Implications for the Future

This book isn't about home knitters, but there are many lesssons to be learned from this episode. First, it's an example of the Reagan administration's drive to lessen government regulation in areas that don't seem to warrant it. Second, many of the arguments that were raised by the knitters and their supporters can translate directly to telecommuters. Specifically, the knitters said they wanted to be able to choose their own workplace and judge for themselves whether or not they were being exploited. Third, it became quite clear how strongly the unions were willing to fight against a change that is contrary to their basic tenet of protecting the interests of workers.

The unions have been victims of declining membership and declining public esteem in the 1980s. Some observers believe their position on work at home is an attempt to stir up some controversy and demonstrate their worth to the American worker. This interpretation has also been given to union attempts to ban telecommuting; if anything, the unions not only want to maintain current FLSA restrictions on work at home, but also to extend them to clerical and white-collar jobs. At its 1983 annual convention, for example, the AFL-CIO passed a resolution against "computer homework," and the Service Employees International Union (SEIU) has banned its members from telecommuting.

Current Regulations

You should note that there are no current federal bans on work at home outside of those few remaining garment occupations under the FLSA. This doesn't mean they aren't possible; you can expect continued lobbying by the unions and by allied groups like "9 to 5" to ban or severely restrict remote work.

Their premise is that we should take a lesson from the history of employer abuses of home workers earlier in the century. They believe that the potential for abuse (because of the inability to monitor employment and supervisory practices in remote work sites) is so great that we shouldn't risk having an "electronic cottage" become an "electronic sweatshop."

The opposing viewpoint is that today's work force won't allow itself to become subject to those abuses and that there are many compelling family and financial reasons (let alone personal preferences) that explain why some people want to work at home. The union response is that in certain labor markets home workers may be captive to a "buyer's market" and thus are fearful about speaking out against abuses because they might not find other employment. Similarly, illegal aliens employed this way supposedly would have no protection; their alternative is to risk deportation if they expose themselves by pointing the finger at the employer.

The arguments on both sides go on and on, and it's up to you to sort them out. The fact remains that employers should be aware of this simmering battle, especially as it relates to clerical-level workers. This group is generally classed as "nonexempt" workers, meaning that by the nature of their work they are not exempt from the FLSA provisions on overtime and other conditions. (In some companies lower-level white-collar workers —such as programmers—are also nonexempt workers.) Also, the clerical (or "pink-collar") work force is perhaps one of the largest opportunity areas for union organizing.

Special Concerns for Nonexempt Telecommuters

You'll need to make sure that your nonexempt telecommuters are treated just as they would be in the office. This includes recordkeeping requirements for regular and overtime hours worked, and making sure that overtime worked is reported and compensated. There's a bit of a paradox in this requirement in the context of remote work, since one of its benefits is the ability to work on a much more flexible schedule in many cases. Don't be lulled into thinking that your nonexempt telecommuters should report their work hours any differently than anyone else.

You may find that you'll need a system for preapproval of overtime work for these employees so they don't just casually extend the work day because they're inclined to do so. This is a good cost control practice anyhow, and is essential for keeping tabs on total hours worked.

It's a good bet that if the unions don't get the legislation they want to control telecommuting, they will work hard to make sure that existing provisions of the FLSA are enforced for remote nonexempt workers. Some employers choose to start their telecommuting programs with exempt-level employees just to steer clear of this red tape. Their rationale is simple: try out the concept with as few complications as possible, and then extend it later to more employees once it has been shown to be effective.

Defining Nonexempt Status

Interestingly, the determination of exempt versus nonexempt status depends on the nature of the job and in part on whether there is supervisory responsibility involved. You could argue that telecommuters working independently for much of the work week are supervising themselves instead of being subject to direct supervision by the manager. If that's the case, some nonexempt telecommuters might more appropriately be classed as exempt.

Be advised that the Labor Department has tended to interpret the FLSA in the employee's favor in borderline cases of exempt versus nonexempt status. It could be risky to change a telecommuter to exempt status without very careful analysis and solid guidance from your human resource and legal staffs. This kind of maneuvering can be detrimental to good employee relations in the long run and is exactly the type of problem the unions point to when they claim that telecommuting invites abuses.

REGULATORY CONCERNS: THE FAIR LABOR STANDARDS ACT

1. Check the provisions of the Act as they relate to nonexempt employees if they are part of your pilot.
2. Treat your nonexempt telecommuters the same as if they were in the office.
3. Don't try to stretch the boundary between exempt and nonexempt classifications.

Employee and Labor Relations

Your remote work program *can* be a model of positive employee relations. This is the best defense against third-party intervention; besides, it's good business in the long run. If your telecommuters feel they get at least as good a deal as they would in the office, there's little reason to expect problems. The employers who risk getting in trouble and creating headaches for themselves are those who try to cut corners on the employee-employer relationship. This is true in general and will be especially true for remote work. There should be enough built-in benefits for both parties that you shouldn't have to squeeze out a few more dollars here and there at the cost of positive employee relations.

If your employees who might become telecommuters are unionized, that's no reason to abandon plans for remote work (except, perhaps, if they belong to the SEIU). Depending on the general tone of your relationship with the union, though, you might not want to move ahead if you think you'll create more problems than you'll solve.

This is an excellent opportunity to collaborate with the union on an innovative work practice if you do go ahead. Even if your contract doesn't require the union's involvement in the planning, it may be sensible to bring them in. You'll want their support anyhow, and their early involvement will help shape the program according to your needs and theirs from the outset. The traditional adversarial relationship between union and management doesn't have to continue. Telecommuting may be a good opportunity for both sides to work with, not against each other.

How to Handle Employment Status

A final topic under the FLSA is the question of employment status. Are telecommuters to be treated as employees or are they more like independent contractors or subcontractors? If they're classed as the latter, there are very different provisions under the FLSA and under most workers' compensation statutes. Some employers do (or would like to) classify remote workers as independent contractors; this often frees the employers from many of the burdens and costs of an employee relationship.

These will be addressed later in this chapter under compensation and benefits. But the FLSA implications of this change in status can be serious. A computer conference on this issue was held in February 1984 on the Working From Home Forum on the CompuServe computer network, and the guest was Daniel Elisburg, former Assistant Secretary of Labor for Labor Standards in the Carter administration. Here's what Elisburg said: "When an employer unilaterally decides to call a worker an independent contractor, that is where the trouble begins. There are fairly well-defined rules on who is an independent contractor . . . including whether the people have opportunity for other work; whether they have substantial investment in the equipment; what kind of restrictions they have on the use of the equipment; whether they are at the mercy of the employer, etc. Saying a person is an independent contractor does not make it so."

This is an area where you'll need to move carefully. A person working as an employee in the office today and at a remote site tomorrow, doing the same job in essentially the same way, just doesn't turn into an independent contractor overnight. Making that switch to cut costs or for other reasons can be risky and may backfire in the long run. The same is true even for new hires who immediately become telecommuters; unless they meet the tests in the regulations, they'll be considered by the authorities to be employees, who are due all of the rights and protections of other employees.

State Labor Laws

Here's where things get interesting, since every state is free to set its own restrictions on work at home apart from the federal guidelines. Many states have statutes on the books prohibiting or restricting work at home, for many of the same reasons as the FLSA does. Some of the regulations apply more directly to businesses at home and won't fit the telecommuting situation. Once again, though, it's a case of the laws lagging behind the old times—and the states will have no choice but to apply the old laws to the new times even if it's an obvious misfit.

Your best bet is to do some research on your state's labor and business regulation laws and, if applicable, those in your city or county as well. Don't give up if you find what seems to be a ban on work at home that would apply to telecommuting. In one case, a large insurance company approached the state labor department to request a waiver of the state law for the purpose of a telecommuting trial. The state officials knew very little about telecommuting and granted the waiver once they understood the concept and its use. You'll probably find that a little bit of education and discussion goes a long way in cases like this; just be sure to do it early, before you're committed to a program.

You should also keep an eye on new legislation in your state affecting work at home. It's often faster and easier for lobbyists and advocates to get laws like this through at the state level. Even if you're only mildly interested in a remote work program, it pays to keep up with and speak out on legislation affecting work at home.

Video Display Terminal (VDT) Legislation

With more and more workers spending increasing time in front of VDTs there is growing concern over the possible health hazards associated with VDTs. These include concerns about radiation from the cathode-ray tubes in the display, potential eyestrain, and muscular/skeletal and emotional stress problems. There has been very little documented proof of a direct causal relationship between VDTs and some of these problems, although there are many reported cases of these problems among people who work with VDTs for most of the work day. The alleged health risks from radiation have not been substantiated and the scientific community has taken the position that there is no danger.

Legislative efforts have been stepped up to write rules on many as-

---

CHECKLIST OF EMPLOYEE RELATIONS CONCERNS

✔ Don't cut corners on the employee-employer relationship; you may pay the price in the long run.

✔ If potential telecommuters are unionized, try to work with the union from the start and head off a "we-they" climate.

✔ Be careful when classing telecommuters as "independent contractors"—this term has a specific meaning and can't be used loosely.

✔ Check into your state labor laws for possible restrictions on work at home. If they exist, consult with state officials and seek a waiver for your pilot.

---

pects of VDT use, including eye exams, rest breaks, transfers for pregnant employees, ergonomic features in the VDTs and in the furniture used with them, and much more. Some states have passed bills mandating study of and/or education about VDT use, and as of early 1985 in well over a dozen states legislators had submitted bills concerning various restrictions or guidelines for VDT use.

This VDT legislation becomes an issue for telecommuting indirectly. According to Charlotte LeGates of the Computer and Business Equipment Manufacturers Association, there is nothing in any of the bills pending in early 1985 to exclude remote work sites from coverage. The potential problem would be the difficulty in complying with and monitoring some of the provisions in these bills (such as those covering rest breaks and lighting and heating standards) at remote work sites. A worst-case scenario for telecommuting would be the passage of these laws and heavy penalties for noncompliance. Employers might be so wary of being unable to comply at remote sites using VDTs that they would forget about telecommuting altogether.

It's impossible to say how likely it is that any of these bills would pass, or whether they'll be superseded by federal legislation. In the short term you should plan to find out what's going on in your state and keep track of legislation that has been submitted. This area is very similar to zoning problems; the statutes weren't created expressly to ban telecommuting, but they may have that result unless the law is changed to exclude or at least account for the different needs of telecommuting.

The "Telecommuter's Agreement"

As you've seen in this chapter and the others, there is a myriad of details involved in remote work. Many of these involve new or different responsibilities of the employee, and there are some significant liability issues for both parties.

One way you can avoid or at least minimize problems is to spell things out in an agreement between telecommuter and employer. This is a form of a contract; as such, you'll benefit from some guidance from your legal counsel. Some of the items covered in such an agreement would include

- Work duties and responsibilities
- Base salary and (if applicable) "pay-for-performance" terms
- Work hour guidelines and limitations, and time reporting requirements (especially for nonexempt employees)
- Restrictions on access to equipment by nonemployees
- Responsibilities for password protection, if applicable
- Responsibility for equipment insurance coverage and protection
- Right of the employer to visit the remote location (especially if in the home) to check equipment and general work area safety, and to retrieve equipment or materials in case of termination or extended illness
- Responsibility for equipment maintenance, supplies, and telephone installation, use, and costs

This list will vary by company, employee, and job. You can rely on your planning group for ideas on what to include. The goal is to put in writing those items that can create legal, financial, or employee relations problems if left to chance or memory. The agreement should be a part of the employee selection process as well; prospective telecommuters have to know what's going to be expected of them as remote workers.

7: COMPENSATION AND BENEFITS ISSUES

Just as there are choices about employee versus independent contractor status, you have choices to make about pay and benefits for telecommuters. These choices fall across a spectrum: one end is to treat remote workers as regular, full-time employees with full pay and benefits, and the other is to carry them as part- or full-time independents with no benefits and pay on an hourly and/or piece-rate basis. The more "casual" your program is (i.e., only a few days a week, at the employee's option, and highly variable from week to week) the more you're committed to the first end of this spectrum. It's not practical for most employers to set up different pay schemes for these fluctuating schedules.

Here are some of the things you'll want to consider as you decide where to place your telecommuters on that spectrum:

- Nature of the work
- Sources of telecommuters (new hires versus existing employees)
- Employee relations and union concerns
- FLSA implications
- Workers' Compensation considerations
- Other state and federal labor and equal employment opportunity laws
- Cost-control objectives
- Precedents from past alternative work arrangements
- Employee preferences

There just aren't any clear-cut answers because of the range of possible applications. You should be sure to consider all the items on this list, even if some of them may seem to conflict with each other.

Risks of Trimming Pay and Benefits

You may be tempted to be as innovative with pay and benefits practices as with the concept of remote work itself, especially today when there's strong pressure to control benefits costs. For example, some people believe it's perfectly reasonable to think about scaling back the pay of telecommuters by 5 percent to 15 percent. Their premise is that the telecommuter has the financial advantage of working at home in many cases, and has lower costs for transportation, clothing, and meals. Even with the scaled-back pay the telecommuter nets out the same, not even counting the less tangible benefits of working remotely.

There's a certain undeniable logic to this option, but it rarely makes good sense in the long run even if your telecommuters would go along with it. First, one of the underlying principles of telecommuting is that you're interested in (and paying for) results. If a telecommuter and an office worker deliver the same results, they should get the same basic compensation. Second, it's likely that many telecommuters in the near future will be women, to the extent that child care creates some motivation for wanting to work from home. Employers are finally beginning to make progress on delivering equal pay for equal work between men and women as mandated under various federal and state statutes. If you pay (women) telecommuters less, you'd be creating a new set of pay inequities to resolve —and nobody needs that kind of problem.

The Nonemployee Option

The biggest issue that has surfaced in this area is at the opposite end of the pay and benefits spectrum: under what conditions do you hire telecommuters on a nonemployee, hourly-pay basis with few, if any, benefits? Part-time work is nothing new and, in fact, is growing across the country (see Chapter 12). The advantage of having employees work less than 20 hours a week is that in many cases it frees you of the costs and burdens of benefits coverage and pension funding, and some other benefits as well.

There's been a lot of speculation about whether telecommuters paid hourly or on a piece-rate basis are better or worse off than if they were employees paid on straight salary in the office. This is a difficult comparison, because of intangibles like the benefits of working at home, the pros and cons of piece-rate pay systems, and the value of the "office" space contributed by the telecommuter in the form of floor space, heating, and electricity.

Unfortunately this is another complex issue with no easy answers. A good rule of thumb is to strive for a pay and benefits plan that meets two objectives. First, it must be attractive enough in your local labor market so you can hire and retain enough of the right kinds of workers to adequately staff your operation. Second, it must be structured so your telecommuters can meet their financial and benefits-coverage needs, and must allow them to see their extra efforts reflected in extra compensation. These are good guidelines for compensating any employees, telecommuters or otherwise.

Merit Pay and Flexible Benefits

Often, the toughest part of the compensation planning is to include "extra reward for extra effort," especially for jobs that don't have unit-based outputs. Pay-for-performance is an important part of many compensation systems, but it's most important in telecommuting where there's room for truly exceptional performance because of the productivity-boosting factors described in Chapter 2.

Clerical-type work is easier to handle because its measurable outputs lend themselves to a piece-rate system. As you move up the organizational ladder, it's harder to create these direct payoffs. The tasks are longer and there are often extenuating circumstances that account for good and bad performance. One of the real risks in telecommuting is that you create a climate where people can and do work harder and produce more, yet you don't pay off for that extra output. Most professional-level workers are used to annual salary review systems where the better performers get bigger raises—and the big jumps in income come from bonuses or promotions for those who contribute the most. But these systems are often flawed in the office, and these flaws can carry over to remote workers as well.

The same alternatives that many firms are exploring to improve salary administration for office workers can be very helpful if not essential for remote workers. For example, flexible schedules for bonuses and raises are often used to create a more timely and rewarding link between effort and reward. If your telecommuters don't see some kind of extra reward for extra work, it won't be long before they figure out that the intangible benefits of working remotely just don't make up for what they're *not* getting in their paychecks. This is a real challenge for paying remote workers; unless you're sure you can create that payoff, you can't be assured of sustaining high performance over time.

Rethinking Benefits Options

One interesting way to tackle this problem is to look at the total compensation package. Some of the traditional assumptions about benefits and their value relative to base pay might come into question under telecommuting. According to Robert McCaffery, a nationally-known compensation and benefits consultant and author, "There's probably no rationale for lessening overall benefits coverage for people at home; in most cases they still will have the same needs for health care and other coverage. But perhaps you can argue that they would need less vacation time. The whole idea of vacations is to provide time away from the office and a break in the routine. If telecommuting provides a less pressured, more varied work environment, maybe those people need less vacation."

Mr. McCaffery isn't suggesting that you do away with vacations for telecommuters. He *is* raising some interesting questions about the mix of benefits. One of the growing trends in pay and benefits administration is the flexible-benefits or "cafeteria compensation" approach in which employees can, within limits, select the types and amounts of benefits they want. For example, a young single person might choose less life insurance and more vacation or tuition reimbursement credits; a married employee with young children might trade off vacation time for more medical and dental coverage.

These plans aren't new, but may have new uses in remote work. Just as benefits and pay needs vary by age and family status, they might vary by work location. Maybe the telecommuter working almost full-time at home might trade off some vacation time for more salary—or for child care assistance or credits toward the purchase of computer software or hardware for personal use. If your firm has or is considering these plans, try to expand the choices to include unique items which may be more appealing to remote workers than to office-based workers. This would also help address the pay-for-performance problem where there are limits on the size or frequency of increases in base pay.

CHECKLIST OF COMPENSATION AND BENEFITS ISSUES

✔ Carefully examine your options for types of employment status, pay levels, and benefits coverage—make sure your telecommuters are treated fairly and equitably.

✔ Don't take a short-term view on salary and benefits cost control— you may lose in the long run.

✔ Look for creative ways to use pay-for-performance methods for telecommuters.

✔ If you have a flexible-benefits or "cafeteria compensation" plan, try to use it or change it to the telecommuters' advantage.

SUMMARY

These are the seven major areas for you to consider as you move ahead with your planning. They are potential problems, not definite obstacles. The success of your telecommuting program depends in part on how carefully you review each one and take the appropriate preventive steps.

12

How to Evaluate the New Options for Employment Status

If you take a quick survey around your organization, you'll probably find a number of people who don't fit the mold of the regular employee working a five-day, forty-hour week. They might be part-timers, retirees, or even job-sharers (two people who divide one job and its pay and benefits). You've seen how telecommuting allows different work *locations*; now you'll see what's going on with the trend toward different work *schedules* and different *employment categories*, both of which dovetail nicely with telecommuting.

It wasn't too long ago that you and your fellow managers might have looked askance at anyone who worked other than a "regular" five-day, forty-hour week. Part-timers, for example, were (and in some cases still are) seen as being less committed to their jobs. People who wanted flexible working hours, or "flextime," were thought to be too disorganized or undisciplined to stick to the same schedule as everyone else. Though these beliefs linger, they're slowly but surely fading away as more organizations see the benefits of a more flexible approach to work schedules and forms of employment. In this chapter you'll learn why it's important to keep an open mind about some of these alternatives and how to tie them in with telecommuting. Two kinds of nontraditional work arrangements will be covered: different work schedules and different employment relationships. **179**

WHY BOTHER WITH
ALTERNATE WORK ARRANGEMENTS?

At first glance, any deviation from the norm might seem to be a problem. After all, think of how much of today's organization life is structured around the assumption that workers will all be full-time, regular employees working on a traditional schedule: pay and benefits programs, facilities planning, and project scheduling tied to "person-weeks" of work involved, just to name a few. But it's essential that you look beyond these traditional assumptions and see why you can't limit your staffing only to those people who can work a "normal" schedule. Here are five reasons:

1: Coping with Changes in the Work Force

You'll be facing a very different type of labor pool in the next 5 to 10 years. Here are some figures taken from an excellent review article entitled "Personnel Trends in the '80s" by Don G. Keown:*

- There will be a 14.5 percent drop in the number of people entering the 18 to 24 age group, the traditional source for staffing most entry-level jobs;

- The percentage of all women who are in the labor force will go up; between 1970 and 1982 it rose from 43.3 percent to 52.6 percent. By 1990, about 58 percent of all women are expected to be in the labor force.

- Similarly, women account for a greater proportion of the work force than ever before: in 1970 they accounted for 38 percent, and in 1984 this rose to 43 percent on the way to over 46 percent projected for 1990. More important, women are expected to account for two-thirds of all new entrants into the labor force through 1990.

- Finally, the number of divorced, widowed, and separated working women with children under age 18 has increased by 74 percent in the past decade.

This all adds up to one thing: you'll have to be prepared to accommodate the needs of many of these working women in order to staff your organization. The use of midday "mother's hours" in banking and other service-type industries is a good example of this. Coupled with the grow-

---

*Excerpted from *Office Administration and Automation*, December 1984 by Geyer-McAllister Publications, Inc., New York.

ing educational levels of many women and the overall decline in the ranks of the 18 to 24 age group, it's clear that many candidates for lower and middle-level jobs will only be available on nontraditional schedules. If you stick with just those candidates who can work "normal" schedules, you're shutting yourself off from many potentially valuable workers.

2: Fitting the Labor Resource to the Task

As more and more office work becomes automated, you'll be able to segment the work and only apply as much labor as is needed to get it done. For example, look at word processing versus traditional typing; with the former it's much easier to allocate the work among several people. You don't have to worry as much about individual typing styles or familiarity with the material being typed. Since various word processing operators can exchange diskettes or files, it's much easier for one person to pick up where another left off.

This means you can better balance your staffing levels against actual workload. This has been done for years in manufacturing operations where volume fluctuates from month to month or even day to day; effective cost control depends in part on the use of part-timers and/or temporary employees.

3: Improving Utilization of Company Resources

Think what would happen if you were a manufacturing manager and went to your board of directors for a capital appropriation to buy a multi-million dollar piece of equipment. You'd be asked to justify the purchase and demonstrate how much use you'd be able to squeeze out of it, usually by making sure it was needed and in use around the clock.

Compare this with how most organizations buy (or even lease) and use other capital assets like computers and buildings. Computers are often used on at least two shifts but not always three; office buildings are generally unoccupied from around 7 P.M. to 7 A.M. Why shouldn't you expect to use these assets just as much as production equipment? Once again, it's tradition staring us in the face and robbing us of potential paybacks.

This doesn't mean you have to put on three full shifts of office workers, but it does make sense to look at off-hours use of these assets. Shifting work away from the standard first-shift hours means money saved by avoiding or delaying planned expansions in office space and computer capacity. Nontraditional work hours (and work locations, as you'll see later) are one way to stretch your available space and capacity.

4: Retaining the Skills of Trained Workers

You saw in Chapter 2 how telecommuting helps you keep qualified workers even though they might otherwise have to resign due to disability or family needs. The same holds for alternate work arrangements; many people have to leave the work force only because they can't handle traditional schedules. They can include retirees who don't want to or can't work a full schedule, those with medical problems, or those who want or need more freedom in work scheduling.

An excellent example of how this works is a program at New York Life Insurance Company in New York City. Faced with the costs and disruption of turnover among women in its programming staff who left after having children, New York Life invited many of these women to come back to work—with a twist. They would be contractors, not employees, and would be hired on a project basis for programming tasks of up to 200 hours. Terminals are installed in their homes for the duration of the project. The advantage to the company is that it can avoid hiring more full-time programmers for workload peaks since this group of almost two dozen women is used to fill these needs. They are trained, trusted workers and the project-type relationship works out well for both parties.

These women are working at a nontraditional location (home) on a nontraditional schedule (self-determined hours) in a nontraditional work relationship (nonemployee contractors). Had New York Life said "We *must* use only regular workers" it would have lost this valuable talent pool. By being open-minded about employment possibilities they and the programmers came out ahead. There's no reason why you can't take a similar approach in your organization. It doesn't have to be with programmers or with women or even with telecommuting. The main idea is to be more flexible in your thinking about finding and using talented people in nontraditional ways to supplement—not replace—your work force.

5: Avoiding the Problems of a Layoff

One of the most difficult jobs a manager can have is to be involved in planning and implementing a layoff. Even though you know it's necesary, you probably cringe at the thought. One strategy that several large organizations use to avoid this is to shrink the "core" of their work force and make up the difference with various kinds of auxiliary workers.

For example, assume you run a manufacturing operation and need between 100 and 200 production workers depending on season or business cycles. One way to handle the swings is to hire 100 more people when you need them, lay them off when you don't, and rehire them when business picks up again. The other approach is to have a core of only 100 regular, permanent employees and fill the other needs with temporary workers or subcontractors. This saves the cost and aggravation of putting people on and off the regular payroll. It also helps stabilize the permanent work force by letting them know that they're not very likely to have to suffer through the hire/layoff/rehire cycle.

This isn't a new idea, but it's not as widely used as you might imagine; it's used even less in office work. Think of the advantages: if managed properly, it allows you to have a no-layoff or minimal-layoff policy—which has to improve morale and loyalty among the work force. Keeping this "core" work force at or near the size needed in the low periods (and filling the gaps via temporary hires) saves everyone the agony of the "boom or bust" cycles.

The only problem with this approach, at least for most office work, is office space: where are you going to put the supplemental workers in the peak periods? Many of them can work at *remote sites* so your core office space only has to be large enough for your core office staff. Even if these telecommuters can't work at home, or you have no other remote space and need to rent space for short periods, it will usually be cheaper than maintaining that space year-round—especially if it's empty a good deal of the time.

WHY YOU SHOULD CONSIDER ALTERNATE WORK ARRANGEMENTS

1. Changes in work force demographics will mean tighter supplies of some job applicants and increased supplies of others.
2. Fitting the labor resource to the task lets you better balance staffing levels and costs against actual workload.
3. More flexible staffing can lead to better utilization of capital assets.
4. Retirees will grow in number and are an excellent talent pool from which to supplement your main work force.
5. Shrinking your core of full-time permanent employees and meeting peak needs with supplemental workers help you avoid the costs and trauma of the hire/layoff/rehire cycle.

In summary, these five background factors are really opportunities and not problems. The use of alternate work arrangements, such as those to be described in detail below, is a natural with telecommuting. Most tasks that lend themselves to part-time work, delegation to subcontractors, or split jobs also lend themselves to remote work.

THE SPECIFIC WORK OPTIONS:
DESCRIPTIONS AND PROS AND CONS

There are seven major alternatives to staffing your jobs with regular, permanent, full-time people in the office. Some are based on changes in work schedules, others on changes in the type of employer-worker relationship, and others on sources of workers not normally considered for the mainstream work force. All seven are suitable for either central-office or remote work. However, this section isn't so much about remote work as it is about an enlightened view of hiring and staffing. If you're willing to take that view, you would also probably be willing to give telecommuting a try either with these workers or with your full-time, permanent employees.

1: Part-Time Employees

Part-time work isn't new, but it certainly is growing. According to the Association of Part-Time Professionals, voluntary part-time workers now represent about 14 percent of the total labor force. The Bureau of Labor Statistics reports that involuntary part-time workers (people who would like to work full-time) make up 5.5 percent of the work force.

Major reasons for hiring part-timers are to cut costs (by trimming or eliminating benefits costs) and to pay only for as much labor as is actually needed for a task. Part-timers can be permanent or temporary employees; in some cases their work schedules vary weekly according to workload and employee preference. You may find that voluntary part-timers are among your most dedicated workers because they can shape their hours around their needs and availability. They can be a real challenge to manage, however, if there's no logical division among tasks and clear starting and stopping points. Finally, if your sole reason for having part-timers is to avoid the benefits and pension funding costs, and you staff almost exclusively with part-timers, be prepared for possible resentment and perhaps even some union organizing interest.

2: Retirees

You might wonder why retirees would want to work; after all, isn't retirement to get *away* from work? For some, the pressures of inflation or boredom with inactivity drive them back to work. Most retirees represent a wealth of knowledge to their own ex-employers and others. They also can complement a much younger work force with their maturity and accumulated experience.

Since they almost always will be working part-time because of income restrictions under Social Security, they have many of the pros and cons described above for part-timers. Retirees may also have something you won't find in many of your younger workers: a complete lack of fear of using computers. The conventional wisdom about why large numbers of senior citizens take computer literacy courses is that they don't want to miss out on the computer revolution. Also, they aren't afraid of admitting ignorance and fumbling around a bit on the keyboard. Contrast this with the attitudes of many younger workers who, for whatever reason, are very willing to let the computer parade pass them by. Some of your best PC or terminal users might be among your retirees.

3: Subcontractors

This term is used interchangeably with independent contractors to refer to people who work on a task or project basis and aren't employees. These range from the clerical person from a temporary-help agency who spends one day with you, to a programmer or engineer who works almost full-time for a year or more. As noted in Chapter 11, you have to be careful about how you define subcontractors; if it's done as a ruse primarily to avoid liability or compliance with labor statutes, you might be in for some problems.

In most cases, contractors are willing to trade off stability and predictability of income for the relative freedom of being on their own, whether or not they've formally set up their own business. Your hourly or weekly cost for their services is likely to be more than what you'd pay them in salary if they were employees, sometimes even considering the cost of benefits. The big advantages in using contractors is the ability to buy only what you need without worrying about a long-term commitment. Most companies in the 1980s are trying to stem the creeping growth in headcount. You can often make the case that it's better in the long run to pay someone more on a project basis than it is to employ someone who then fades into the overhead—or becomes a layoff statistic—when the project is over.

The criticism often raised about contractors is lack of loyalty. There's the fear that they'll just go to the highest bidder, or skip off for the ski slopes when the first snowstorm arrives. This risk is always there, but you can protect against it in two ways. First, be as diligent in hiring a contractor as you are in hiring an employee. A thorough interview and a careful check of work history and references should separate the skiers from the workers. Second, consider using a contract to bind the person (and yourself, of course) and make it harder for him/her to leave abruptly.

4: Flexible Work Hours

This is second only to part-time work as a widespread option. Flexible hours, or "flextime" as it's often called, had its big growth in the 1960s and 1970s and has tapered off in popularity since then. There are some interesting parallels between flextime and telecommuting: both require a basic rethinking in many assumptions about work and supervision and both are (or were) somewhat trendy in nature.

One of flextime's problems is that it was sometimes implemented without careful thought about its impact on business operations; also, it was done without a clear need in mind. You can learn a lesson from those problems as you go ahead with telecommuting—if you do it with adequate planning and in response to clear business needs you'll be better off in the long run.

You're probably familiar with most of the pros and cons of flextime: it gives employees more freedom and discretion, within limits, can help ease the load on mass transit or roads, but also can create coordination problems when people aren't around when they're needed and can be an administrative burden. These hold for telecommuting to some extent with one big difference: the employee usually gains more from flextime than the employer. When telecommuting is implemented correctly, the employer stands to gain at least as much as the employee. In that sense, telecommuting is the best of both worlds: it offers the worker the benefits of flextime (plus some more) *and* has real payoffs for your organization.

Taken on its own, flextime undeniably is attractive to most employees. The situations where it offers benefits to you as the manager are limited to jobs where there's value in providing service to clients or customers beyond the normal work hours. For instance, if flextime lets a bank employ tellers all on eight-hour shifts, but some start at 7:30 A.M. while others don't end until 6 P.M., the bank's customers can be served over those longer hours. If that gives the bank a competitive advantage, then flextime is very attractive to the employer as well.

5: Compressed Workweeks

This is another idea that's been with us for some time; in one popular form it's the four day/forty hour schedule. This parallels flextime in its relative value to employees over employers. The theory is that people will gladly work an extra two hours a day in return for an extra day off. But what's in it for the employer? One big advantage is the extended service hours described under flextime, though in some cases those last two hours of the day can be far from peak work times for most people. Also, if you manage an operation with significant daily startup time or cost, you get a better return on those daily investments if you run for two hours longer each day.

Don't shy away from this option or flextime just because their benefits may be skewed toward your employees. If you can use this to your advantage to remain competitive in your labor market, or if it responds to a strongly expressed preference from your people (and doesn't create other problems) you might find it worthwhile. The big risk with both options and the next one comes when you misuse them to appease your people. If they're upset with more fundamental issues (like pay, quality of supervision, or the work itself), they might feel you're just throwing them a bone if you implement these options.

6: Job Sharing

Oddly enough, this option has probably gotten most use at the very top of some organizations. It was fashionable several years ago to create an "office of the president," for example, staffed by two to four top executives. This was done as a management development exercise, to allow them to focus on different aspects of the business, or as an outcome of a merger or acquisition. These job-sharing applications have a mixed record; the biggest problem is to split up what is usually a single focal point for decision-making. Also, these job sharers were *not* splitting one paycheck.

Below these executive levels the concept has had more success, but is much less widespread than any of the other options. (Note: One force behind job sharing is New Ways to Work, a San Francisco-based organization that promotes the concept and publishes how-to manuals.) The fundamental challenge in job sharing is maintaining coordination and consistency. The two people sharing the job have to carefully plan the work and make sure they overlap enough, but not so much as to duplicate effort.

One advantage is that you might get more than your money's worth. Even though you pay for one full person, in most cases you get the benefit of two people's thinking, and you face much less disruption based on absence due to illness or vacations. Also, if the shared job is a supervisory one, the subordinates stand to gain more by having two coaches and counselors—as long as they're not getting conflicting signals.

7: Disabled Workers

Finally, there's the potential for hiring workers who have physical or emotional handicaps that normally keep them out of the traditional work force. Providing meaningful employment for these workers—especially at the professional level—has been a problem for years. Two reasons why there's been more success recently is the impact of rules under affirmative action legislation and the growing number of adaptive devices that take advantage of or are linked to microcomputer technology.

Your ability to hire and properly use the skills of the disabled depends on five factors:

- The degree and type of disability;
- The absence of architectural barriers at the workplace;
- Your willingness to help make accommodations where needed;
- The person's motivation and personality;
- The availability of suitable public or special transportation if needed.

There are many private, state, and federal agencies that can help you work through these issues. Also, the Job Accommodation Network in Morgantown, West Virginia was set up in 1984 as an information and referral clearinghouse and has been very helpful to many employers.

Telecommuting and the Disabled: A Good Match?

Some people feel that telecommuting is a natural for this group, especially for those whose mobility is restricted. One of the first telecommuting applications was Control Data Corporation's use of its PLATO computer-based instruction system to train the homebound handicapped to be computer programmers. Other similar programs have been in place for several years, but the merits of this application aren't as clear-cut as you might expect.

While telecommuting can help solve the mobility problem, it runs counter to the thinking of some specialists in the field (and some of the disabled themselves) who stress the value of "mainstreaming" the disabled as much as possible. They believe that putting people to work in the office with everyone else is much better than keeping them in their homes or special centers. There's no doubt that today's technology can play a big role, but employers shouldn't overlook the human factors.

No matter where they're employed, however, there is a great deal of expertise among the disabled population. They have been overlooked in many cases simply because managers don't understand enough about various disabilities or how to accommodate them. If you want to take advantage of this hidden talent, your best bet is to get in touch with referral agencies in your area and find out what skills are available to you.

CHECKLIST OF SEVEN MAJOR WORK OPTIONS

Think about ways to use these options selectively to supplement your staffing efforts. Many of them are well suited to remote work.

✔ Part-time workers

✔ Retirees

✔ Subcontractors (or independent contractors)

✔ Flexible work hours

✔ Compressed workweeks

✔ Job sharing

✔ Disabled workers

SUMMARY

This has been a quick tour through seven of the most popular work force options. While they've been described separately, you'll probably find that you can and will mix and match them—such as retirees working part-time or flexible hours for the handicapped. Most important, they should be examined against the backdrop of telecommuting since all can be a part of remote work in one way or another.

13

How to Identify and Manage the Productivity Issues

It's almost amazing to realize that it took several years of inflation and then a recession (in the late 1970s and early 1980s) plus an awakening to the gains made by Japan before American business really started addressing the need to increase productivity. While our workers have been the most productive in the world for many years, our rate of productivity growth is falling behind that of several countries, according to Bureau of Labor Statistics data:

AVERAGE ANNUAL RATES OF CHANGE IN OUTPUT PER EMPLOYEE HOUR

Country	1960–1973	1973–1983	1983 Alone
United States	3.0%	1.9%	4.3%
Japan	10.7%	7.4%	5.0%
France	6.7%	4.6%	5.9%
Canada	4.5%	1.7%	6.4%
United Kingdom	4.4%	2.0%	6.6%

The meaning of somewhat abstract figures like these is brought home quickly to managers who learn they have to do as much or more with fewer people. If your organization was trimmed down, especially in the middle-management ranks as so many were in the early 1980s, you know what it's like to try getting more output from your staff—without turning the office into a sweatshop.

In Chapter 2 you were shown the seven major sources of increased productivity with telecommuting. You might want to go back and reread that section now that you have a fuller understanding of how telecommuting should work. To quickly recap, they are

- More hours worked per day
- More work done per hour
- Faster access and turnaround time
- Ability to work at peak times
- Freedom from group norms that limit productivity
- Less incidental absence
- Use of more productive tools

UNDERSTANDING THE SOURCES OF INCREASED PRODUCTIVITY

There's also an eighth item on this list—the amount of attention normally paid to telecommuting programs and the excitement and willingness of the participants. Because telecommuting is still something of a novelty, it is watched carefully; anything observed that way is changed just due to the observation itself. This is the well-known "Hawthorne Effect" first documented in experiments at a Western Electric plant starting in 1927.

In most cases, everyone involved *wants* telecommuting to work. The employees want to continue enjoying the personal benefits of remote work, and managers who suggested (and others who approved) the implementation are anxious to see it live up to its promises. This is good because it provides encouragement and motivation to make things work. But being in the limelight can also confound the implementation; it becomes hard to say whether the productivity gains come from the seven factors above, the high attention level, or some combination of these factors.

You might say to yourself, "Who cares—if productivity from telecommuting is up, let well enough alone. Let's not look a gift horse in the mouth." The problem with this response is that if you're not sure why things have improved, it's hard to make sound decisions about further implementation—and hard to find the right cause and solution when problems come up.

However, one encouraging outcome of many remote work applications is *sustained* productivity gains. After the initial hoopla is over and the novelty is gone, the gains are still there. In some cases, the output measures even show some early declines before the later increases. This seems to be due to an initial shakedown period when everyone (telecommuter, coworkers, manager, and family) tries to get into a new routine and work out the bugs in the system. These two findings help support the notion that the productivity gains are due to more than the added management attention and initial surge of enthusiasm by the telecommuters.

MEASURING PRODUCTIVITY: AN OVERVIEW

This all adds up to a need to carefully track productivity as part of your implementation. This takes some finesse because of the difficulties of measuring white-collar productivity in general and in remote sites in particular. According to Carl Thor, Vice-President of Measurement at the American Productivity Center, you should consider these points:

1. *Mix of Tasks.* Most office work, especially at the professional level, consists of individual tasks and group-oriented tasks. For the former, productivity measurement at a remote site is the same as in the office. But measuring the group work gets a little more complicated because you need to look at whether the telecommuters are effective—a much broader concept than output alone. According to Mr. Thor, some of the reported productivity gain in telecommuting might be because the remote worker can focus almost exclusively on the individual aspects of work.

2. *Mix of Indicators.* You can't really separate productivity, quality, and timeliness as indicators of output from so-called "knowledgeable workers." You have to look at all three in the office setting, and examine the impact of remote work on all three as well.*

Productivity Measurement Planning

It pays to keep these four points in mind as you plan to measure productivity changes with telecommuting:

1. *Develop Solid Measures.* Productivity measurement for telecommuters can only be as good as it is for their counterparts in the office,

---

*NOTE: If you're looking for general information on productivity and its measurement, the American Productivity Center is an excellent resource. Contact them at 123 N. Post Oak Lane, Houston, TX 77024.

assuming that the jobs are done the same way in both locations. If you don't have meaningful ways of tracking productivity for the job in the office you won't be able to do it remotely either. Your first step is to set up a good measurement system and *then* adapt it to remote sites.

2. *Measure the Whole Job.* Don't mislead yourself into thinking you can generate big productivity gains via telecommuting by removing the group-oriented tasks so the telecommuter just does the more measurable individual tasks. This change would give you an apples-and-oranges comparison of remote versus office work output. Also, you'd probably accomplish little in the long run because the work you took away from the telecommuters would fall on the office workers, decreasing *their* productivity.

3. *Don't Overmeasure.* Don't develop a measurement fetish. In jobs that are tough to measure in quantitative terms, it's tempting to try to reduce everything to a number. That can not only distort the measurements, but even change the way the work is done. As an example, consider the personnel manager whose job is to provide sound employee relations guidance and administration. Nobody would quibble with that definition, except that nobody knows how to tell if it's happening.

The result is that someone tries to measure some of the events that are proxies for "sound guidance," for example. Counts are made of the number of new policies generated, the number of managers and employees counseled, or the average time it takes to resolve employee complaints. These certainly are important issues but don't show the whole picture. Also, the more those measures are emphasized, the more the personnel manager is tempted to shape his/her activity to look good based on those statistics. Simple questions from managers that could be answered in a two-minute hallway chat now get shunted to more formal meetings—because the meetings get counted but the hallway chats don't.

4. *Measure All Job Dimensions.* Remember Carl Thor's advice: you have to look at output *and* quality *and* timeliness for knowledgeable workers. As you look at your potential telecommuters, think about the full range of ways of finding out how well they're doing. One good source of information might be your performance appraisal system. If well designed, these systems often capture many aspects of a person's job beyond the ones that can be counted.

The advantage of linking your productivity measures to the performance appraisal system (or vice-versa, if your measures are in better shape than the appraisal system) is that you can put your payroll money where your measures are. You can talk about productivity and quality until you're blue in the face; if the workers don't believe those measures have any bearing on their pay raises or chances for promotion they probably won't pay much attention.

Pinning Down the Measures

Another way to get at the quality and timeliness issues is to discuss them with the potential telecommuters and the people they work with or serve. Don't be afraid to ask your people how they judge their own work; their answers probably won't be self-serving because they know you'll be tempering them with your own judgment.

It's an unfortunate irony that some managers aren't as close to their subordinates' work as are the workers, peers, and inside or outside customers. There's a logical explanation for this: if you have a lot of people reporting to you, manage a highly technical staff, or are in a true service-type function, you can't be expected to have a complete grasp of what's going on. Also, the comments about quality and timeliness measures from these "outsiders" are almost essential for telecommuting applications. These other people will be the first to complain if they think your remote workers are delivering less than they should be. It's better to be aware of their expectations *before* you start—and build them into the productivity tracking—than to get blindsided three months into the program.

CHECKLIST OF POINTS
ABOUT WHITE-COLLAR PRODUCTIVITY

- ✔ Productivity gains from telecommuting, while welcomed, must be understood.
- ✔ Office workers work alone and in groups; look at the overall effect of telecommuting on both parts of the job.
- ✔ Look at productivity, quality, and timeliness together—quantity alone isn't a complete measure.
- ✔ If you can't track productivity for people in the office, you probably can't do it for remote workers either.
- ✔ Don't get measurement-happy—everything can't be reduced to a number.

THE ROLE OF CONTROL GROUPS

You read earlier in this chapter about the need for evaluation and measurement as a way of understanding the true sources of improved productivity. An important part of a top-notch evaluation process is a control group. This is a group of employees who are closely matched to your telecommuters in every respect but one: the control group works in the office five days a week.

Using a control group is the only truly reliable way to figure out the effects of remote work on productivity. A control group also lets you track other information, such as absence (yes, telecommuters *do* miss work!), illness, and turnover that may have bearing on the overall success of remote work. There can be many subtle changes that occur with telecommuting and you have to be able to separate their impact.

For example, let's take the issue of management style. In Chapter 7 you saw the importance of setting clear goals with specific timetables and giving ongoing feedback on progress. Most managers of telecommuters will also be managing in-office workers; if these managers are coached in those skills, isn't it possible that they'll apply them to *all* their employees? This is why many managers of remote workers report that the act of managing from a distance makes them better managers of the in-office staff; they use managerial skills and tools that serve everyone well.

The Productivity Guessing Game

If that's the case, and if the telecommuters show well-documented productivity gains, you won't know if it's due to the benefits of remote work as outlined in Chapter 2, the manager's improved skills, or a combination—unless you have a control group. If a control group's productivity showed gains similar to the telecommuters', you'd have to assume that improved managerial skills were the key. However, if the telecommuters showed even higher gains than the office workers, that incremental difference would be attributed to remote work in itself.

Here's the same question posed earlier in the chapter: if the gains are there, why should you look a gift horse in the mouth? There are three reasons. First, you want to be able to give (and even take) credit where credit is due. Second, you want to be on firm ground if your management asks you to demonstrate why you should continue or expand a remote work program. Third, you want to have the right kind of information to be able to dig into problems if they occur.

How a Control Group Can Help

Let's say your initial telecommuting project involves a group of ten programmers working remotely, out of a department with 100 programmers. Several months into the project (at a point when everything is going well) you introduce a new software package for the group. It's intended to streamline programming by greatly reducing some of the tedious and repetitive aspects of the job. After some initial training sessions all the programmers begin to use this tool.

Two months later, seven of the ten telecommuters start to have serious problems with it and their productivity plummets instead of rising as expected. Your first hunch (supported by your boss, who's always been a little lukewarm about remote work) is that the telecommuters are having problems because they don't have easy access to coworkers who can help answer their questions.

If you're like most managers, your mind was working as you read this scenario: some of the questions you're asking yourself are

- Why are only seven out of the ten telecommuters having problems?
- What's happening with all the other programmers in the office—how are they doing?
- How well were those seven telecommuters doing before the new tool was introduced?

You can't begin to find the real cause of the problem unless you've been tracking relative performance of both groups of workers. The cause can be any of the following:

- Some programmers were trained by a poor instructor;
- Some programmers have more experience and can adapt to the new package more easily;
- The different projects assigned to various programmers require different use of the new language;
- Some programmers are more likely than others to ask for help when they're having problems, thus cutting down on the time they waste trying to muddle through on their own.

The real cause can be any of these—or it *could* be the fact that it's harder for the remote programmers to pick the brains of their counterparts. Having a control group that's set up as described in the next section will help you shortcut the search for the solution. The worst thing you could do is try to fix the wrong problem in a case like this. Reassigning projects to different programmers would be a mistake if all that's needed is to give everyone a more detailed reference manual. In summary, a control group helps you manage a remote work program more effectively by giving you a way to verify what's going on and thus be more sure of the conclusions you draw from the program.

CHOOSING A CONTROL GROUP

In its strict sense (such as in laboratory experiments) a control group should be a perfectly matched group of people. The only thing that differs is the experimental factor. If you're trying to assess the effects of a new drug, you want the control and trial groups to be mirror images so that any changes have to be a result of the new drug. These trials are usually done in "double blind" fashion: neither the subjects nor the experimenters know which group gets the real drug and which gets a placebo.

For better or worse, you're running a business and not a medical experiment. You don't have the luxury of this kind of strictly disciplined testing. Also, it's impractical to think that you could come up with two perfectly matched groups of employees. You also have to think about the potential problem of what to do with the results of any comparisons. If you have a control group in the office and the pilot group of telecommuters, there are two chances out of three that one group will perform better than the other. No matter in which group it is, the "losers" might take it hard, and then you have a morale problem on your hands.

Safeguards for Control Groups

Fortunately, there are ways to guard against this, assuming you believe in the basic advantages of having some kind of control group for comparison purposes. You can avoid a lot of problems by keeping three points in mind as you design and discuss the project and the use of a control group:

1. *This Is a Pilot Program.* The company is trying to learn how well the concept of telecommuting will work, and *one* (but not the only) way to find that out is to compare the productivity of both groups. You're not out to pit one group against the other; there's a subtle but important difference between comparing the results and setting up a competition.

2. *The Concept Is Being Tested, Not the People.* If you make this clear, no one should fear for his/her job and there should be no relationship be-

tween the results of the comparison and any future salary, transfer, or promotion possibilities.

3. *The Manager Is a Key Player.* What you're comparing across the two groups is the performance of the *managers* as much or more than the individual employees. The manager is, as always, the critical linking factor between the staff and the organization.

You have to decide if these three points make sense in your own mind for your people in your organization. If they do, and you can convincingly discuss them with everyone involved, then by all means establish a control group as part of the program. But if there are circumstances where the risk outweighs the benefits, then consider two other options.

First, you can scrap the idea of a control group and simply rely on the telecommuters' results and your instincts to let you know how well everything is working out. Or, you can run your comparisons confidentially. There's no reason why you have to advertise the fact that you've set up a control group, and you're not obligated to share the results with the participants. If you take this second option, be prepared for the possibility that someone above or below you might ask whether you're making these comparisons. You can have your cake and eat it, perhaps, by doing this on the sly—but don't do it in a way that's devious or misleading to those involved.

Control Group Selection Criteria

If you select a control group, you'll want to have as close a match as is practical; here are some of the factors used to make the choice. Since you're trying to mirror the makeup of the telecommuters' group, you'll have to select them before you choose the control group.

1. *Work Characteristics.* Type and difficulty of projects assigned, level of training needed to do them well, special resources needed, and mix of individual versus interactive requirements.

2. *Personal Characteristics.* Education, total years of experience, time with the company, time in current job, overall performance rating, absenteeism history.

3. *Equipment and Services.* Type of equipment and services available, level of training in their use, and availability of backup resources when needed.

It's probably unrealistic to think you can match the groups exactly. For one thing, it's very hard to do for small pilot groups; for another, there may be some things that are purposely different for the telecommuters than the office workers. For example, if your telecommuters have access to electronic mail and most of your office people don't, that gives the telecommuters a built-in edge. But if you know about this and other differences from the start, you can take them into account when comparing the results of the two groups.

TIPS ON USING AND CHOOSING CONTROL GROUPS

1. A control group is the best way to thoroughly measure and understand the specific outcomes of telecommuting.

2. Benchmark data from a control group can help you get to the bottom of performance or other problems among your telecommuters.

3. You won't be able to have a perfectly matched control group; settle for as close a match as you can get.

4. Base your selection of control group members on work and personal characteristics and on available equipment and services.

A final benefit of control groups is to help insure that you build in periodic checkpoints to see how your program is going. In most cases, it makes sense to set a timetable for your pilot program—perhaps three, six, or nine months. If you have the comparative results available, you'll be reminded to call "time out" at some checkpoints along the way before you hit the end of the formal trial. These data will help you decide how to modify the trial if needed and whether and how to expand it beyond the first stage.

HOW TO SUSTAIN THE PRODUCTIVITY GAINS

Let's optimistically assume that you have a control group and that the results show real productivity gains for the telecommuters. Your challenge now is to keep everything rolling along so the early success isn't just a flash in the pan.

Here are four methods for converting your early pilot program gains to more permanent improvements:

1. *Keep Up the Momentum.* Make sure you can pinpoint what led to the productivity gains and make sure they continue, whatever they are. More than likely this will be a series of things the telecommuters, their coworkers, and their managers have done. Encourage them, commend them, and reinforce them for a job well done.

2. *Cope with Plateaus.* Watch for and deal with plateaus that often show up in productivity improvements. It's hard to sustain a steady gain; a graph of the change might look like a set of stairs, with a gain followed by a rest period and then another gain. These leveling-off points show up because people simply need a chance to get used to the new, higher levels, and because the incremental gains beyond the early ones may take longer to show up. Be sure you reinforce the gains—don't criticize or be impatient with the plateaus.

3. *Don't Overdo the Praise.* There's a risk of overdoing the reinforcement and praise for improvements. You can create resentment among others who aren't involved in the gains, and you also might be giving the high performers an excuse to rest on their laurels. Let them know that you're pleased with the results *and* that you have every hope they'll continue to contribute more. Don't go overboard and draw so much attention to the telecommuters that they become uncomfortable. It's one thing to be a novelty but quite another to feel as if you're in a sideshow.

4. *Handle Gain-Sharing Questions.* Be prepared to deal with the question of "what's in it for me?" from the telecommuters. If in fact they're able to show reliable, measurable gains in productivity and are worth more to the company, they're probably going to want a bigger piece of this bigger pie.

How you'll handle this depends on the telecommuters' job levels, the way they're paid, your salary administration guidelines, and your philosophy about gain-sharing. Either extreme is no good: if there's no extra reward you might quickly see the productivity gains slip away, and if you give away the shop you lose the value of the gains themselves.

Also, it might be hard to change their salaries without creating inequities with others in the same job categories. If so, you'll need to consider some forms of reward that are one-time events—such as a three-day weekend vacation or cruise, or a gift for the home. Finally, go back and take a second look at the section on merit pay and flexible benefits in Chapter 11 for more ideas.

WAYS TO KEEP THE PRODUCTIVITY GAINS GOING

1. Commend and reinforce the telecommuters, their coworkers, and managers for what they've done that led to more productivity.

2. Be patient if the gains level off—plateaus are natural and not necessarily a sign of trouble.

3. Don't overdo the praise and reinforcement—too much can cause others to resent the whole program.

4. If the gains are obvious, don't be surprised if your telecommuters ask "What's in it for me?" Do some research and planning to see how to answer them and still stay within policy.

POSSIBLE SPILLOVER TO OFFICE-BASED WORKERS

The best of all possible situations is when you have real gains in productivity among your telecommuters *and* in your office-based staff. This really isn't impossible although you may see less of a gain in the office than at the remote sites. One reason this might happen is the improved skills of the managers who supervise people at both locations. In that case, telecommuting prompted the skill development but in itself wasn't directly responsible for the gains shown by the remote workers.

There are three other ways that your remote work program might pay some unexpected dividends in the office:

1. *Borrow from the Best.* Look for methods, systems, and techniques used by your telecommuters that can be transferred to the office workers. One good example is electronic or voice mail; if you're using them remotely, consider expanding their use if some or all of their benefits would also apply in the office.

The same is true for less formal systems used by the remote workers. Perhaps they've found some shortcuts to save time or steps in methods that are taken for granted in the office. If they apply remotely maybe they can be used in the office, though they may have to be modified.

2. *Look for Subtle Changes.* Encourage your telecommuters and their managers to examine their work methods and work relationships. If they can verbalize some of the subtle changes they've made in how they operate, you might be able to apply them more widely. For example, if they're using those low-tech "speedy memo" forms to get short messages back and forth (instead of relying on face-to-face contacts that inevitably drift into other topics), maybe others can use them as well. Or perhaps it's something as simple as writing down a response to a memo in the margin and returning it to the sender instead of writing a reply memo and having it typed.

3. *Adopt Pieces That Work.* Give some thought to applying some of the methods used in the remote work environment for your office workers. Let's say you learn from your telecommuters that one of the major plusses of remote work is the flexible schedule. They find that they produce more when they can work at their own peak times. If you don't have

a formal flexible work hours (or "flextime") program, this could be a good reason to start one if you think the benefits will spread. As noted in Chapter 12, don't go into this without careful planning. You can approach this like telecommuting—on a pilot basis initially before committing to wide-scale use.

In summary, you have to be realistic about how much you can borrow from your telecommuting program in these ways. Don't overlook any opportunities, but remember that it's the characteristics of the remote site itself that often account for the gains. You can't transfer those to the office no matter how hard you try.

14 *Empty Skyscrapers? What Does the Future Hold?*

You've been thoroughly immersed in the details of telecommuting for most of this book—the how-tos and the day-to-day issues involved in adopting the concept of remote work. Now it's time to step back from these details and get a glimpse at what's ahead in more general terms. Some of this crystal-ball view of the future will take you beyond the boundaries of your organization into society in general, since widespread telecommuting will have profound, pervasive effects on almost every aspect of our lives.

As you know from your own planning activities in your job, there's no such thing as *the* future. There are several different scenarios and the "real" future is a blend of them. That's why it's more important that you understand some of the overall trends and changes that are possible as a result of remote work; their final scope and form will always be changing.

The premise for this chapter is that telecommuting *will* grow, and that large numbers of office workers will work at remote sites for two or more days a week. It's almost impossible to say exactly how many people and how many days a week, other than by making some educated guesses.

POSSIBLE LIMITS ON TELECOMMUTING'S GROWTH

There's little reason to believe that telecommuting won't flourish. The driving forces you learned about in Chapter 1 will continue to intensify for the rest of the decade. However, there are three factors that could slow the rate of implementation of remote work if they gather steam:

1. *Regulatory Limits.* Very restrictive labor laws or zoning ordinances could almost stop telecommuting in its tracks before it even got started. The likelihood of these depends on:

- The strength and persistence of organizations working for such limits, and the opposing strength of groups responding to this threat;
- The uncovering of as yet unknown widespread abuses of remote workers (or perhaps of even one truly tragic situation) that would trigger a flood of legislation to prevent similar abuses;
- A regulatory challenge from unexpected quarters: highly punitive treatment of remote workers by the IRS, for example, could also mean all but the end of telecommuting.

2. *Social Limits.* There's no way to know what will happen to our society and some of our institutions (like the family) if a big part (up to 25 percent) of the work force is dispersed to sites away from the office. For many people, the central workplace (or the immediate vicinity) is the focal point of their lives—their social life, professional development, recreation, entertainment, and shopping, for example.

Also, what will happen if a family can work, shop, be educated, and have access to entertainment all through a computer or terminal in the home? This creates new opportunities, but also new challenges for families used to heading away from the home (and from each other) for the entire day. There are several research projects underway that will begin to expand our knowledge about these changes, but it will be several years before we understand the full impact.

3. *Organizational Limits.* Finally, there's the question of how quickly large employers can get used to a new way of life. The pace of adoption of innovations in large organizations is usually quite slow. In some cases this is because the innovation is based on technology being promoted for its own sake—technology in search of applications. Slow implementation in these cases is a good defense against overcommitment of resources.

PROJECTED NUMBER OF TELECOMMUTERS

One way to estimate the absolute upper limit on the number of remote workers is to look at the population of information workers. According to government figures roughly 55 percent to 60 percent of today's work force is involved in information work—they make, use, change, process, or otherwise build their jobs on information. Some estimates project that this number will rise far higher toward the end of the century.

Information workers aren't just typists, clerks, and writers. Look around your organization and see how many office workers at all levels fit into this category. Many managers and executives are information workers—they manage and rely on data and information about sales, projects, plans, and resources. Even if you slash the government figures *in half* you still come up with over one-fourth of the work force in true information-based jobs.

Rates of Change: the Big Unknown

Every one of these people is a candidate for telecommuting, since ideas and information can be moved almost anywhere. The rate at which we move from today's number of remote office workers (well under 5 percent) to this conservative number of 25 percent will be based largely on how fast organizations can shed their old traditions. Technology is also a factor here although most organizations haven't even scratched the surface of telecommuting's potential using mid-1980s technology—which is impressive but will be downright antiquated by 1990 standards.

When it comes to adopting innovations—even those that have been proven elsewhere—most organizations just don't move that fast. Whether it's office or factory automation, telecommuting, or even "radical" ideas like new dress codes, there are few leaders and many, many distant followers. The question is whether your organization can afford to wait for dozens of others to take the first step—without paying a serious price in efficiency, profitability, or competitive position. The regulatory limits could be a make-or-break factor, but the social and organizational limits will only slow down implementation, if they have any effect at all. The question isn't *whether* telecommuting will catch on, but *how soon.*

An Assumption for 1990

The rest of this chapter is based on a conservative assumption about the number of telecommuters as follows: using today's total work force of roughly 100 million people and assuming that 55 percent of them are in information work, there are roughly 55 million potential remote workers. Allowing for no increase in the size of the work force or the proportion of information workers (though both *will* grow) it's possible that by 1990 five million people will be telecommuting, or just under 10 percent of the potential population.

This doesn't mean five million people working at home five days a week in front of a terminal or PC, although that scenario isn't impossible by any means. Rather, it means five million people spending at least two days a week at some remote site. You can see that even a very limited projection involves a lot of people. Apply that 10 percent to your work force and see what the numbers are; you'll see that this is not going to be an oddity or novelty.

In the rest of this chapter you'll look at five types of projections for the future: effects of remote work on urban structure, effects on business, an A through Z excursion into the offbeat and unexpected effects, a look at new technologies coming down the road, and a perspective on the office without walls—one that is truly location-independent.

URBAN STRUCTURE

One of the most apparent physical changes resulting from widespread telecommuting will be in the design of cities and metropolitan areas. Here are some of these changes.

Home Versus Local Telecommuting

You learned in Chapter 3 that there's a variety of remote work locations. Many telecommuters might work at home, but it's just as likely they'll spend time at some kind of local office—perhaps a miniaturized clone of the downtown headquarters.

If these satellite centers were located strategically around an urban area, automobile commuting could be cut by one-third to two-thirds depending on the number of centers and actual driving patterns. The best way to visualize this is in terms of shopping malls: if you plot all the malls in a 25-mile radius from the center of most cities, you'd have a good picture of this network of satellite office centers.

The central business district might become a business-residential area surrounded by this network of satellites that now locate workspace near housing and shopping areas. This isn't going to happen overnight, and it would probably look quite different from city to city. The point is that dispersing a good portion of work away from the central core would result in new definitions of urban and suburban land uses.

Mass Transit and Highways

Think what would happen if over time 10 percent or even 20 percent fewer people commuted to the central business district. The transportation systems in most cities are overloaded and need other major repair or expansion. As telecommuting grows, there's a chance to save some of this money or at least redirect it to uses that will equalize the flow of people. Most roadways and transit systems are built and funded with the two daily rush-hour peaks in mind, yet are underutilized at other times. Wouldn't it be nice if we could get away from this peaking problem and the financial and personal problems it creates?

Urban planners in southern California are already beginning to think along these lines. The Southern California Association of Governments, representing over 200 cities and counties, is building its regional plan with the assumption that 12 percent of the area's work force will be telecommuting by the year 2000.

Cities Versus Suburbs

One fear sometimes expressed about telecommuting is that it will turn the center city into an empty shell. A much more likely scenario is the shift to multipurpose downtown areas, as noted earlier. The revitalization of rundown areas in Boston and Baltimore is a good example of what these might look like.

Even though many professionals are moving into new housing in these downtown areas, many also continue to move out of the cities into rural areas. New rural cities begin to develop as housing, office parks, and shopping centers all pop up. This is good if it takes some of the burden off the downtown area, but could be disastrous if it leads to an unlimited urban sprawl. If everyone wants to move closer to the lake, mountains, or ocean, the city that people wanted to escape from begins to reappear in their backyards.

This is another argument for a mixed model of home-based and small-office-based forms of remote work. This model would tend to foster the development of clusters in less densely settled areas, instead of one uniform urban/suburban landscape.

EFFECTS ON BUSINESS

The effects of telecommuting on your particular business may differ from this list depending on the numbers of telecommuters, the work they do, and your office space situation.

Widespread Productivity Gains

If as little as 10 percent of your work force increases its productivity by 15 to 30 percent, you can look forward to lower labor costs. Also, you might see customer service improve if the telecommuters' work is closely linked to service levels. Lower costs mean higher profits and improved customer service can lead to higher sales or, at minimum, better customer relations.

Cheaper and More Reliable Staffing Methods

Earlier chapters noted that you pay a high price in recruiting costs and vacant jobs when you can't find the people needed for key openings. Whether this is due to high demand for certain workers or structural changes in the labor force, you need an alternative to the traditional methods for finding workers.

As telecommuting grows into an effective recruiting method, you can look forward to lower costs and, more important, a more reliable way to find the people you need when you need them. Except for direct personal-service businesses (like consulting, where you can measure the value of lost contracts), most managers don't have a good way to estimate the cost of a job remaining unfilled. In many cases, it far exceeds the salary alone since you pay a penalty for lost sales or delayed projects. If you *can* quantify these costs, you'll begin to see the potential payback of telecommuting.

Employee Relations and "Telescabs"

Chapter 11 addressed the concerns of some union leaders about potential abuses under telecommuting. Consider this twist: what if your firm was faced with a union organizing drive among office workers (or this group was already unionized) and you wanted to take a stand against the union but still needed to keep the work going? You could conceivably hire non-union telecommuters (or "telescabs," as Jack Nilles of the University of Southern California has named them) and disperse this work away from your central office.

This tactic could be used to break a strike or even break a union's hold on your employees. This is one of the less attractive sides of telecommuting, and it's definitely not suggested. It goes against what most managers believe about the long-term value of positive employee relations.

U.S. manufacturers have often moved work from highly unionized areas of the north to southern states with little or no union activity. They've also exported work overseas to get away from the unions and from high wage rates. This practice is also used in information work—there are clerical and data entry "factories" in several Caribbean countries, India, Korea, and other countries. The "raw materials" (forms and records) are shipped over (or, increasingly, transmitted via satellite) and the "finished goods" sent (or transmitted) back. Just as offshore manufacturing has had profound impact on the U.S. labor force and business structure, the same pattern might emerge in the growing information-oriented sectors of our economy. If it does, it probably won't happen without creating employee relations problems.

Juxtaposed Job Duties

As more office work becomes computer-based, some observers believe it will become highly routinized, leading to "deskilling." This is most likely to happen in lower-level jobs but could also carry over to managerial slots. You could see a curious combination of tasks and duties when these jobs are done remotely: your staff's *work* might become more routinized and less discretionary, but their *self-supervision* (especially for in-home telecommuters) might mean they'll end up with more, rather than less, diversity in the work.

One thing to look for when choosing telecommuters is the ability to handle a wide range of problems independently. Even if parts of their jobs are less demanding, they'll probably be handling more varied tasks with fewer resources around them to fall back on. What will this mean for job descriptions, titles, and pay grades? You might find that a telecommuter with a bachelor's degree and two years of experience in a low-level professional job will have to exercise the judgment of a manager several rungs up on the ladder in a traditional office-based structure. If so, should this telecommuter get the pay and title of a manager because he/she is now worth more? This isn't an easy question to answer, but you'll have to address it as the telecommuting concept spreads.

Our whole view of organization structure and titles may have to be overhauled to match this new kind of division of labor. One good example of how this happens (though not for telecommuters) is PeopleExpress Airlines. This highly successful firm gives everyone a "manager" title, and it's not just a cosmetic ploy. The airline has built its job structure and operating methods around delegation of authority deep into the ranks, and decision making by those most qualified to do it because they're closest to the task. This closely parallels the telecommuting scenario described above.

Information Entrepreneuring

Be prepared to expand your thinking about employer-employee relationships. Today's computer technology means that someone can buy a powerful PC, modem, software, and printer for under $3000—and that figure will drop each year. Put this package together with some extra space in the home, add to this the person's experience, and an entrepreneur is born.

This is happening all over the country today as people look to use their skills and their computers at home to get into business on their own—this old-fashioned dream isn't a casualty of the computer age. If anything, it has intensified: the Working From Home Forum on the CompuServe computer network had almost 2000 members in early 1985. One of the most frequent messages found on its electronic bulletin board is "I work as a (whatever) during the day, have (whatever) skills, own my own PC and want to start up a business at home. Does anyone have any suggestions?"

If you've seen some of your better employees follow this route, or think they might, why not try to arrange the best of both worlds? Maybe you and the employee can continue the relationship as supplier and customer. You might keep your people (though on different terms) if you can harness this innovative and entrepreneurial bent. Their earnings on an hourly or daily basis will be higher than their current salaries but you'll be saving three big costs: office space, equipment (they'll use their own), and payroll overhead costs (benefits, vacation, pension funding).

The truly creative employers might even carve out new kinds of work relationships that fall in the middle between employees and independents. While it might be more difficult to work out these special deals, you have to consider the alternative (and the cost) of losing key staff.

Your *own* performance suffers when your best people walk out the door to work on their own. With remote work there *is* an alternative for keeping some of them.

Redefinition of Office Space

Finally, you can expect changes in how office buildings will look in the years ahead. This is partly due to the growing number of terminals and PCs in use already, requiring different kinds of work areas, lighting, and storage. But as telecommuting takes hold and more workers work remotely, the overall allocation and use of space will change.

The obvious change is that less space will be needed, though not in direct proportion to the number of telecommuters. If they'll still be coming into the office for part of the week, you won't see a one-for-one reduction in number of cubicles or offices. But think about what your telecommuters will be doing on those days they *are* in the office—most likely they'll be doing less individual work and spending more time in meetings or conferences.

These won't necessarily be large meetings; your telecommuters will be with two or three other people, some of whom will be other telecommuters. What will be needed is a hybrid office/conference/workstation area that includes several walk-up workstations for individual access, a few small conference tables, and several small private desks or work surfaces. This would be a "drop-in" center where nobody has his/her individual desk, but just takes over whatever space is needed for the duration of the visit to the office. Some future office buildings will look like a mix between today's spaces with highly individualized work areas and a kind of high-tech public library reading room. For example, the design firm Environetics International has prepared a design for an "instant privacy igloo" that creates a free-standing conference room in the middle of an open office.

SUMMARY

These six changes are some of the major ones in the offing as telecommuting spreads, but they're far from the only ones. Perhaps the major change affecting business is one that's harder to see—the change in attitudes about supervision. The transition from an approach that stresses observing and monitoring activity to one that relies on planning for and tracking progress on results is a big step for many managers. But this transition must occur, because all the technology in the world by itself won't facilitate remote work.

AN A THROUGH Z LIST OF EFFECTS
ON EXISTING BUSINESSES

As we continue to gaze into the crystal ball, here are some educated guesses about the impact of telecommuting on existing businesses. Once again the specific changes in some of the businesses will depend on how much and in what form telecommuting grows. This admittedly random (and somewhat tongue-in-cheek) list is included simply to help you see the scope of the implications of remote work for virtually every aspect of our lives:

Advertising: New market for employers and individuals buying office equipment, supplies, furniture, and services for remote sites.

Architects: More demand for homes that also work as offices, for renovation of existing homes to include offices, and for new forms of office space and/or mixed-used residential-office space.

Auto leasing: The company car may no longer be a worthwhile benefit, even aside from the tax deduction issues.

Auto sales: Less need for cars to handle regular commuting. Perhaps the small electric car will serve for close-in household errands, public transit will provide the inter-city link, and daily rentals will replace full-time ownership.

Banks: Greater demand for in-home banking services and widely distributed automatic teller machines, especially in satellite or neighborhood centers.

Bars: The after-work gathering might be a less common occurrence.

Builders: More demand for retrofitting existing housing with compact, functional office spaces.

Cable manufacturers: More demand for traditional and fiber-optic cables as we build a growing and widespread telecommunications network.

Child care: Continuing demand for this service, although perhaps linked to neighborhood centers and in the telecommuters' homes instead of at separate day-care centers.

Cleaning: Demand for house-cleaning services may grow if this becomes a new employee benefit for telecommuters.

Clothing: Less demand for office "uniforms" as more people work in casual clothes.

Computers: Another reason why this market will grow; perhaps there will be different models for in-home use—with cases in designer colors or to match the furniture style in the home?

Copying: New demand for small, cheap copiers for certain telecommuters' homes, and for contract operation of copy centers at neighborhood or satellite centers.

Couriers: Increased demand for local courier services; new routing needed for fleets that now have to cover a wider area; perhaps needed for cars or station wagons instead of trucks for deliveries to telecommuters in residential areas that ban trucks?

Dentists and diet organizations: Demand for both will grow for telecommuters who can't keep their snacking under control; as part of their corporate fitness programs, employers will purchase remote-controlled refrigerator locks for telecommuters' homes.

Detectives: More requests for corporate loyalty checks as employers wonder if their telecommuters are holding down two or three remote jobs.

Disposal: A new combination for the in-home paper shredder, or combination food and paper disposal units for the kitchen sink.

Electricity: Demand for "clean" (filtered and reliable) electricity to power computers and other devices sensitive to power fluctuations.

Employment: Employment agencies may shift their role to being real-time brokers for remote workers' services. Also, temporary-help agencies may start providing "telesecretaries"—remote workers who take dictation by phone and then transmit finished work to client's site for printing on company printers.

Fire equipment: Demand for additional smoke detectors and fire extinguishers as protective devices for home offices.

Food service: Less demand for corporate cafeterias; more demand for mobile kitchens that deliver prepared meals to busy telecommuters at home for their own use or to cater in-home meetings.

Gambling: Office football pools will have to be run electronically with losses automatically deducted from employee's checking account. State lotteries will enable remote ticket purchases via home computer or face extinction.

Graphics: Increasing need for low-cost full graphics capability in computer applications and transmission so remote workers have full access to nontext materials.

Health care: Changes in nature and extent of illness as workers are no longer subject to accidents in or while commuting to office. Market for cold and flu remedies drops off as fewer people get sick from being close to ill coworkers.

Hotels: New market for hourly or daily room rentals for telecommuter meetings. Drawing on the concept of the Murphy bed, these rooms would have fold-down conference tables and other facilities so they could be used for short meetings during the day and rented as sleeping rooms at night.

Insurance: New market for different kinds of insurance needs for remote workers and their employers.

Interiors: Demand for interior designers specializing in creating offices at home or renovating schools to look like offices. The designer's services for converting an extra room into an office might be a new kind of employee benefit.

Kitchen equipment: New market for larger sinks to handle dishes piled up through the day by telecommuter.

Labor unions: Need to find ways to reach remote workers—perhaps organizing cards to be sent out as electronic mail?

Lawyers: More guidance needed for as-yet undefined legal and regulatory areas in remote work.

Mail: New volume/distribution patterns for U.S. mail and growing use of electronic mail.

Mass mailers: Confusion reigns as these groups can't decide where to send mailings—home, central office, satellite center?

Movers: Expensive corporate-paid employee relocations may decline as firms let employees take new jobs in old areas via telecommuting. Also, less need for office moves as firms scale back building plans because remote work cuts down floor space needs.

Newsstands: May suffer as fewer office workers are around to pick up magazines or papers while at work downtown. Innovative ones may expand to provide services (such as shoe repair or dry cleaning) for telecommuters who now are in town only infrequently.

Office equipment: Demand for office furniture suitable for home but still up to corporate standards; new market for scaled-down versions of standard office equipment.

Paging: Demand for cheap, reliable, wide-area paging systems to reach telecommuters who may not always be near phones. (Cellular radio phones also will be affected in the same way.)

Paper manufacturers: Less demand as more information flows electronically.

Payroll: Direct-deposit of paychecks becomes almost mandatory.

Printers: More need for ink-jet, laser, or other similar printer technologies that are suited to high-quality graphics output.

Quail farms: May suffer because fewer executives are around to frequent classy restaurants for gourmet lunches.

Real estate: New types of housing required, new valuation basis of housing as proximity to employer's office becomes less important, blurring of distinction between commercial and residential agents.

Safes: More need for in-home safes for highly confidential materials, or perhaps even armored car service that acts as safe-deposit vault on wheels.

Schools: New market for abandoned elementary schools, thus helping solve budget problems for school boards. Less need for teachers' aides as some telecommuters are available to come in to child's school during the day.

Solar energy: Solar heating becomes more practical in homes where people will be present during prime sun hours.

Telephone: Much more demand for all forms of services, and broad implications for capacity planning as former downtown volume shifts to residential areas.

Time clocks: Will either fade into the sunset as relics of another era, or someone will develop one that can be accessed remotely perhaps by touch-tone phone for firms that want to continue their use.

Universities: May have to adjust staffing and course offerings since telecommuters will no longer be limited to attending evenings classes after traditional work hours.

Vending: Office vending machines will be used less, but there will be new market for convenience shopping by telecommuters to replace lunchtime or to/from work stops; possible demand for a convenience store on wheels?

Video: New market for in-home or remote-office teleconferencing facilities, probably tied into local cable TV systems.

Watercoolers: Market for units with miniaturized tape recorders to capture and then transmit office gossip to telecommuters.

Xylography: This craft of engraving on wood will enjoy a resurgence as telecommuters now have more time to enjoy such spare-time activities.

Yearbooks: A new market for office yearbooks; like the high-school and college versions, these will serve as a common bond among those who become geographically dispersed.

Zymurgy: Many telecommuters will enroll in courses in this subject (the chemistry of fermentation processes, as in brewing) as they develop interest in homemade wines and beers.

Maybe the ideas started running thin toward the end of the alphabet, but you still get the picture. Many parts of our economic system have been based on the traditional commutation and work patterns that have been developing for close to 100 years. When those patterns change there's a tremendous ripple effect, and this list just scratches the surface. This kind of speculation is fun, but it's also a little unsettling. There might be large numbers of businesses and jobs changed, created, and lost due to the relocation of work through telecommuting.

Fortunately, this isn't going to happen overnight and the organizations affected should have plenty of time to switch gears—*if* they're attuned to the change. The same holds for *your* organization: ask yourself how the market for your firm's products or services will be affected as telecommuting spreads. You might find there's an entirely different set of changes you'll have to cope with and plan for other than those affecting you as an employer.

THE IMPACT OF NEW TECHNOLOGIES

Very few telecommuting applications today are hampered by the lack of suitable technology, although in some cases it may not be cost-effective to use that technology. Looking ahead to 1990, there's a number of new or enhanced technologies that will make it even easier for you to use remote locations. This isn't the definitive statement about what the marketplace will offer. It's just a selected list of developments that, in the eyes of industry experts and observers, should be available at reasonable cost by 1990. Many of these items obviously aren't intended just for telecommuting and have many other applications.

Voice Recognition

This is probably at the top of everyone's wish list and could truly revolutionize office work. Today there are systems that recognize a limited number of words or commands but must be reprogrammed for each speaker's voice. The dream, of course, is a system that can cope with many speakers and accurately capture long messages. The application most people think of first is replacing typing—being able to dictate a memo or letter and have the computer print it out perfectly.

The obstacles are the computing power and memory required to instantaneously understand and encode many different voices, and the software that lets the machine tell the difference between words that sound alike ("read" and "red") and choose the right one in the context of a sentence. It's impossible to tell how well these challenges will be met by 1990, but it doesn't seem likely that you'll be able to dispense with your secretary entirely by then.

The implications for telecommuters are significant: as for in-office workers, voice recognition frees them of the keyboard and makes the telephone a primary computer access tool. You can begin to see this now in systems that allow remote access to databases via instructions punched out on the pushbuttons, with replies coming from speech synthesizers. Also, there are applications where easy access to corporate files would make remote work life much easier. For example, you could tell your office computer "Give me the sales results for products A and B for the last six months" if you were in the middle of planning a budget and needed those figures. Finally, you could handle a lot of administrative details on your own—you could call your travel agent's computer and say "Tell me the schedules for flights tomorrow from New York to Atlanta" and then make your reservation, all without touching a keyboard.

The most far-reaching effect of voice recognition could be a wholesale reshuffling of jobs and duties, and with it some new ideas about remote work. If one reason telecommuters have to come to the office is to get information or have administrative work done, will those trips still be necessary? Also, what happens to our concept of secretarial work and the need for centrally located secretaries? On the surface it seems that voice recognition will be a shot in the arm for telecommuting, but the specific outcomes won't be known until we learn more about its capabilities and costs.

Image Transmission

This has been referred to several times so far and continues to be a big factor in remote work. Look at your desk: there's probably as much printed material that's in color, with pictures or graphs, and that comes from outside your organization as there is straight text and data. Everyone relies on this variety and few remote workers (especially in professional or managerial jobs) can exist only with the things that are printed out on a terminal or printer today.

Three of the keys to more diverse image transmission are image input devices (to "see" drawings or photos and then store and transmit them as easily as words or numbers), more sophisticated printers, terminals, or other display units to show the materials (perhaps linked to videodisk storage units), and videoconferencing systems that allow quick, high-quality meetings or displays of three-dimensional items (like products, tools, or packages). All three are available today but almost always suffer from high cost, bulkiness, or technical limitations that hamper their use in remote work.

You can look forward to big advances in these and related technologies by 1990. Costs for the equipment will drop, it will become more versatile, and competition and new developments should lead to better and cheaper communications systems to link remote sites. The more that remote workers can *see* in addition to just *read*, the better they'll be able to do all parts of their jobs remotely.

As you begin to see and take advantage of these technologies for your telecommuters, you'll have to guard against their overuse. One thing that helps remote workers stay effective is coming into the central office from time to time. If it's technically possible for them to do their entire job remotely, there's a risk that their ties to the office will be lost or distorted. Telecommuters shouldn't be hermits even if it's technically feasible.

Telecommunications

The broad impact of this field has been stressed throughout the book because it's at the heart of telecommuting—which has been defined, in large part, as the substitution of telecommunications for travel. This substitution will grow as the telecommunications network grows and improves.

Some of the changes you'll see are:

- Widespread fiber-optic cabling (to increase transmission capacity and reliability);
- Digital switching and protocol conversion in telephone company facilities (to facilitate faster, better service, and blur the distinction between voice and data transmission);
- Increased use of satellite transmissions (to cut costs and get around some of the limitations of the existing installed cable-based network).

The AT&T divestiture changed the ground rules in telecommunications and the dust is still settling after the January 1, 1984 breakup. To a large degree, telecommuting is at the mercy of the telecommunications rate structure, especially for local service. If this rises as much as some say it could, the use of the local network for some telecommuters might become cost-prohibitive.

Working against this are lower long-distance rates (though there's been less of a drop than predicted) and the use of alternative or "bypass" technologies to get around the local network. It's possible (though it would be ironic) that long-distance telecommuting at satellite offices far from the central site can become the most cost-effective. If so, this would affect some of your plans for selection of remote workers and methods for managing them. It's very hard to make any reliable predictions about the rate structures for 1990 at this time, but the added competition in the marketplace should work in your favor in the long run.

PCs and Software

Most observers will tell you that the machines and programs you're see-ing today are light-years behind what you can and should expect by 1990. Stop and think about it: if these are the wonderful executive tools they're made out to be, why is there such a flourishing industry in training every-one how to use them, and why are the manuals getting longer instead of shorter? This isn't to take anything away from today's PC and software; com-pared to what was available five years ago they are exceptional products.

Arcane commands, mystifying manuals, inscrutable error messages, and hard-to-use keyboards simply don't help inspire confidence. They also make it hard for someone whose job is otherwise suited for remote work to think of working with a PC in the den on a sales forecast without the department computer expert nearby to answer questions. You can't expect a successful manager to calmly accept the prospects of looking silly while trying to figure out how to do something his/her ten-year-old child probably did last year in the school computer lab.

There's a difference between the PCs and software suited for office use versus those for remote use, though this gap is quickly closing. As equipment costs drop and you start to see "industrial-strength" process-ing power in smaller and smaller boxes, the machines will take over many of the more onerous aspects of their use. Coupled with advances in artifi-cial intelligence and "smart" systems, you'll be able to have almost anyone work remotely without fear of failure. Also, the issue of PC to mainframe links should become a nonissue; with appropriate security controls and software, your telecommuters will have easy access to corporate files that will replace the file cabinets of today.

Storage Media and Systems

The systems on the drawing boards today will do for computer files what microfilm and microfiche did for paper files—and then some. Optical storage systems—not unlike, but advanced beyond videodisk systems—will allow rapid access to many times more material than can be stored on today's disk systems. The optical systems starting to appear today show the signs of any early entry in a new market—they are far ahead of the technology they replace, but high in cost and limited in versatility, compared with what you can expect in only a few years.

These or similar systems will add another level of freedom for your telecommuters. First, they'll be able to have fast, easy access to almost unlimited amounts of material (including text, data, and all kinds of images) from a remote location. Second, more jobs will be suited for remote work because the need for access to paper records or for special terminals hard-wired into the mainframe will be eliminated.

These storage facilities and the image transmission methods described earlier will combine to make your satellite and/or neighborhood centers far more versatile than you might imagine. If these facilities are to be partial or total clones of your central office, they have to offer the remote workers almost everything they'd have at the central office. Providing easy access to a full range of corporate files is one way to do this; coupled with high-quality telecommunications links, you'll have the basis for fully equipped remote offices that function on a par with the central office.

Videotex

Videotex is a system for distributing diverse kinds of information and services to wide audiences, either in businesses or in homes. Originally intended to carry both text and graphics, it has been hampered by technical problems, purchase of expensive dedicated terminals that have no other use, and by the chicken-and-egg problem of lack of commitment to its use by both information providers and users. Much-heralded trials in Florida, New Jersey, and California were less successful than planned, and new ventures (such as a major one planned jointly by CBS, IBM, and Sears Roebuck) are subjects of much speculation and will be slow to develop.

Let's assume for now that the technical, content, and marketing issues get worked out somehow by the late 1980s and there are systems in place to deliver text-only information and services to PC users. According to estimates from LINK Resources, there will be over five million users of videotex (via PCs) in 1989, up from just over one million projected for 1985. That's a lot of people with access to news, sports, and banking information, shopping, financial data, and perhaps dozens of other types of information and services.

An Information Pipeline?

What does this mean for telecommuting? First, it helps the telecommuter efficiently get access to services or information via PC that otherwise would have required a trip to the bank, store, or newsstand. This means that remote sites of all kinds become less remote (and thus more attractive) because the telecommuters won't be shut off from the outside world. Second, many of these videotex systems may well be in-house systems for a company's own use, perhaps piggybacked on the public services. As such, these services might replace (and improve on) communications vehicles like company newspapers and bulletin boards. This means your telecommuters could be even more closely linked to the office by having a richer, more diverse, and perhaps more reliable information flow than if they were at the central office as you know it today.

Videotex has a long way to go, but it could turn out to be an integral part of telecommuting. One of the greatest fears of telecommuters and their managers is being out of touch and out of the mainstream; if videotex can be the kind of broad information pipeline that its supporters envision, that fear will quickly go away.

This has been a quick tour through six developments that will become part of the telecommuting landscape by 1990. There will be countless others, and these six may take forms very different from those described here. As someone interested in the prospects for remote work, it pays to keep your ear to the ground and follow these and related technologies. When you see a news report of some new equipment, software, or service, ask yourself "What will this mean for remote work?" With luck, you'll find that the relatively few technical obstacles will fall away as Silicon Valley and its counterparts around the world churn out new offerings.

WORKING FROM ANYWHERE:
THE "VIRTUAL" OFFICE

Telecommuting as it's been described in this book is really only one form of what's labeled "the virtual office." This term is taken loosely from the term "virtual memory," a method of easily exchanging space in and out of a computer's memory to expand the working area without adding more physical storage devices.

The "virtual office" means that the office is wherever the person is; his/her presence in itself, together with the appropriate tools, defines the office. Everyone is used to thinking of an office in physical terms as something with walls that's part of what's called an office building. But when you open up your briefcase on a train or plane and start working, isn't that space your "office?"*

You and your peers have been working for years in cars, planes, trains, hotel rooms, dining rooms or dens, and even more exotic places. You think nothing of opening this "office" for an hour or two, and using your office equipment like files, dictating machine, calculator, and (for some) lap-top PC.

The next step is telecommuting as defined in this book, where the home or other remote site partially supplements or replaces the central office. As technology develops, these supplemental sites will lose their "almost an office" status because you'll have access to the *same information* in the *same form* as you do in the traditional office. Just as you'll call up a file on your PC screen in your office on the 32nd floor, you'll call up the same file on same kind of PC and get the same information at home, at a neighborhood center, or in other locations as yet undefined.

Consider some of the things that are in place now or planned for the next few years:

- Small, powerful modems to fit in cars that will be used to link a small PC to cellular radio telephones; a more compact version will include a portable cellular phone, modem, and PC all in a standard briefcase.

- Hotels are experimenting with outfitting certain rooms with terminals or PCs for traveling managers; some hotels will couple these with small suites that include a conference/dining table, a TV that doubles as a computer monitor, and other business amenities.

- Public-access videotex terminals will be located in airport lobbies and will work like pay phones; you'll be able to call up your central computer and transmit or receive information—and charge it on your telephone credit card.

---

*See "The Office: Here, There, and Everywhere" by Vincent Giuliano in February 1983 *Today's Office* for an excellent description of this concept.

CONCLUSION: LESSONS FOR THE FUTURE
FROM THE PAST

We are living today with organizational structures that are artifacts of years past when there was no alternative but to bring everyone to one central location. You could easily argue that the two inventions with the greatest impact on these existing structures were copying machines (that had to fight for respect among dedicated carbon-paper users) and the telephone.

Both began to free business people from the need to be located next to each other. These aren't exactly new technologies, yet they're the most recent ones to have widespread impact on your organization life, short of the PC. Both have certainly developed far beyond their early forms but there have been no fundamental changes in their use. Whether you had to crank your phone to get the operator to make a call or push a few buttons on today's high-tech models to do the same thing, the basic purpose served by the phone hasn't changed much at all.

As you look ahead to the future of remote work, you should take a lesson from these important yet "stretched" technologies, and from the lowly typewriter. The "QWERTY" keyboard (so named because of the first six keys on the top row of letters) was designed because other keyboard layouts caused early typewriters to jam up when typists became proficient. The typewriters weren't designed to accommodate the faster typing that was possible using other keyboard layouts.

The QWERTY layout was developed to slow down typing speeds because of the pattern of letter placement relative to the frequency of letter use in the English language. Typists have paid the price for this for years; even the software-based typing instruction packages for today's PC users can't compensate for that poor layout. August Dvorak patented another design in 1936 that took advantage of letter use and was estimated to increase typing output by up to 50 percent. It's only now in the 1980s that serious interest in the Dvorak keyboard (and other alternate layouts) is developing, although it's far from a groundswell of change.

Instead of taking advantage of an obviously improved method, business limped along for years because of the investment in equipment and (more important) the tradition of the QWERTY layout. Interestingly, the PC might turn out to be what's needed to spur the conversion since it allows an electronic (and thus changeable) link between keyboard and the printing process.

The challenge for you as you think of telecommuting is to learn from the QWERTY experience. The "virtual office" idea is a mindset *and* a physical change, as is the Dvorak keyboard. Your challenge is to move beyond the office buildings that have been used for close to a century—the architectural equivalents of the QWERTY keyboard—to a more flexible design where bricks and mortar are no longer the prime determinants of an "office."

Index